New Standards. Together

AIRBUS

Hospitality at the highest level, celebrated above all.

Best Cabin Crew in the Middle East, now onboard Qatar Airways.

Every journey is a rewarding experience. That's because each one of our dedicated crew endeavours to make every flight a voyage to remember - for every single passenger. So step onboard today, you'll soon see why we've won Best Cabin Crew in the Middle East for seven years running.

World's 5-star airline. qatarairways.com

QATAR AIRWAYS القطرية

Contents

The World in 2010

EDITOR: Daniel Franklin
MANAGING EDITOR: Harriet Ziegler
DEPUTY EDITORS: John Andrews, Leo Abruzzese
EDITORIAL ASSISTANT: Jennifer Quigley-Jones
COUNTRIES EDITOR: Alasdair Ross
INDUSTRIES EDITOR: Carla Rapoport
DESIGN AND ART DIRECTION: Mike Kenny, Bailey and Kenny
ART DIRECTOR: Anita Wright
CHARTS: Phil Kenny, Michael Robinson, Peter Winfield
ILLUSTRATIONS: Steve Carroll, Kevin Kallaugher, James Sillavan
PICTURE EDITOR: Juliet Brightmore
RESEARCH: Carol Howard, Jane Shaw
EDITORIAL ASSISTANCE: Ingrid Esling, Caroline Carter
ADVERTISING MANAGERS: Harry Whitbread (UK), Natalie Henault, Sarah Jane Lindsay (Europe), Sadia Aman (MEA), Suzanne Hopkins (North America), Kelly Jang, Terrie Lam (Asia)
CIRCULATION & MARKETING DIRECTORS: Lisa Jamal (UK), Grace Hahn (Asia)
CIRCULATION MANAGERS: Isaac Showman (UK), David Smith (Europe)
PRODUCTION: Sharon Simpson, Michael Mann, Andrew Rollings, Amy Brown, Katy Wilson, Nick Ormiston, Robert Banbury
WORLDWIDE LICENSING & SYNDICATION: Rebecca Cogswell, Mark Beard, Jay Abai
PUBLISHER: Des McSweeney

The Economist
25 St James's Street
London SW1A 1HG
Telephone: 020 7576 8133
E-mail: worldineditor
@economist.com

11 **From the editor**

Leaders

13 **The hard slog ahead**
A year of small advances for the West
14 **Now for the long term**
Business can once again think of the future
18 **Europe's chance**
The EU must make use of the Lisbon treaty
22 **Not so fast**
Disappointment for the global economy
24 **Chill, China**
How to adjust to great-power status
26 **Smart states**
As government gets bigger, can it get better?
30 **Wanted: green engineers**
The world needs more of them
32 **More than a number**
What to call the next ten years

35 **Calendar for 2010**

Britain

37 **Regime change**
The Tories take over
38 **The slimming cure**
Britain's bloated state faces strict rations
39 **Recessionomics**
Previous downturns suggest: don't panic
42 **Advantage, Hong Kong**
Can the City of London regain its edge?
42 **On yer bikes**
London follows the cycles-for-hire fad
43 **A history lesson**
Paul Kennedy assesses the old country

Europe

45 **More than a museum?**
A year that will test the EU's new treaty
46 **Europe isn't working**
Tackling unemployment
48 **Chameleon Bonaparte**
Nicolas Sarkozy unloved, yet unrivalled
50 **Beyond the crisis**
José Manuel Barroso on Europe's priorities
51 **The eternal leader**
Italy's Berlusconi phenomenon 
51 **Coolissimo**
An Italian view of the must-haves for 2010
52 **Changing the colours**
Germany's new coalition proceeds with caution
53 **A scent of history**
Eastern Germany has a fresh allure
54 **A still darker Russia**
Once more into the unknown
56 **New twists in an old saga**
Europe's dependence on Russian energy
58 **No need to weigh the past**
Poland's election year
59 **Russia's role in turbulent times**
Dmitry Medvedev on co-operation

United States

61 **Mr Obama's unpromising year**
The president will be blamed for bad times
62 **Square-root reversal**
America will recover, but weakly
63 **The Fed's next battle**
This time, with politicians
64 **Found(er)ing Fathers**
California's new constitution
66 **Counting heads**
America's census means political mischief
68 **Thirty-somethings**
Three youngsters to watch in 2010
70 **All the news that's fit to pay for**
Michael Kinsley on newspapers

The Americas

71 **After Lula**
Brazil's presidential election
72 **Bolívar's continent**
Two hundred years of solitude for Latin America
73 **Canada's northern goal**
The Arctic: no more the forgotten frontier
74 **Greenland, the new bonanza**
Hoping to become oil barons
75 **Sí, se puede**
Shakira on universal education

Asia

77 **Bring on the new generation**
Getting Japan out of its fiscal black hole
78 **Political football**
Not just a game for North and South Korea
79 **The cautious leap forward**
China prepares a new plan 
80 **Peak labour**
Chinese workers will become scarcer
81 **The dragon still roars**
Is China's economic boom sustainable?
82 **An imperfect storm**
Manufacturing overtakes farming in India
83 **Worryingly fragile**
Don't bet on Pakistan's stability
83 **A grim prospect**
NATO may lose in Afghanistan

Beyond the crisis
A hard slog, says **John Micklethwait**, page 13. Disappointment ahead for the global economy: leader, page 22. A weak recovery in America, page 62. Heading for the exit, page 135. The crunch ripples on, page 133. Meanwhile, China overtakes Japan, page 81, and India's factories overtake its farms, page 82. A Chinese bubble? page 134. **Dominique Strauss-Kahn** suggests ways to avoid another crisis, page 138.

Regime change
David Cameron prepares to govern in Britain, page 37. Brazil after Lula, page 71. Bring on Japan's new generation, page 77. Testing Europe's new treaty, page 45. **José Manuel Barroso** outlines the EU's priorities, page 50, and **Dmitry Medvedev** explains Russia's, page 59. A regime change for the internet: expect a dot.surge, page 125.

More than a game
Africa's World Cup, page 90. The continent should shoot for exponential growth, says **Jacob Zuma**, page 92. Political football between the Koreas, page 78. Competing for 2018 and 2022, page 99. The 2010s name game: leader, page 32.

50% engineer
50% entrepreneur
100% father
One Credit Suisse
for all you are

People are not made of numbers. They are made of hopes and dreams, passions and partnerships, talent and tenacity. We strive to see beyond the numbers and understand what success means to our clients, to deliver what really matters. Credit Suisse, working to help its clients thrive since 1856.

credit-suisse.com

CREDIT SUISSE

Contents

84 **Australia set fair**
The election has an odds-on winner

85 **Islam and the West**
Susilo Bambang Yudhoyono on tolerance-building

Middle East and Africa

87 **Mission not quite impossible**
Israel is not alone in confronting Iran

88 **Struggle and strife**
Iran's threats

89 **Iraqis rule Iraq**
Hope laced with danger

90 **The year of African football**
The FIFA World Cup

91 **The worst country on Earth**
Somalia takes our unwanted prize

92 **The world's eyes on Africa**
Jacob Zuma on the continent's potential

International

95 **A modern guide to G-ology**
The clubs that would rule the world

96 **Our greatest hits...**
...and misses for 2009

97 **Nuclear non-proliferation entreaty**
A busy year for nuclear diplomacy

98 **Predicting the swine-flu pandemic**
Margaret Chan on the global response

99 **The Madagascar model**
Conflicts over natural resources will grow

99 **A World Cup double**
England for 2018, America for 2022

100 **Today London, tomorrow the world**
Young people gather to save the planet

101 **Delayed explosion**
Will 2010 be a year of social unrest?

102 **Where survival is at stake**
Mohamed Nasheed on climate change

The world in figures

103 **Forecasts for 81 countries**
113 **Forecasts for 15 industries**

Business

119 **Coming out of the dark**
Light at the end of the tunnel for business

120 **The jargon of 2010**
Way beyond English

122 **The plot thickens**
E-books will move to the mainstream

122 **Can e-readers save newspapers?**
Eventually, maybe, but not in 2010

124 **Search me**
Tracking consumers' online habits

125 **Change of addresses**
Prepare for a dot.surge

126 **Big SIS is watching you**
With ubiquitous technology

127 **Leadership in the information age**
Carol Bartz on management

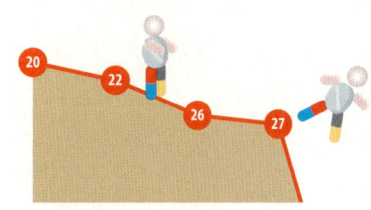

128 **Generically challenged**
Big Pharma faces a precipice

129 **The end of the affair**
Falling out of love with business

130 **Asia's green-tech rivals**
Clean-energy competition will be intense

131 **Rethinking the car industry**
Sergio Marchionne on accelerating change

Finance

133 **In the wake of a crisis**
The credit crunch ripples on

134 **Blow, then burst**
China may be inflating the next bubble

135 **Looking for a way out**
The search for "exit strategies"

136 **The lure of Africa**
Bond markets will discover its attractions

138 **Reshaping the post-crisis world**
Dominique Strauss-Kahn on stability

140 **The big boys' game**
The bankers are ready to play

141 **Ups and downs**
The gap between weak and strong banks will grow

142 **People power**
Stephen Green on the developing world

Science

145 **Introducing the transparent ocean**
The Census of Marine Life

146 **On thin ice**
An answer to the Arctic riddle

147 **The new NUE thing**
The next green revolution

148 **The fiscal frontier**
Elon Musk on commercial space travel

150 **The crisis in human genetics**
Some awkward news ahead

152 **The coming alternatives**
Novel technologies continue to advance

153 **Where have all the sunspots gone?**
The sun will surprise scientists

Obituary

154 **Bringing space down to Earth**
America's space-shuttle programme

Small world

Shakira champions education for all, *page 75*. The swine-flu pandemic will starkly reveal the gap between rich and poor, predicts **Margaret Chan**, *page 98*. A clash between Islam and the West is not inevitable, says **Susilo Bambang Yudhoyono**, *page 85*.

The long view

Time for business to emerge from survival mode: leader, *page 14*. Light at the end of the tunnel, *page 119*. **Carol Bartz** reflects on the art of leadership in the information age, *page 127*. The plot thickens for e-books, *page 122*. End of the affair for MBAs, *page 129*.

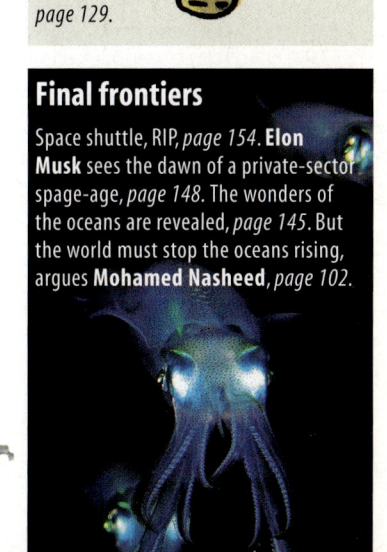

Final frontiers

Space shuttle, RIP, *page 154*. **Elon Musk** sees the dawn of a private-sector spage-age, *page 148*. The wonders of the oceans are revealed, *page 145*. But the world must stop the oceans rising, argues **Mohamed Nasheed**, *page 102*.

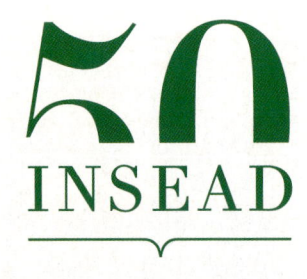

50 INSEAD
The Business School for the World®

For the past 50 years, INSEAD has done more than just research globalisation - we have lived it.

With campuses in Europe, Asia and the Middle East, alumni of more nationalities in more cities, and more customised business education programmes than any other business school, INSEAD truly is The Business School for the World.

www.insead.edu

Understand the world.
Expand your world.

The World in 2010 online

The past is prologue

How well—or badly—do our past predictions stand up? In *The World in 2006* we asked an historian, Niall Ferguson, to review our first 20 years of publication:

"It is an axiom among those who study science fiction and other literature concerned with the future that those who write it are, consciously or unconsciously, reflecting on the present. Could the same be said of The World in? *Of course."*

You can read the rest of his two-page essay, and browse an archive of editions starting with *The World in 2004*, on our website:
Economist.com/theworldin

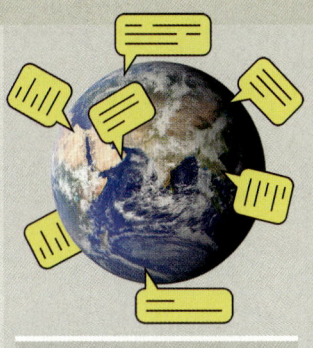

What do you predict?

All the articles in *The World in 2010* are published online, and are open to comment. What do readers think of our predictions? What are their own forecasts? Find out, and have your say.

Articles and comments:
Economist.com/theworldin

Watch out

In December 2009 we will be publishing a number of video interviews on the year ahead. Watch out for them in our multimedia player.

Video interviews:
Economist.com/audiovideo/worldin

Play time

Interactive versions of *The world in figures* pages allow you to zip from country to country and industry to industry.

Countries and industries:
Economist.com/theworldin

Now you see it

A blog on *The World in 2010* starts shortly before publication of this edition and runs until mid-December 2009. Catch it (and comment on it) while you can.

The World in 2010 blog:
Economist.com/blogs/theworldin2010

What really happens

As the year unfolds, you can find out how the forecasts in this edition fare by following analysis of global events, and debate about them.

Daily analysis and debate:
Economist.com

Listening to the future

Two end-of-year programmes of our regular podcast on the week ahead focus on the year ahead.

"The week ahead":
Economist.com/weekahead

For the first time you can also listen to the complete edition. Details are online.

The World in 2010 in audio:
Economist.com/audioedition

NYSE TECHNOLOGIES.™
TOGETHER WE POWER THE EXCHANGING WORLD.

NYSE Euronext
Powering the exchanging world.™

GLOBAL MARKET DATA • EXCHANGE SOLUTIONS • GLOBAL CONNECTIVITY • CO-LOCATION • TRADING SOLUTIONS

©2009 NYSE Euronext. All rights reserved.

We've found ways to enrich life through communication.

Today, more than one third of the world's population uses Huawei's products and services. And they talk, write, laugh and love without a hitch because our constant innovation aims to keep people connected seamlessly anytime, anywhere, on any device.

www.huawei.com

HUAWEI

The World in 2010

From the editor

The good news about 2010 is that the world will emerge from recession and the post-crisis economic landscape will become clearer. Less cheerful is what that landscape will look like.

The rich world, burdened by debt and high unemployment, faces a long, hard slog. Governments will confront difficult decisions on how fast to start withdrawing the huge support they provided to keep the financial system going. Voters will vent their anger when given the chance at the polls—kicking out Labour in Britain in May and perhaps even depriving Barack Obama of a Democratic majority in the House of Representatives in America's mid-term elections in November. Businesses will hardly feel much better, but they can at least begin to focus on strategies for future growth, rather than tactics for short-term survival.

Those strategies will place an increasing emphasis on emerging markets, many of which will power ahead. India will mark an historic transition: manufacturing will at last outweigh farming. It and other emerging giants will also make their presence felt in the G20, now the pre-eminent club for global decision-making. The presidents of three of these countries—Indonesia,

> China will be central to just about every global issue in the coming year, from the economy to climate change and nuclear diplomacy

Russia and South Africa—offer their views on 2010 in this edition.

Then there's China. It is identified as central to just about every global issue in the coming year, from the economy to climate change and nuclear diplomacy; it is becoming, with America, an "indispensable nation". In 2010 not only will China once again host big, eye-catching events (after Beijing's Olympics in 2008 it will be Shanghai's turn, with its World Expo expected to draw 70m visitors, and Guangzhou hosts the Asian Games). It will also reach two statistical landmarks: it will overtake Japan to become the world's second-largest economy; and it will arrive at the peak of its "demographic dividend", after which its dependency ratio of young and old to people in work will rise. Whether China, with its multiple growing pains, proves to be a relaxed power or a prickly one will be a central issue for 2010 and beyond.

If China is a leitmotif, readers may also detect a second running theme—or a pervasive tension. For every article about the world's woes (economic distress, environmental doom, nuclear threat) there is another about the prospect of astonishing progress (leaps in farm productivity, the take-off of private space travel, the power of ubiquitous technology). Sometimes, as with the outlook for the swine-flu pandemic, progress and distress compete in the same story. Which prevails will determine whether "the tens", the decade that begins in 2010, prove to be terrible or triumphant.

One triumph is assured in 2010: on July 11th the world will watch a proud team win the FIFA World Cup in South Africa. Off the football field, Qatar will be a champion: the only country expected to achieve double-digit growth, it will also boast the largest man-made structure in centuries when it completes its Ras Laffen gas plant. At the other end of the league Somalia, plagued by poverty, piracy and civil war, wins our unwanted award as the world's worst country.

Some of the predictions in this volume are safe: we know that 2010 will be the 300th anniversary of Meissen porcelain, the 200th of Frédéric Chopin and of independence for several Latin American countries, the 100th for Girl Guides and the 50th for the laser. Others are more speculative: we suggest bicycles and white wine, among other things, will be cool, whereas MBAs won't be. We identify thirty-somethings to watch in America and where to find twenty-somethings who want to save the planet. Right or wrong, this collection of forecasts offers a flavour of the year ahead—or, given the economic outlook and that one curiosity in 2010 will be efforts to cut bovine flatulence, perhaps a whiff of it.

Daniel Franklin
editor, *The World in 2010*

ADVERTISEMENT

❯ You have the chance to power your own city.

How will you do it?

There are lots of ideas about how to meet a growing energy demand. Here's a chance to try out a few of your own.

Energyville is an online game that lets you choose from a wide range of energy sources to meet the demands of your very own city. Alternatives. Renewables. Oil. Gas. What should be developed? Is conservation the answer? What about safeguarding the environment? See the effect your choices have, then share those results with others.

Energyville is a lot more than just a game. It's a chance to better understand and discuss the energy challenges we all face, then find the inspiration and know-how to solve them.

Put your ideas to work at willyoujoinus.com

Energyville, from Chevron
An energy game developed by The Economist Group.

Chevron | The Economist Group

CHEVRON and the CHEVRON HALLMARK are registered trademarks of Chevron Intellectual Property LLC.
© 2009 Chevron Corporation. All rights reserved.

The hard slog ahead

It will be a year of small advances for the West, argues **John Micklethwait**; better that, though, than big retreats

"The commercial storm leaves its path strewn with ruin," Alfred Marshall, a Victorian economist, once observed of financial crises. "When it is over, there is calm, but a dull, heavy calm." That sounds a pessimistic way to approach 2010, a year which promises recovery. But think again. Not only does subdued growth seem the most likely path next year; it is enormously better than the alternative—heading back into the storm. This is a year in which politicians, especially in the West, will do better to err on the safe side, and not just with the economy. Both America and Britain in particular could see some fairly storm-tossed politics.

A weak, jobless recovery should set the scene in many countries. In 2009 world output probably shrank by more than 1% (on a purchasing-power-parity basis)—the first time since 1945 that the global economy actually got smaller. By the second half of the year all the world's big economies had stopped shrinking, and optimists hope this will build into a sharp v-shaped bounceback. Sadly, the signs point towards a more gradual recovery (see leader, "Not so fast").

True, there will be patches of perkiness in the emerging world. During this crisis India and especially China have powered ahead; there are even worries about a Beijing bubble, of rising house and share prices, helped by the undervalued yuan.

Others have done well too. An increasingly confident Indonesia may well replace sluggish, kleptocratic Russia in the club of emerging superstars: the BRICs could become the BICIs. But even in the emerging world much of the growth will still come from government stimulus, rather than sustained private demand. And these economies, though growing fast, are not big enough to haul up the rest of the world.

The American consumer, who selflessly provided so much of the demand in the previous boom, will surely keep her hands mostly in her pockets in 2010: American family balance-sheets are weighed down with debt and there is the spectre of still-rising unemployment. By the end of the crunch as many as 25m people may have lost their jobs in the rich OECD countries: unemployment rates of "one in ten" could be the norm. In continental Europe personal debts are relatively low, but the banks look sickly. Japan, worn out by years of deflation, hardly seems ready to lead the way.

Indeed, Japan serves as a warning: it takes a long time to recover from balance-sheet recessions, and policymakers have to pull off some difficult tricks. Fighting deflation first, but keep-

> For Barack Obama, the calm looks likely to be especially onerous

John Micklethwait: editor-in-chief, *The Economist*; co-author of "God Is Back: How the Global Rise of Faith Is Changing the World" (Penguin/Allen Lane)

ing an eye on inflation; cleansing the banks rapidly, but keeping credit lines open; providing fiscal stimulus, but spelling out a way to cut public debts. Do all these things well and the recovery could be more v-shaped; get them wrong and a w soon appears. Given the record of central banks and treasuries thus far—a little slow and clumsy, but far more systematic than Japan in the 1990s—the best bet is somewhere in that dull heavy middle. Western economies will grow, but struggle with large deficits, heavy public debts and stubborn unemployment.

Politics will also play a role. For Barack Obama, the calm looks likely to be especially onerous. Even if he has a health-care reform bill before the year starts, that carries risks. In political terms, he will "own" health care: suddenly every shortcoming in America's system—each delayed appointment, insurance wrangle or botched operation—will be his fault. And in 2010 Afghanistan will be "his" war, its miseries laid at his door.

The delights of dullness

This hard slog will surely bring some joy for Republicans in the November mid-terms; but it will also reveal more about this opaque president. In 2009 there was plenty of flam—symbolised by the meaningless Nobel peace prize, awarded for good intentions. Can he be tough, not just with Iran, Russia and North Korea but also with allies such as Germany (over troops in Afghanistan) or Israel (over settlements in Palestine)? Can he lead the way on climate change, the ultimate hard slog? Will he drift to the left, as businesspeople fear? Will he stand up to the protectionists in his party—or can we expect more sorry populism, such as the tariffs on Chinese tyres?

For British politicians the going will be even heavier. Gordon Brown faces the grim prospect of probable defeat in a May election. For David Cameron, any joy in the Tories regaining power after 13 years will soon be muted by the fiscal mess Mr Brown will have left behind. Huge spending cuts beckon. At its best this offers a chance to reinvent government; but, given the vulnerability of Britain's economy, the timing will be tricky.

The Anglo-Saxon distress will doubtless prompt *Schadenfreude* across the English Channel. But Europe too has its woes: inflexible labour markets withstand recession well but are slow to recover. For all their banker-bashing rhetoric, Angela Merkel and Nicolas Sarkozy are likely to push ahead with mild deregulation. After eight years of wrangling about the Lisbon treaty, the European Union would be wise to find a few opt-outs for Mr Cameron (to shut up his more rabid Eurosceptics), and then focus on the single market and further enlargement.

None of this will be quick. After two years of drama—economic collapse, rollercoaster markets, Mr Obama's election—2010 may feel rather dull. Better that than the alternative. ■

Now for the long term

It's time for businesses to think about the future again, says **Matthew Bishop**

For companies, the past year has been first and foremost about short-term survival. In 2010 the challenge will be to refocus on the long term. In many ways, this will be the harder part of the recovery. Keeping the show on the road during a period of turmoil required certain skills, but setting a company on the right course afterwards will provide the true test of corporate leadership.

A focus on the short term became essential as the global economy slumped in the aftermath of the financial panic that followed the collapse of Lehman Brothers in September 2008. With even blue-chip companies such as General Electric struggling to get the funds they needed, cash became king, and firms slashed any costs that were not essential to keeping the profitable—or at least cash-flow-generating—parts of their business going. True, the stronger, better-run firms took care to cut fat rather than muscle, and may as a result emerge from the crisis with a new edge over their less surgical rivals. But even for them the economic shock and massive uncertainty about the future ensured that prudence and risk-aversion trumped any loftier long-term ambition.

To survive the crisis, there may have been no alternative to this obsessive concentration on the short term, yet it was the endemic short-termism of the business world that got it into the mess in the first place. As it piled up debt to fund ever riskier bets, the financial system put itself in a position where only massive intervention by the world's governments kept it going. In its dealings with companies, the financial system spread the same short-termist virus that led to its own undoing, creating in the boardrooms of too many firms a belief that nothing mattered as much as the next profit announcement and the next day's share price.

In 2010 there will be much debate about the first, and most politically charged, step in shifting the entire system to a longer-term focus: redesigning how corporate executives are paid. In finance, short-term bonuses paid for doing a deal long before ▶

> If business leaders do not act decisively in 2010 to redesign pay to encourage long-termism, they are likely to regret it

Matthew Bishop: American business editor, *The Economist*; co-author of "The Road from Ruin: How to Revive Capitalism and Put America Back on Top" (to be published by Crown Business in 2010)

Reading. Writing.
And redefining the classroom.

Intel has trained more than 6 million teachers to promote problem solving, critical thinking and collaboration in the classroom. Using these skills, students at one school in India educated their village about polio and provided vaccinations for underserved children. Learn more at intel.com/inside.

(intel®)

Sponsors of Tomorrow.™

Advertising feature

*Health reform: a global issue

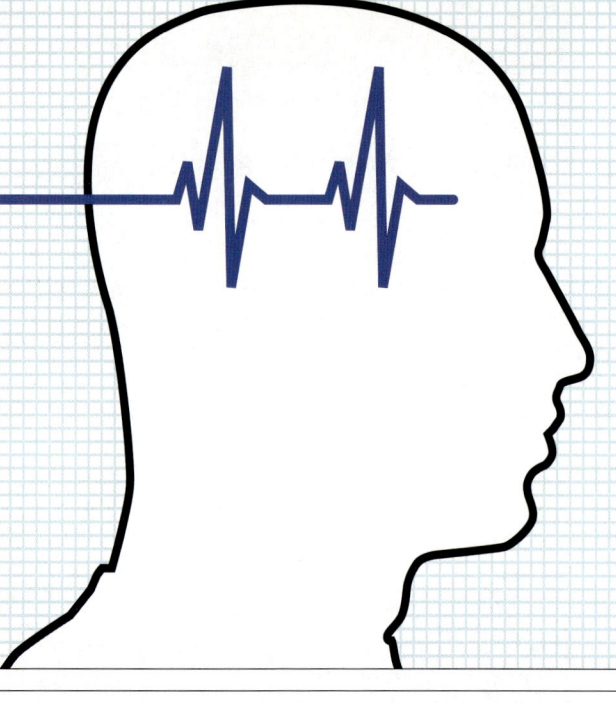

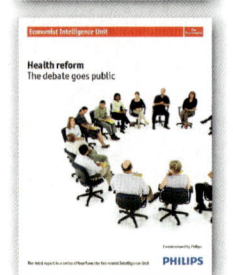

Healthcare systems around the world are creaking under the strain of rising demand. In the US, the president, Barack Obama, is pushing for reform on a massive scale. The UK's 60-year-old National Health Service is overstretched, presenting a huge challenge for whichever party comes to power in 2010. In developing countries such as India and China, citizens' expectations are forcing governments to undertake a radical review of the way healthcare is delivered. And after the crisis, constraints on public finances will create the need to achieve more with less.

The Economist Intelligence Unit has conducted a major programme of research, commissioned by Philips, to explore this hugely important issue.

Understand the issues.
Read the in-depth reports, stakeholder surveys and case studies from the Economist Intelligence Unit exploring future directions for healthcare systems. Download the reports free at *www.GetInsideHealth.com*

Hear the experts.
Watch interviews and discussions with a wide range of experts, Dr James Rohack, the president of the American Medical Association, Sir Liam Donaldson, the UK's Chief Medical Officer, and the Clinton Global Initiative, on why health reforms are crucial.

Have your say.
What do you feel should be the focus of health reforms? See how your views compare with the insights of more than 2,000 citizens and healthcare professionals in special benchmarking surveys on the site.

For more exclusive content and analysis on health and wellbeing from the Economist Intelligence Unit and other leading commentators, including research, news, videos and more, visit *www.GetInsideHealth.com*

PHILIPS

it became clear whether the deal was a good one fostered a culture of irresponsibility known as IBGYBG: "I'll be gone, you'll be gone." That needs to be replaced with a bonus formula that ensures dealmakers retain some skin in the game until the merits or otherwise of the deal are clear.

Likewise, too many share and share-option schemes encouraged short-termism, rewarding bosses for doing things that boosted their firm's share price long enough for them to cash in, but at the expense of investing in the long-term value of the company. Although it makes sense for senior executives to receive a large part of their compensation in shares of the firm they lead, to ensure their interests are aligned as closely as possible with those of the majority of shareholders, they should be required to retain those stakes until at least a year after they leave the company.

If business leaders do not act decisively in 2010 to redesign pay to encourage long-termism, they are likely to regret it. Politicians have already responded to public anger at overpaid executives, especially those who got rich while bringing the global economy to its knees. The longer compensation remains unreformed by the corporate world, the more politicians will intervene—probably in ways that discourage wealth creation by simply capping the amounts that executives are allowed to earn. The far smarter way is to design schemes that pay well those who perform well but do not (unlike much existing executive compensation) reward failure.

Let this be the start of a beautiful relationship
Reforming pay alone will not guarantee a more long-term approach. That will require a transformation of corporate governance more broadly, both in the boardroom and in the relations between senior executives, directors and the institutional shareholders who increasingly dominate the ownership of companies. These institutional owners—pension funds, mutual funds and the like—deserve much of the blame for short-termism, because of their obsession with today's share price, their preference for frequent buying and selling of shares over building lasting relationships with firms they invest in and their unwillingness to

It's nuts to eat it now

vote their proxies thoughtfully, especially when that means going against the wishes of management.

In 2010 the public should turn its attention to how to get these institutions, which manage the retirement savings of most people, to focus on long-term value creation, including by redefining what it means to be a responsible fiduciary. It would help if business leaders, who have as much to gain as anyone from a better long-term relationship with shareholders, played a positive role in this debate, instead of indulging in knee-jerk opposition to all attempts to improve corporate governance.

Strategy and seismic shifts
A longer-term focus will see companies change in three ways that ought anyway to follow from the structural shifts in the global economy that have been accelerated by the crisis. One is more investment in innovation, not least in developing cheaper products that address the needs of the new "frugal consumer". Another is an even greater concentration on emerging economies such as China, which are already returning to strong growth, something unlikely to happen soon in the big developed markets. Forward-thinking rich-world multinationals will relocate more of their bosses to developing countries, so that they can better understand those markets. There will also be a growing emphasis on good corporate citizenship, especially on strategies that aim to "do well by doing good", as firms try to convince the public of their newfound long-termism by demonstrating that their activities are not just making money but are also building a better world.

If all this sounds simple, it won't be. There is a danger that long-termism, as it has often been in the past, will be used by bosses as an excuse for avoiding tough but necessary short-term decisions. Equally, bosses will be tempted to avoid costly or difficult long-term decisions on the ground that, as John Maynard Keynes put it, "In the long run we are all dead." Yet, as executives shape their strategies for 2010 and beyond, one lesson from their recent experience should be clear: unless the business world takes a more sustainable approach, it is unlikely to be long before the next crisis comes around. ■

Europe's chance

The European Union must use the Lisbon treaty, not abuse it, advises Edward Carr

The moment when the Lisbon treaty becomes law, probably around the start of 2010, will seem to many in the European Union like a blessed relief—a halt to eight years of haggling, to the repeated rejection of a European constitution and to an obsession with the union's internal pipework. The treaty's ratification is all of those things. But it also marks the beginning of something. Armed with the treaty, Europe could pack more of a punch in the world, or it could suffer from a trial of strength between the European Parliament and the union's other centres of power. Which will it be?

You do not have to be a British Eurosceptic to break out in a rash at the very mention of the Lisbon treaty. The exercise was supposed to make the EU more democratic and to help its 27 members work together. In fact the treaty's hundreds of baffling, jargon-strewn pages seem designed to punish any citizen unwise enough to take an interest. Worse, the treaty ended up being forced through, after voters rejected the overall project in France, the Netherlands and (first time round) Ireland.

Despite that, the Lisbon treaty matters—for what it does, what it fails to do and what it leaves ambiguous. Chief among its provisions are a charter of fundamental rights, a tighter limit on countries' vetoes, a say over almost all legislation (though not a veto) for the European Parliament, and two new top Eurodogs: a permanent president for the council that contains Europe's 27 government heads, and a new foreign-policy supremo.

Lisbon is also remarkable for what it leaves undone. The treaty drops an embarrassing attempt to echo the rousing words of America's constitution. On grand, anthem-worthy occasions Europeans will be spared having to stumble through Beethoven's "Ode to Joy". And unlike all the EU's other treaties—Maastricht, Nice and so on—Lisbon contains no plans for the next great piece of reform.

This absence, and all those lost referendums, carry a message: the great treaty-drafting machine that has kept European integration pressing forward for decades has, for now, seized up. Federalists who sought integration by pursuing first a grandiose constitution and then, by hook or by crook, the Lisbon treaty have won a Pyrrhic victory. As the EU has enlarged towards the east, it has ended up defining itself as a club of nation states.

Behold the Lord High Representative

What those states now make of it depends partly on the treaty's ambiguities. In Britain large parts of the Conservative Party, which looks set to take power in 2010, would like to sabotage the whole business. That will not happen. The new prime minister, David Cameron, will take great pains to avoid a row that could wreck his government. He has greater ambitions and indebted, troubled Britain faces greater problems.

Instead, the disputes are more likely to take place in Brussels. The European Parliament, bent on extending its own influence in spite of its weak democratic mandate, will fight with the commission and the council of ministers—rather as it did in the summer of 2009, when it delayed the approval of José Manuel Barroso as head of the commission. Members of Europe's parliament tend to believe in regulation and intervention. They will seek to inject soggy corporatism into financial reform, the promotion of high-tech industry, climate-change policy and the other areas the EU wants to address in 2010.

> Unlike all the EU's other treaties, Lisbon contains no plans for the next great piece of reform

So a vital task for the EU in the year ahead will be to defend Europe's beleaguered economy against this and against attacks on the single market by states keen to be seen protecting jobs amid rising unemployment. The other task is foreign policy, perhaps the treaty's main achievement.

Europe's foreign policy is chaotic partly because 27 countries often want different things, but also because of the poor organisation of teams that rotate every six months. The new president of the council and the "high representative" for foreign affairs may sound as if they have wandered off the set of "The Mikado", but they could have clout and resources. They could boost the EU's place in the world—if only EU governments let them. Having bungled the creation of the Lisbon treaty, Europe should now strive to make it work. ■

Edward Carr: foreign editor, *The Economist*

Royal Bank of Canada

Strength
to move forward.

For over 140 years, we've made it our business to focus on the fundamentals and consistently deliver results.

That's why RBC is one of the top 10 largest financial institutions globally, with a market capitalisation over USD70 billion and net income of USD4.4 billion in 2008.

This strength allows us to continue to build our client relationships in the current market and deliver focused expertise, insightful thinking, and proven execution, every day.

It's time. Put our strength to work.

www.rbc.com/moveforward

Capital Markets – Banking – Wealth Management – Insurance

® The Lion & Globe design and RBC are registered trademarks of Royal Bank of Canada. © Copyright 2009.

Not so fast

Robin Bew sees mostly disappointment for the global economy in 2010

Chinese exceptionalism
2010, % change on previous year

	US	EURO ZONE	CHINA
GDP	2.4	0.6	8.6
Personal spending	1.2	0.4	8.8
Investment	1.9	-0.2	11.1

Source: Economist Intelligence Unit

Since April 2009 journalists have been writing of green shoots, economists have been reporting rising output and investors have gleefully pocketed big gains on their equity portfolios. But for many households the good news seemed to pass them by. Millions of jobs disappeared, home-loan defaults mounted and corporate restructuring made the workplace distinctly unsettling. Will the recovery that started in the final months of 2009 bring wider relief in the year ahead?

Perhaps not. Much of the lift in 2009 came from two sources. First, factories that shut down when global demand slumped reopened to restock nearly-empty shelves. Second, massive public-spending programmes began to feed through, taxes were cut and central banks slashed interest rates.

But what happens in 2010 when the warehouses are full again? Production could grind to a halt unless sales of fridges, cars and clothing pick up. There is little chance of that happening until battered consumers shed debt and recover their nerve, and that seems unlikely as long as unemployment remains high. Governments, meanwhile, can't fund the recovery for ever. Most central banks have cut interest rates as much as they can and flooded the financial system with cash. Public spending can stay high, but further increases would be unaffordable in most countries. So 2010 could be a disappointment. The recovery will be a longer slog than many expect.

> The recovery will be a longer grind than many expect

The dragon's tail

As usual, the story is brighter in the emerging world, although even here there are nuances. China remains the place to watch. The collapsing American and European economies flattened China's exports, but the government produced the mother of all stimulus packages. That, combined with a lending boom (when China's bankers are told to lend, they lend), was enough to keep the economy purring along at 8%: slower than before, yes, but still impressive. Unlike most other countries, China can afford to do it again in 2010, if necessary. To be sure, a state-directed spending boom does not inspire deep confidence, and China's economy remains unbalanced—too much saving, too little consumption. But those long-term problems will not prevent another year of 8%-plus growth in 2010.

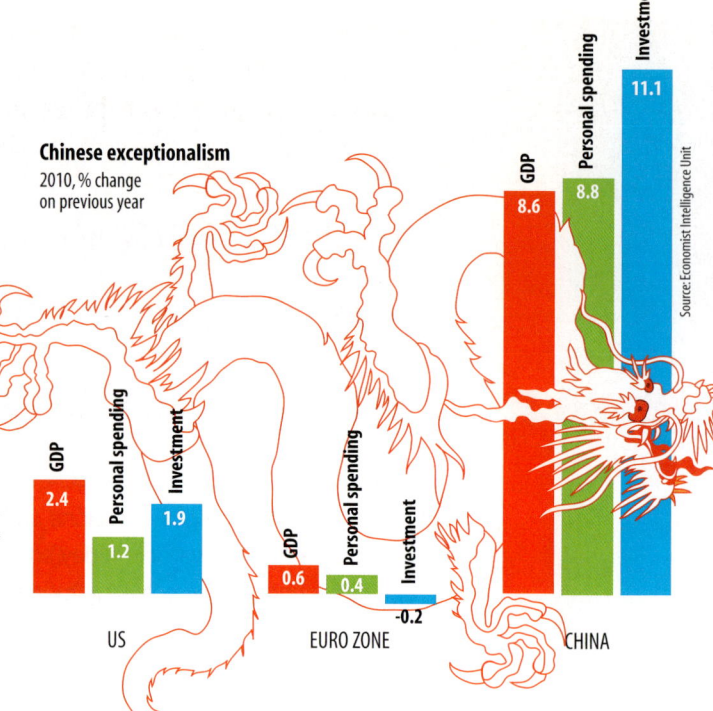

Plenty of other economies will benefit from China's success. Its state-backed infrastructure projects are boosting demand for the exports of other Asian countries, and commodity producers from Australia to Brazil will be dragged along by the dragon's tail. India should also pick up, assuming a better harvest than in 2009. Eastern Europe is a real worry, burdened with too much debt and with too few solvent customers in their west European export markets.

Two things will become clearer in 2010. First, in the rich world hopes of a v-shaped recovery will be laid to rest; the excesses of the past seven years will take more than a few good months to fix. Second, in the developing world, government spending will keep the factories churning while policymakers try to rebalance their economies for long-term growth. In China, that means more pressure for reforms that will help persuade consumers to start spending their hard-earned savings.

Policymakers in the West will mostly have to content themselves with not making the situation worse. Take trade: the global economy would benefit from a trade-liberalising Doha deal, but as unemployment rises governments will have their work cut out just to keep protectionism at bay. Similarly with public spending: much as governments might love to pump more cash into their fragile economies, ballooning national debts will make that hard. And central bankers will struggle to do more than raise interest rates modestly, as worries about recovery trump fears of inflation.

So, after hectic crisis-management, 2010 will be a quieter time for policy. With luck that will allow governments to focus on their next big task—drawing up credible plans for bringing their bloated budget deficits under control. ■

Robin Bew: editorial director and chief economist, Economist Intelligence Unit

For healthy growth, just add Bahrain.

low operating costs

world-class financial centre

zero corporate tax, 100% foreign ownership

zero income tax, one-stop shop for start-ups

gateway to the Gulf, excellent transport links

strong central bank, advanced telecoms infrastructure

low labour costs, highly skilled workforce

US free trade agreement

Even in a climate of fiscal aridity, delicate seedlings have to be tended. Bahrain provides an ideal environment in which to do just that; a complete economic ecosystem, in fact, providing business with essential support and sustenance. This is perhaps why so many multinationals – from Microsoft to Citibank to Kraft – have already planted themselves on Bahraini soil. The track record – theirs and ours – demonstrates what fertile ground it is. Ground where green shoots of recovery stand the best possible chance of not mere survival, but of a blooming future. For gardening tips, visit bahrain.com

business *friendly* **BAHRAIN**

Smart states

Government is getting bigger. Can it get better as well, asks **Adrian Wooldridge**?

The world will need smart government more than ever in 2010. The state is becoming bigger, thanks in large part to the emergency measures taken to avert economic collapse. But the resources to support the Leviathan are limited, with tax revenues shrinking and public debt ballooning. This is raising a question with increasing urgency: can governments learn to do more with less? Can they, in other words, become smarter?

Their expansion has been dramatic. Governments intervened to prop up capitalist Goliaths, such as Citigroup and General Motors, and to boost falling demand. The American Recovery and Reinvestment Act represents 5.4% of GDP, 70% of which remains to be spent. Fourteen years after Bill Clinton announced that the "era of big government is over", big government is back with a vengeance.

Happily, the crisis has given states some of the tools they need to improve their jobs. A big constraint on smart government is the difficulty of getting smart people to work for the public sector. But with so many of the private sector's great hiring machines sputtering, governments have been given a once-in-a-generation chance to hire the best and the brightest.

Governments have plenty of models to draw upon. During the Swedish economic crisis in the mid-1990s the government succeeded in shaving 11% off its budgets without any apparent damage to performance. The British government boasts that it has squeezed £26.5 billion ($43.4 billion) in "improved efficiencies" out of the civil service.

The apostles of smart government also have the ideological wind in their sails. Barack Obama, America's most glamorous president since Kennedy, preaches a brand of post-ideological pragmatism. "The question we ask today is not whether our government is too big or too small," he said in his inaugural address, "but whether it works." He wants to use government to fine-tune the market rather than to strong-arm it: to look after the losers in the health system, to encourage green investment and curb America's appetite for sugary drinks.

But there is mounting evidence that governments have missed a trick. They have hired a few smart people: central banks and regulatory agencies have been scooping up business-school graduates who would normally not have given them a second glance, for example. The money flooding into the economy will create some green jobs. But they have squandered more than they have achieved. Emergency spending is funding a huge number of make-work projects. Government hiring has been slow. Companies chafe at the bureaucracy involved in acquiring government funding for green jobs.

Attempts to reform government have always had a mixed record. States are lumbering dinosaurs that take years to adapt to change. And they are plagued by rigidities that make it hard to hire the best or sack the worst. When competing for the best people, most governments have a "tool belt but no tools", to borrow a phrase from the director of the United States Office of Personnel Management.

What a waste

The depth of the crisis has forced governments to focus on the short term. They have also been more interested in preserving jobs than in structural reforms. Construction companies with shovel-ready projects are swallowing up a disproportionate amount of the stimulus money. Mr Obama made the fatal mistake of sub-contracting a great deal of policymaking to Congress, which loaded his stimulus package with pork.

All this suggests that 2010 will be another year of disappointment: instead of getting smarter, governments will succumb to the old cycle of bloat followed by retrenchment. And the recovery of the private sector will rob them of their chance to restock their talent pools. During the economic slump the Obama government liked to say that "a crisis is a terrible thing to waste." Over the next year it will become increasingly obvious that, when it comes to getting smarter, governments almost everywhere have wasted this particular crisis. ■

Adrian Wooldridge: management editor, *The Economist;* co-author of "God Is Back: How the Global Rise of Faith Is Changing the World" (Penguin/Allen Lane)

www.barcap.com

EARN SUCCESS EVERYWHERE.

At Barclays Capital our world revolves around expanding yours. Centred on your business, our integrated approach to client coverage gives you access to a wide range of expertise across geographies, industries and investment banking products. As a leader in all asset classes in the Americas, Asia Pacific and EMEA, we deliver worldwide financial solutions combined with seamless execution – all to extend your global reach. From global portfolio offerings to cross-border advisory, we can help you get wherever you need to go to succeed.

Earn Success Every Day

BARCLAYS CAPITAL

Issued by Barclays Bank PLC, authorised and regulated by the Financial Services Authority and a member of the London Stock Exchange, Barclays Capital is the investment banking division of Barclays Bank PLC, which undertakes US securities business in the name of its wholly-owned subsidiary Barclays Capital Inc., an SIPC and FINRA member. ©2009 Barclays Bank PLC. All rights reserved. Barclays Capital is a trademark of Barclays Bank PLC.

IT'S ALWAYS

Next-Generation 737. Continually

BOEING

THE NEXT-GENERATION.

advancing technology to advance your success. Find out more. www.boeing.com

737

Wanted: green engineers

The world needs more of them, notes **Oliver Morton**

Regardless of the outcome of the Copenhagen conference in December 2009, one of the most pressing anti-climate-change needs will be the ability to get things done in 2010 and beyond. The commitments already made by some large economies require an extremely large capacity to get new energy systems in place quickly. That includes making sure that there are the people around to design and build them.

The infrastructure needed to make a large dent in the world's emissions is daunting. What is unusual is not the scale of investment, but that much of it has to be spent on new capabilities. With the use of coal worldwide expected to double by 2030, for example, carbon capture and storage (ccs) technologies will be crucial. The amount of pipelining, geological surveying and chemical engineering needed for this is not unprecedented compared with what already exists in the oil, gas and mining industries. But it is vastly larger than today's ccs capacity, and the people needed cannot just be borrowed from the current fossil-fuel industry.

The nuclear industry is also bedevilled by labour-force issues, at all skill levels. For the past few decades very few Western countries have been producing nuclear engineers; if the nuclear industry is to expand again, over the next decade it will need thousands of engineers who are at present nowhere to be found. And if the supply of expert engineers is tight for builders and operators, it will be tight for regulators, too—regulators who will be sorely needed if a new generation of nuclear-power plants is to enjoy, and deserve, public confidence.

Renewables do not face these issues in quite so pressing a form; the solar and wind industries reap the benefits of the production line in ways that nuclear and carbon-capture technologies, with their large installations, do not. This is one of the reasons that governments like renewables: they provide jobs. Retrofitting homes for greater energy efficiency also offers this advantage on a large scale (which makes one wonder why it is not a higher priority). Even so the renewables sector will also be competing for designers and engineers.

To a large extent this is a market problem that markets can solve; if the demand is created, companies will find ways to get the work done. But there are some specific things that governments can do to help. One is to fund research with a strong emphasis on energy engineering and science. New breakthroughs, however welcome, are not the point here; though new technologies will be a boon in the 2030s and 2040s, the realities of large-scale change mean that, for the moment, energy transformation is a come-as-you-are party. But breakthroughs are not the only thing research produces. Nuclear engineers are scarce in part because there has been little ongoing research to captivate students.

> The people needed cannot just be borrowed from the fossil-fuel industry

Isambard's kingdom to come

Another smart policy will be to re-examine the extent to which governments subsidise high-tech jobs in other industries, notably defence, tying up talent. There are a lot of opportunities in green technology for laid-off missile designers. A third idea, for those who can afford it, is to reap the benefits of the educational successes of other countries by importing people from places where many aspire to become, and qualify as, engineers.

Who wants to be an engineer?

And it would be nice to find ways to spread that aspiration more widely. In a number of countries (Britain is an example) engineering does not carry much cultural cachet. A pride in the engineered past—remember Isambard Brunel—is accompanied by apathy towards the engineering of the present. It is neither fruitful nor desirable for governments to meddle in broad cultural attitudes. But leaders of the environmental movement, and politicians who aspire to such leadership, might do well to encourage the young to apply their idealism to their choice of career path.

It's all very well to recycle, pester your parents about fuel efficiency and aspire to holidays that need no flights. But the best thing a bright young person can do to help rid civilisation of fossil fuels is get an education in engineering. ■

Oliver Morton: environment editor, *The Economist;* author of "Eating the Sun: How Plants Power the Planet" (Harper/Fourth Estate)

FOR THE NEW ENERGY FUTURE
WE NEED TO TURN MORE IDEAS INTO ACTION.

The world needs more energy and less CO_2. To meet that challenge we need to turn bright ideas into workable solutions – and then make those solutions a reality.

We're working on a range of innovative projects. Some are still on the drawing board – like developing ways to produce fuel from algae and straw. Others are already being delivered to our customers in many parts of the world – like cleaner coal technology.

At the same time we are making our existing fuels cleaner and more efficient, and working on technology to manage CO_2 emissions.

To find out how Shell is helping prepare for the new energy future visit
www.shell.com/newenergyfuture

More than a number

What to call the next ten years, muses **Adam Roberts**

The beginning of wisdom is to call things by their right names, advises a Chinese proverb. A little wisdom would be welcome now, as the world turns its back on the naughty noughties and its years of economic calamity, ill-judged war, terrorism and man-made climate change. So here is a challenge for the forthcoming decade, beginning in 2010 and ending in 2019: find the right name by which to call it.

Despite a human fondness for sticking labels on all that moves (Adam started it), this is not a task to be entered into lightly. A namer takes on a heavy burden, as any new parent could report. Blunders with names may stick for life. The Dwyers will not be forgiven by their teenage daughter, Barb; the Balls are blamed for a lack of foresight in christening young Crystal. Some mistakes are so grave that officials step in. A New Zealand judge ordered that a miserable nine-year-old girl be allowed to drop her given name, "Talula Does The Hula From Hawaii", in favour of something less awful. And officials in the same country also stopped the parents of newborn twins who had tried to register one as "Fish" and the other as "Chips".

All names carry baggage. A survey in 2009, for example, exposed the prejudice of British teachers, who admitted to judging children long before their arrival in the classroom. From a glance at the register they routinely expect particular pupils to be mischievous (they tremble at a list of Chardonnays, Caseys, Jacks, Daniels and Callums, apparently) and others to be angelic swots (the Alexanders, Charlottes and Rebeccas). Perhaps this reflects a British obsession with class, but the study demonstrates how your name flies ahead of you, helping to establish a first impression, for good or ill.

Businesses know this well. Slip up with branding and giggling consumers are unlikely to part with their money, however attractive your latest product might otherwise be. Pity carmakers, for example, who are compelled to dream up new names for their many models. The Dodge Swinger (launched in 1969) surely appealed only to a few broad-minded buyers.

> The next decade, with its awkward teen years, presents a special challenge

Spanish speakers were never keen on Mazda's Laputa ("the whore" on wheels).

The broad lessons are clear: steer away from the silly, the double-entendre, names associated with trouble and anything that might get the courts involved. Less clear is what specific label to pick for an era. Few time periods are honoured with descriptions, the odd *annus mirabilis* or *horribilis* aside. Neither a century nor a lustrum is typically graced with any special moniker. Yet decades, for some reason, are usually thought worthy of a name and an attached adjective. For most of the century this should not be too hard: the 20s, 30s and so on will arrive, each judged to be roaring, sinking or swinging.

But the next decade, with its awkward teen years, presents a special challenge. How about an adjective without a connecting name? One commentator on modern events, Timothy Garton Ash of Oxford University, has already written off the first years of this millennium as the "nameless decade", rather as experts on Japan lament its recession in the 1990s as the "lost decade". Or what about a new noun? The economic legacy of the past few years means that in the 2010s much of the world faces a dour "debtcade".

Tense, tentative yet tenacious

Another approach is to play with numbers. The "teens" might prove popular among younger trend-setters (even if purists protest that these begin in 2013 not 2010). The "tens" would give an audible hint of anxious times ahead; the "twenty tens" is more neutral; the "two thousand and tens" is a mouthful. Perhaps the "decas", "dekkas", or—fingers crossed for the economy—the "decadents", could prove more appealing.

Yet uncertainty hangs heavily today over geopolitics, economics, the climate and more. All this points to "tentative" 2010s. But cheer up. A lot will change over the next ten years. Sooner or later, the current angst will surely lift, giving way to a gritty optimism. So here's to the "tenacious tens". ■

Adam Roberts: online news editor, *The Economist*

Bob Greifeld, NASDAQ, said:

You're going to see more of these over the counter instruments being driven to a true market price discovery mechanism.

Larry Tabb, TABB Group, said:

The industry can't lose a half trillion dollars because of faulty risk models and do nothing about it.

WHAT HAPPENS NEXT?

We asked the finance industry's leading experts what they think will happen next to the global financial landscape.

Have your say. Join the conversation at sungard.com/whn, follow us on Twitter @SunGardFS or tweet #WHN.

©2009 SunGard
SunGard and the SunGard logo are trademarks or registered trademarks of SunGard Data Systems Inc. or its subsidiaries in the U.S. and other countries. All other trade names are trademarks or registered trademarks of their respective holders.

SUNGARD®

*References the 2008 Forbes Tax Misery & Reform Index

WEALTH YESTERDAY
TODAY TOMORROW

Qatar. A place that's changing everyday. With its world class regulation and secure and transparent rule of law, the QFC has helped Qatar to become the region's most dynamic economy, and its perfect access point. Benefit today from the lowest tax in the world.* 100% ownership, repatriation of all profits, and an onshore trading environment. And tomorrow, why not experience one of Qatar's oldest treasures?   www.qfc.com.qa

BUSINESS ENERGY

Qatar
FINANCIAL CENTRE

Calendar for 2010

Our selection of events around the world

JANUARY

Spain assumes the rotating presidency of the European Union and Pécs (in Hungary), Essen (Germany) and Istanbul (Turkey) become European capitals of culture.

The great and good from business, politics and the media puzzle out the state of the world at the World Economic Forum in Davos, Switzerland.

President Barack Obama delivers his first state-of-the-union address, telling Americans how it is.

Mr Obama's self-imposed deadline arrives for the closure of the Guantánamo Bay detention centre.

FEBRUARY

Chinese around the world welcome the Year of the Tiger, symbolising power and sensitivity (but also short tempers), just as the world's lovers, actual or would-be, celebrate St Valentine's Day.

After legal battles, controversy surrounds the 33rd America's Cup, a yachting contest for fractious billionaires.

Rio de Janeiro's hedonists revel in the world's most famous carnival. Trinidad and New Orleans do their best to compete.

American giants confront each other in Miami in football's 44th Super Bowl. Lesser mortals, by their millions, watch the game, and ads, on TV.

Costa Rica holds its presidential election.

Snow-loving athletes compete in the Winter Olympics in Vancouver, Canada.

MARCH

Musicians delight in the music of Chopin, born 200 years ago.

Hollywood rolls out the red carpet for the 82nd Academy Awards. Oscars for the film world's best come after Golden Raspberries for the film world's worst.

French-speakers around the world wax eloquent on the international day of *la francophonie*.

Canada upsets seal-lovers as it begins its annual seal hunt.

Southern-hemisphere naturists, from Australia to South Africa, celebrate their nudity with a naked bike ride.

APRIL

April Fools make fun around the world.

American households answer (supposedly) the once-in-a-decade census questionnaire.

Tiger Woods attempts to win the US Masters golf tournament in Augusta for a fifth time, just one behind Jack Nicklaus's record.

Austria holds its six-yearly presidential election, and Hungary elects a parliament. With luck the Sudanese vote in presidential and general elections—the first for many years in their war-torn nation.

Coffee-makers from around the world gather in London for the World Barista Championships.

MAY

The 189 signatories of the Nuclear Non-Proliferation Treaty meet in New York to review it.

Spare a grin for World Laughter Day.

The Philippines elects a new president and Congress.

Britain holds its general election this month, if not next.

The six-month World Expo 2010 begins in Shanghai, China.

Norway hosts the kitsch-filled Eurovision Song Contest; France hosts the star-studded Cannes film festival.

Macedonia assumes the leadership of the Council of Europe, promoting democracy and human rights.

JUNE

France celebrates the summer solstice with the Fête de la Musique: free music played outdoors, from Paris to the smallest village.

Canada hosts a summit of both the G8 and G20 in Huntsville, Ontario.

Soccer's best nations convene in South Africa for the month-long FIFA World Cup.

The tennis elite moves from the red clay of the French Open to the green grass of Wimbledon.

JULY

Belgium takes a six-month turn as president of the European Union.

Cycling's Tour de France, three weeks of athletic agony, begins, confusingly, in the Netherlands.

At the San Fermín festival, macho types—both Spanish and foreign—taunt stampeding bulls in the Pamplona bull run.

America celebrates independence on the 4th and France celebrates revolution on the 14th.

Strong men compete in Finland's wife-carrying world championship. The winner gets his wife's weight in beer.

The fashion world crowds the catwalk for the Paris Haute Couture week.

AUGUST

The deadline arrives for American combat troops to leave Iraq. Others will stay to train Iraqi soldiers and police.

Much of Europe takes a month-long holiday.

Free-flying aesthetes in the skies of Russia conclude the World Artistic Skydiving Championships.

Thousands gather in London's Notting Hill district for Europe's biggest street carnival.

Post-genocide Rwanda holds its second presidential election, with the winner in office for seven years.

SEPTEMBER

Bookworms salute International Literacy Day, designed to increase their number.

Intrepid rally-drivers meet in Beijing for the start of the Peking to Paris Motor Challenge.

The world's diplomats gather in New York for the UN General Assembly.

OCTOBER

Beer-lovers end the Munich Oktoberfest, having downed enough gallons to keep it as the world's biggest beer festival.

America's best travel to Wales to compete with Europe's best for golf's Ryder Cup.

Hawaii challenges the fittest to survive its Ironman triathlon.

Germany celebrates 20 years since unification.

The Nobel peace laureate is proclaimed in Oslo; other laureates are announced in Stockholm.

Egyptians elect a 518-member People's Assembly, with 64 seats now reserved for women, and Brazil holds presidential and general elections.

Athletes from 71 nations compete in the Commonwealth Games in Delhi, India.

NOVEMBER

Americans elect a new 435-member House of Representatives and a third of the 100-seat Senate. Some 39 states choose a governor, too.

Guangzhou in China hosts the Asian Games.

Seoul, South Korea, hosts a G20 summit.

Burkina Faso elects a president, and Azerbaijan a parliament.

Japan hosts heads of government at an Asia-Pacific Economic Co-operation summit in Yokohama.

Beautiful women and their male admirers travel to Nha Trang, Vietnam, for the 60th Miss World contest.

DECEMBER

Tanzania holds presidential, parliamentary and local elections.

Google announces the most-searched items of the year.

The Kluge prize, worth $1m, is awarded in Washington for lifetime achievement in disciplines (such as linguistics and anthropology) not covered by the Nobel prizes.

America celebrates the 390th anniversary of the landing of the Pilgrim Fathers.

The illustrations on this page, by Kevin Kallaugher, are from The Economist 2010 Wall Calendar, which is available at www.economist.com/2010calendar

With the help of contributions from foresightnews
www.foresightnews.co.uk

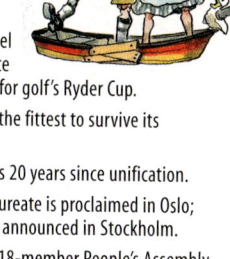

Britain

2010 IN BRIEF

Britain applies an EU-wide **art levy**, providing royalties to artists or, for 70 years, to their descendants.

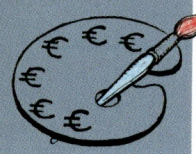

ought to inflict the worst pain immediately, so that the country feels better by the time they have to renew their mandate, Mr Cameron and boyish George Osborne, his chancellor of the exchequer, will raise VAT, a sales tax. Lots of people in Whitehall will be made redundant.

A more upbeat priority for the new government will be Swedish-style school reform, the most radical and interesting of its campaign pledges (even if the policy was actually first mooted by Mr Blair). Michael Gove, the impressive new schools secretary, will introduce legislation to allow charities, groups of parents and others to set up new secondary schools with state funding. Take-up will be slow to begin with—and there will be squeals about the diversion of funds from other bits of the education budget—but the Tories will be able to point to this one positive, potentially transformative achievement amid all the axe-wielding and tax-hiking.

That leaves the issue of Labour's next leader. Mr Brown's exit will bring a contest featuring plenty of unpalatable contenders but no obvious front-runner.

Clement Attlee used a cricketing metaphor to describe the effect of Winston Churchill's pre-eminence on the subsequent generation of Tory politicians. "It's the heavy roller," Attlee remarked. "Doesn't let the grass grow under it." The heavy rolling by Messrs Blair and Brown, dominant in the Labour Party for 16 years, means that few of their colleagues have developed independent political identities. One who has, Lord Mandelson, Mr Brown's grandiosely titled First Secretary, will be among the kingmakers in the leadership contest.

The winner will be a Miliband: David, the elder of the two brothers and hitherto the foreign secretary; or Ed, the energy secretary. But, after a humiliating election rout, as factions within the party bicker over its causes and as recriminations break out, Labour's crown will seem a shabby one to inherit. ■

The slimming cure

Paul Wallace

Britain's bloated state faces strict rations

If the Conservatives win power, as is likely, their first step will be an emergency budget. A tough budget will be essential. In 2010 Britain will run a deficit almost as high as the one in 2009, which was easily the biggest since the second world war. Public debt will reach 82% of GDP, nearly double its share in 2007.

The rise in debt is from a relatively low starting-point, but the deterioration is so rapid that bond investors are uneasy. They are expecting a new government to deliver a credible programme to get the deficit under control. If they are disappointed, Britain could lose its triple-A borrowing status and face higher interest costs, exacerbating the fiscal crisis.

George Osborne, replacing Alistair Darling as chancellor, will inherit an already unpalatable plan to rein in the deficit. As Britain's borrowing surged in 2008 and 2009, Mr Darling set out a strategy for mending the public finances after the recession ends. That entails measures to cut borrowing by over 3% of GDP by 2013. Higher taxes were to make up only a fifth of the reduction. The rest would come from lower spending, with investment in particular facing deep cuts.

But even with help from a recovering economy, the government would still be borrowing 5.5% of GDP in 2013. The Tories will want to set a lower target for the deficit and to get started earlier than Labour, whose plan essentially starts in 2011. Spending will bear the brunt of the additional cuts, although David Cameron has ringfenced the National Health Service from real cuts. There will be a public-sector pay freeze in 2011 and sharp cuts in the budgets of the other big-spending departments providing public services. The Tories will also look for big savings in the welfare bill.

The precise make-up of the emergency budget will depend upon what Mr Darling himself does in his own budget in spring 2010, with revised Treasury forecasts and details on how he will squeeze spending. This will set a new baseline against which the Tories will have to find extra economies. The good news is that the lean years will follow ten fat ones: the long expansion of the public sector has left plenty of flab that can be drawn down without biting into muscle and bone.

Even so, Mr Osborne will have to raise taxes as well as cut spending. Labour is already planning to raise nearly 1% of GDP from higher national-insurance contributions and a tax raid on higher earners, including a top rate of income tax of 50% from April 2010. But the Tory chancellor will have to raise probably another 1% of GDP in higher taxes to make up for the loss of the "bubble revenues" that poured in during the credit boom from the finance sector and buoyant asset markets.

The Conservatives have an electoral mountain to climb, so they may not win a clear majority. That could unnerve bond investors, who fear they would lack the will to do what is necessary. The health of the economy will also be crucial. The more entrenched the recovery, the earlier a fiscal clampdown can begin. But, assuming the Tories do win, their emergency budget will put Britain's bloated state on a slimming cure during the first half of the new decade. ■

Paul Wallace: Britain economics editor, *The Economist*

Brown's bulge
Public borrowing, % of GDP, financial years starting April 5th

Year	% of GDP
2010	11.9
2009	12.4
2008	6.2
2007	2.4
2006	2.3
2005	2.9
2004	3.3
2003	2.9
2002	2.3
2001	0.0
2000	–1.9
1999	–1.6
1998	–0.5
1997	0.7

Source: HM Treasury
2008-2009 estimates, 2010 forecast

Recessionomics

Anatole Kaletsky

Look at previous downturns, and stay calm

Britain, with its large financial sector and its love of property speculation, was supposed to be the big economy most vulnerable to the global financial crisis, and in terms of the government's own budget this turned out to be true. But looking at the economy more broadly, and especially at the surprising resilience of both consumer spending and business sentiment, Britain's performance has come quite close to the rosier of the two scenarios outlined here a year ago: "a common-or-garden recession, followed by a decent recovery in the second half of the year, driven by ultra-low interest rates and a competitive exchange rate."

The four main questions for the year ahead are whether this recovery can continue, what policies will be applied to help sustain it, what permanent damage has been caused and what damage-limitation policies will be adopted by the new government.

A positive answer can be offered to the first question with reasonable confidence because this recession has turned out to be surprisingly similar to previous ones. Although the decline in GDP of 5.9% from peak to trough was much deeper than the 2.5% dip in 1990-91, the present downturn was marginally shallower than the 6.0% fall in 1979-81 and it has done less damage to employment, retail sales, business confidence and even inflation-adjusted house prices than previous recessions.

Although unemployment will go on rising, as it normally does after recessions are over, the jobless figures are unlikely to reach the shock-horror 3m-3.5m considered inevitable by many economists when 2009 began. Assuming the jobless rate peaks at around 9%, Gordon Brown's recession will have been less painful for the public than the Thatcher recession of 1979-81, after which unemployment more than doubled to 11.9%, or even the Major recession of 1990-91, when it peaked at 10.7% (in 1993) and far more people lost their homes.

Economic recoveries, once they gain momentum, almost always continue unless some external force suddenly intervenes. In fact, there has never been a case of recovery spontaneously aborting in Britain (or America) through lack of consumer demand. (Germany and Japan, by contrast, have experienced several such interrupted recoveries, largely because of employment arrangements that stretch out job losses over many years.) On the rare occasions when British recoveries have aborted, the reason was clear: interest rates were drastically increased, to ward off inflation or to "defend" sterling.

Which leads to the next question: what policies will Britain see in 2010? On the monetary side, the Bank of England has made its intentions unusually clear. Interest rates will be kept at exceptionally low levels, not just until economic growth is firmly re-established but until there is significant shrinkage in the very large "output gap". This is a measure of spare capacity and unemployment—and hence of potential deflationary pressures—favoured by many central banks. Since no big reduction of the output gap is likely until 2011, interest rates will remain very low into 2011 and probably beyond.

The main damage done by the crisis, the collapse of government finances, is ironically another reason why British interest rates will remain at rock-bottom levels much longer than businesses and homeowners generally expect. If the new government has the courage to attack the deficit, it will expect low interest rates as a quid pro quo—and the Bank of England will be happy to oblige, since its internal models suggest monetary stimulus really will be needed to offset the deflationary effects of serious budget cuts. Moreover, such is the size of the hole in government finances that many years of fiscal retrenchment will be required. Thus a combination of ever-tighter fiscal policy with surprisingly low interest rates will dominate British macroeconomic policy until the middle of the new decade.

> There has never been a case of recovery aborting in Britain through lack of consumer demand

What us, panic?

The imperative of long-term fiscal retrenchment raises the final, and most interesting, question about Britain's prospects: will politicians dare to undertake the fiscal tightening needed to stabilise public debt at a reasonable level? The retrenchment required can appear impossibly daunting. But the British government remains one of the world's most creditworthy borrowers, so it has the luxury of tackling its budgetary problems over several years. If the directors of any private company sent their department heads an instruction to cut costs by 2% a year without sacrificing customer service, this would hardly be considered a managerial nightmare. Any leader who could instil private-sector attitudes towards productivity growth and cost control into the management of the public sector would be hailed as the saviour of the British economy. ■

2010 IN BRIEF
After a two-year refurbishment, London's luxurious **Savoy hotel** reopens for business.

Anatole Kaletsky: partner, GaveKal Research; editor at large, the *Times*. Author of "Capitalism 4.0: How the Global Economy Evolves Through Crises" (to be published by Bloomsbury/Public Affairs in 2010)

JOY IS TIMELESS.

Joy is now and forever. New yet eternal. Joy is desire that shouts out loud. Design that stands the test of time. Joy knows that what you make people feel is as important as what you make. It's what is yearned for. It's what BMW was born for. Joy doesn't waste a second. The story of Joy continues at bmw.co.uk/joy

JOY IS BMW.

BMW

www.bmw.co.uk
Tel. 0800 777 120

The Ultimate
Driving Machine

Advantage, Hong Kong

Merril Stevenson

The players' spirits are reviving in the City, but the game is not what it was

In the effort to restore Britain's economy in 2010, few measures will matter more than those touching the battered City of London. Because financial services loom so large—accounting for about 8% of national output and 14% of government revenues—a City on its pinstriped knees has contributed heavily to the appalling slide of the public finances.

The worst seems over. In March 2009 share prices began a long bull run. Mergers and acquisitions are stirring; house prices have risen in the bits of London bankers favour; and—controversially—bonuses are back. The City is emerging from the crisis.

Yet it is not to business as usual. For two years, bankers, hedge-fund managers, private-equity whizzes and the like have been blamed for the excesses that led to taxpayers' money being poured into bad banks. Where once it was seen as an international money-spinner to cherish, today there is talk of slimming the City and rebalancing the economy. The rules are being tightened. London is losing the distinctive "light-touch" regulation that helped make it the centre it was.

Three things in 2010 will affect whether the City manages to retain its pre-eminence. The first is the general election. The Tories, the likely winners, want to return bank supervision to the Bank of England. But as important as the regulatory (and tax) regime they put in place is the general climate. Though the Tories have done their share of talking tough about bankers' bonuses, and will accept for now Labour's new 50% top rate of income tax, they may reassure financial folk of their benevolence in a way that Labour no longer does. A Tory victory may mean fewer removal vans on the road to Switzerland.

A second factor will be how aggressively the European Union exploits Britain's loss of regulatory reputation to push rules that discourage financial businesses traditionally based in London. One proposal, to make alternative investors borrow less and reveal more, has prompted two-fifths of the hedge-fund managers surveyed to tell pollsters they would move if it were adopted unaltered. Lastly, how well Britain's economy does will also matter. Though the City serves the world, the health of its hinterland affects its own wellbeing—and Britain's outlook is hardly glowing.

Whatever the Brussels shenanigans, the City will not lose much to continental Europe or America. The qualities that have made it an international financial centre for centuries remain: an open economy, a cluster of relevant disciplines, reliable laws and a skilled English-speaking workforce open to additions from abroad.

But a broader change is under way as the economic centre of gravity shifts eastwards. Until now the City has been the Wimbledon of finance: the players may be foreign but they play on Britain's court. The decision late in 2009 of United Company RUSAL, a big Russian aluminium producer, to consider floating its stock in Hong Kong rather than London may reflect specific factors, but it is also a sign of things to come. ■

> The City has been the Wimbledon of finance

Merril Stevenson: Britain editor, *The Economist*

2010 IN BRIEF

In a trial scheme British passengers arriving at Heathrow with non-biometric passports can register their details (for a fee) and use an **automated clearance system** to bypass immigration queues.

On yer bikes

Jennifer Quigley-Jones

London follows the cycles-for-hire fad

In 2010 Boris Johnson will give London cyclists something to smile about. The mayor plans to launch a bicycle-hire system modelled on similar ones in Paris, Barcelona and a growing number of other cities around the world. With some 6,000 bikes and 400 docking stations, the scheme, at first covering about 17 square miles (44 square kilometres) of central London, should allow quick and relatively cheap access to rental bikes.

There will be difficulties to overcome. Securing land for bike stations in the busiest parts of London will need strong collaboration between Transport for London (TfL), which is commissioning the scheme, the Royal Parks and the nine boroughs involved. Then there's the cost: £140m ($229m) over six years. The aim is that over time the project will pay for itself.

BIXI, the company which will provide the bikes and run the programme, has assured TfL that its lab-tested bikes have withstood the equivalent of 15 years' use; it is offering a five-year or 40,000-mile guarantee. To deter theft, they are fitted with a security gizmo and users will have to pay a credit-card deposit.

A bigger worry may be safety. The bikes will encourage large numbers of new, tentative cyclists to ride—or wobble—onto some of London's busiest roads. The scheme is expected to generate an extra 40,000 journeys a day. TfL is supporting numerous cycle-training and safety initiatives throughout London. Plans to have 12 "cycle superhighways" by the end of 2012 should help eventually. Oddly, the rate of accidents appears to decrease as the number of cyclists rises: since 2000 London has had a 107% increase in the number of cycle journeys and a 21% drop in casualties. But drivers in the capital can still reckon on close shaves galore with inexperienced cyclists.

Despite the worries, the goal is to provide a green and healthy way of getting around London—an alternative to the all too frequent misery of the tube and traffic jams. Londoners may agree with President John Kennedy that "Nothing compares to the simple pleasure of a bike ride." ■

Jennifer Quigley-Jones: editorial assistant, *The World in 2010*

A history lesson

Paul Kennedy

A British historian of empire assesses the old country

In one of his more mordant reflections during the mid-1930s, George Orwell suggested that, were the British empire to be lost, England (sic) would be reduced to "a cold and unimportant little island where we would all have to work very hard and live mainly on herrings and potatoes."

Well, the empire has gone, but the cold little island is not as diminished as Orwell predicted. It is much shrunken since Winston Churchill's day, yet a mere ten years ago, at the height of Tony Blair's New Labour regime, it actually looked a pretty successful mid-level player in international issues. At present, however, it looks battered: a rather shabby mid-level player, if that.

It would be tempting to blame Gordon Brown, and more generally a Labour Party slowly dissolving into its various regional and socio-economic components. But that would miss a larger and more interesting point: that almost all medium-to-large powers are having a problem figuring out who they are, what their priorities should be and how to move on.

So battered Britain is not alone; it sits alongside battered Italy, battered Spain, battered Japan and so on. They have all come a long way down from their imperial zenith, and they are not like the Big Guys in world affairs (such as the United States, China, India, perhaps Brazil). But of all these middleweight nations, Britain is the one that has been reduced the most since 1945. Handling the politics of relative decline is never easy. And alarmist politicians and doomster academics may, in pointing to the state of decay, miss a nation's continuing strengths and attractions, which have to be weighed against its problems and worries.

The parliamentary scene, after all, is not a great cause for concern; it is as messy and inefficient and democratic as it ever was, but it is nowhere like as tense an arena as in, say, the 1909-10 crisis over reform of the House of Lords, or during the strains of the late 1970s and the early Thatcher years. The National Health Service is buckling under pressures, but it is not close to collapse; try living in a country like America, where 46m people have no health insurance. Public transport is not nearly as bad as the British think. The much-maligned BBC has no match across the world. The British treatment of their countryside is astounding. It is taken for granted that you can drive out to a village pub for a Sunday lunch, wander into the medieval church, stroll through the churchyard, climb a stile and cross a whole array of farmers' fields without someone shooting you. Do not stroll across a farmer's fields in Kentucky without armour.

So what are the items to worry about? Boiled down, they are two.

The first is whether the polity can keep the complex, mixed fabric of British society together when it is fraying in so many ways, notably in the general sense that a yobbo/hooligan culture is taking over more and more public space, so that smaller and milder people are not eager to go to town on a Friday night. Unsurprisingly, the top professional classes have been moving themselves and their families into private schools, private health-care systems and holidays abroad, thus widening the socio-economic gap. Mr Blair, to his credit, caught this sense of the fraying of English civic culture (much extolled by Orwell as English "decentness"), and tried to alert the nation. It still needs alerting. The growing coarseness needs to be headed off.

The second, perhaps even greater, issue is whether or not this small, cramped, magnificent island-state is still "punching above its weight"; that is, whether its real resources fall short of its ambitions and strivings in world affairs. The answer to that is a straight yes, and probably has been since 1918, though its recovery as a claimant Great Power between 1940 and 1945 fooled almost everybody. This presents a problem. Given Treasury limits on defence spending, the British government is overstretching its armed forces, certainly not as much as Philip of Spain did to his, but getting close. In consequence, all the military services are underfunded.

Back to the future

As the British look ahead to 2010 they should pause to remember the recent 500th anniversary of the death of King Henry VII, the first Tudor monarch, the real founder of this realm, the smartest king the English-Welsh were lucky to enjoy, the founder of financial and political stability, and a man who knew that England's military resources were limited and acted accordingly. Politicians now contending for the parliamentary "throne" might be advised to read about this Henry VII guy. They would not be wasting their time. ■

This Henry guy made ends meet

> All the armed services are underfunded

2010 IN BRIEF
Penguin Books celebrates 75 years of highbrow appeal.

Paul Kennedy: J. Richardson Dilworth professor of history, Yale University

IG INDEX

get thinking

financial spread betting

igindex.co.uk

Free online seminars to develop your financial spread betting skills.

- View our free seminars online, on demand
- Ideal for all levels of experience; topics range from understanding forex to advanced charting strategies
- Join live online sessions with in-house expert David Jones

Register now to learn more at igindex.co.uk

Spread betting can result in losses that exceed your initial deposit.

THE WORLD IN 2010

Europe

Also in this section:
Unemployment rising 46
Sarkozy unrivalled in France 48
José Manuel Barroso: Europe's policy priorities 50
Berlusconly 51
The must-haves for 2010 51
Germany's new coalition 52
Eastern Germany's new allure 53
A still darker Russia 54
Europe's dependence on Russian energy 56
Poland's presidential election 58
Dmitry Medvedev: Russia's role in turbulent times 59

More than a museum?

David Rennie BRUSSELS

A year that will test the European Union's new treaty

After years of institutional wrangles, the European Union will in 2010 have new rules on decision-making, its own diplomatic service, a quasi-foreign minister and a new "president" to represent national governments—all the tools needed for the 27 members to speak with one voice on the global stage. At this moment of triumph, however, a doubt has set in: what if Europe speaks to the world, and nobody listens?

The fear of irrelevancy will haunt European leaders in 2010. They devised a new rule book, the Lisbon treaty, to come into force in 2010 and give their union the political heft to match its might as a trading and regulatory power. Its first year will reveal whether the design really does the job.

Spain will hold the rotating presidency of the EU for the first half of 2010, chairing meetings in all fields except foreign policy (which will come under the union's newly installed foreign-policy chief, or "high representative"). Setting out priorities for the presidency, Spain's prime minister, José Luis Rodríguez Zapatero, says Europe has to become an "indispensable power". The challenge, he says, is to find a new economic model that is globally competitive and yet retains the European ideals of social "solidarity". If Europe fails at that hard task, it risks becoming "a sort of huge museum of no weight in the world."

For a few heady months in the early days of the global economic crisis, back in 2008, Europeans felt they were leading the world. The EU proclaimed itself a leader of global efforts to combat climate change, and European governments first demanded and then drafted new rules for global finance. Politicians in France, Germany and elsewhere announced the death of the "ultra-liberal" Anglo-Saxon economic model.

In 2010 those memories of European hubris will seem cruelly distant. Government intervention and protective labour-market rules limited a surge in European unemployment in 2009, but EU bosses fear jobless numbers will explode in 2010 (see next story), putting pressure on battered public finances and tempting governments to indulge in protectionism. There will be sharp debates among countries that use the single currency, as some, such as the Germans and Dutch, push for an early exit from fiscal-stimulus policies that have sent public debts soaring, while others, such as the French, continue to call for borrowing and state investment.

Early 2010 will see increasing attention paid to Britain, and the prospect that the election there will be won by a deeply Eurosceptic Conservative Party. A British demand (assuming the Tories win) to "repatriate" employment policy and opt out from chunks of EU social legislation will prompt furious accusations of "social dumping" from continental politicians.

The European Parliament will throw its weight around, using new powers from the Lisbon treaty to oversee almost all areas of EU regulation. Debate will begin in 2010 on the future shape of the EU budget ahead of actual budget negotiations two years later, and the parliament will want a big say. Spending on

> Talks will resume on enlarging the union

2010 IN BRIEF
According to the "Lisbon agenda", agreed upon in 2000, the EU should in 2010 be the **world's most competitive economy**. Reality disappoints...

David Rennie: Brussels bureau chief, *The Economist*

2010 IN BRIEF

Ireland helps its postmen by sorting its addresses into **postcodes**—the last country in the European Union to do so.

farm subsidies will provoke a fight.

It will not all be gloom. After a two-year pause, talks will resume on enlarging the union still further: a policy that has proved to be the EU's most successful source of soft power across central and eastern Europe. Croatia could become the club's 28th member at the end of 2010, or soon after. Tiny, recession-hit Iceland will open entry talks in early 2010. Success may hinge on how much autonomy the EU is prepared to give Iceland in managing its rich fish stocks.

Spain will try to breathe new life into Turkish entry talks with the EU, which have slowed to a crawl amid rows with Cyprus about direct shipping and trade links, and vocal hostility from leaders such as Nicolas Sarkozy of France. Mr Zapatero calls Turkey a "great country" that has waited too long at Europe's gates.

This may be the last time a country uses the presidency to shape the agenda so visibly. Federalist-minded Belgium takes the chair in the second half of 2010, and intends to "break" for ever with the idea of a powerful rotating presidency. It wants to give the new treaty a chance to work, its diplomats explain: the new president and high rep must become Europe's true spokesmen. That is, if anybody's listening. ■

Europe isn't working
John Peet

Governments will be tempted by the wrong policies to tackle unemployment

A spectre will haunt Europe in 2010: not communism, but the return of mass unemployment. The European economies will recover slowly during the year. But unemployment is a notoriously lagging indicator. The OECD, a think-tank of rich countries, expects it to reach a post-1945 high of 10%, or some 57m people, for the whole OECD club in late 2010; by then some 25m jobs will have been lost since 2007. In several countries—Spain, Ireland, France, Germany and Poland—the rate will rise above 10%.

The last time that joblessness was a big scourge in Europe was in the early 1990s. But the boom of the past 15 years helped to reduce it, even in countries like France, Germany and Spain where it had seemed entrenched. Falling unemployment made it easier for some countries to loosen the regulations that gummed up their labour markets, helping to push the jobless numbers down further as well as making economies more competitive.

This virtuous cycle will go into reverse in 2010. Rising unemployment will make it far harder to push through labour-market reforms. It will make it politically impossible to scrap or blur the divide that exists in many countries between protected "insiders" on permanent contracts and unprotected "outsiders" stuck with temporary ones. This means that the first and biggest sufferers from rising joblessness will be outsiders, a group disproportionately made up of the young, women and people from ethnic minorities.

Governments will not be able to weaken job-protection laws any further. Because most will be struggling in 2010 to contain big budget deficits, they will also find it impossible to mop up private-sector unemployment by spending more public money and creating more public-sector jobs.

The risk is that many governments will instead react much as they did in the 1980s, when they encouraged schemes to promote early retirement, to shorten working hours and to reduce part-time working. These policies betrayed an atavistic belief in the "lump-of-labour" fallacy, which holds that as there is a fixed amount of work to be spread around, easing some people out of jobs generates additional jobs for others. Both experience and economic theory have shown this to be false.

Another policy response from the 1980s that many governments may try again is to shuffle some of the unemployed off the dole and into state disability schemes. Countries such as Britain, the Netherlands and Sweden made extensive use of such gimmicks to hold down published unemployment figures. Fortunately, they will find this harder to do in 2010 because of the greater need to restrain public spending.

The best answer to unemployment is neither more regulation, nor pushing people into early retirement, nor massaging the numbers down. These either do not work or they tackle the symptoms, not the disease. They are also perverse given Europe's demographic future, in which working populations in most countries will be shrinking, not expanding. In the short run Europe may experience high unemployment; in the long term it will suffer from labour shortages.

A much better policy response is training and other measures to ensure that those thrown out of work stay in touch with the labour market so that they can quickly rejoin it as growth picks up. The Scandinavian countries have proved much better at this than most. They explicitly seek to protect and educate workers rather than preserving existing jobs and factories. Such investment in human capital is also likely to raise productivity, generating higher growth and more employment in the long run. Unfortunately the policies that are most likely to be pursued by many European governments will do precisely the reverse. ■

The lengthening lines
Selected countries' unemployment rate %, 2010*

Spain 20.5
Ireland 15.1
Poland 12.0
EU 11.0
France 10.9
Germany 10.8
Sweden 10.7
Hungary 10.5
Britain 10.0
Italy 9.4
Netherlands 6.2

EU unemployment rate, %
2008: 7.2
2009†: 10.1
2010*: 11.0

Source: Economist Intelligence Unit   *Forecast †Estimate

John Peet: Europe editor, *The Economist*

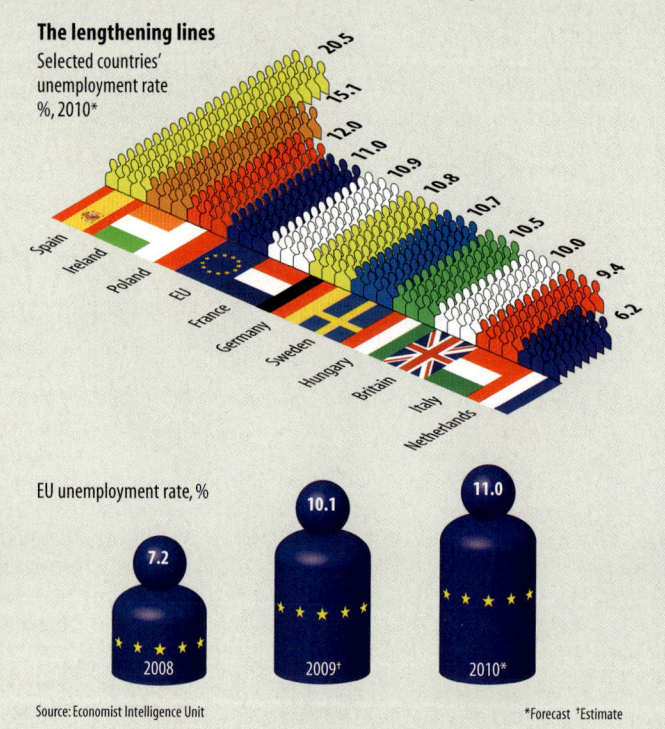

Carbon

Others may copy, but we are first

first direct has become the first bank to be awarded the Carbon Trust Standard for carbon footprint reduction.

It's this sort of thing that makes **first direct** unique. We really do go the extra mile to make a difference. Solar power heats part of our building. Our PCs shut down automatically when they're not in use. More of us are cycling to work and all of us recycle when we get there.

It's the little things that matter. And they all add up to make **first direct** a better place to bank. Maybe that's why we've been voted number one for customer satisfaction*.

Our friendly people are on hand to help day or night, 365 days a year. So why not copy 1,000s of happy customers and join **first direct** today?

first direct
banking's better in black and white

CARBON TRUST STANDARD
REDUCING CO2 YEAR ON YEAR

0800 24 24 24
firstdirect.com

Member HSBC ◆ *Group*

Source: Institute of Customer Service, 2009.
Because we want to make sure we're doing a good job, we may monitor and/or record our calls. We hope you don't mind. © HSBC Bank plc 2009. All rights reserved. 40 Wakefield Road, Leeds LS98 1FD.

Chameleon Bonaparte

Sophie Pedder PARIS

Nicolas Sarkozy will emerge unloved, yet unrivalled

A curious paradox will reveal itself during 2010 in France. As he enters the second half of his five-year term, President Nicolas Sarkozy will remain unpopular in the polls. His critics, and the left-wing media, will demonise him. The slightest faux pas will be derided. Joblessness, and social tension, will rise. All will contribute to a sense of a president under pressure. And yet Mr Sarkozy will emerge stronger than ever.

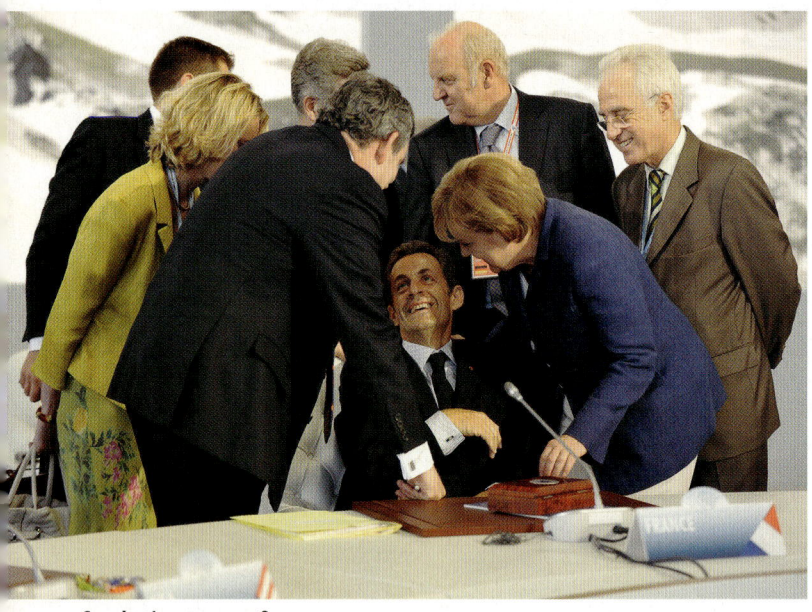

So what's your secret?

How so? The centre-right leader will put the finishing touches to a project that, for the first time under the fifth republic, has united the political right under a single umbrella. Barring the far-right National Front, which Mr Sarkozy has in effect crushed, this movement will reach from right-wing nationalists to Socialist defectors from the moderate left. Within this broad church he will face not a single credible rival.

By occupying such a wide political space, and borrowing both ideas and manpower from the opposition, Mr Sarkozy will deny his opponents breathing room. The Socialists will be marginalised by their internal rivalry. Ever flakier, Ségolène Royal, who is not the party's leader, will behave as if she is already its candidate for the 2012 presidential election. Torpedoing her own party bosses, to project an outsiderish quality, Ms Royal will establish herself as Mr Sarkozy's foremost opponent—but will not be an immediate threat.

To curb the rise of the ecologists, Mr Sarkozy will apply his suffocation tactics to them too. His carbon tax will come into effect, and he will press for a similar tax at Europe's borders, prompting cries of protectionism from free-traders. He will push the development of the electric car, and non-biodegradable plastic bags will be banned from supermarkets from January. Four new TGV high-speed rail lines will be under construction at the same time. The government will launch a "super bond" to retail investors, with investment in the carbon-free economy as one of its themes.

A test of Mr Sarkozy's strength will be elections in France's 22 regions in March. The Socialists, who swept the board last time, are set to lose control of several regions—though Ms Royal is likely to hang on to hers. If Mr Sarkozy's party can win back even half of them, that would be a strong springboard from which to plan for 2012. Unless François Fillon gets a big European job, Mr Sarkozy may not need to change his prime minister: Mr Fillon's patrician discretion complements the president's showmanship. If a new prime minister were needed, candidates could include surprises, such as Christine Lagarde, the finance minister, or even Eric Besson, a Socialist defector, as well as old-time Sarkozy chums such as Brice Hortefeux.

Although the economy will start to revive, Mr Sarkozy will not return to his one-time liberal discourse in a hurry. This will disappoint those, including his own business friends, who thought they had elected a liberal reformer. He will clash with European friends over running a high budget deficit. But he will try to make some structural changes. The retirement age will be raised. Hospital charges will increase. A big administrative reform will halve the number of elected departmental and regional representatives.

Sharm offensive

There will be further scattered unrest at the factory gate, yet France's generous welfare provision will keep spending buoyant and café trade brisk. The unions will find it harder than in the past to draw vast numbers onto the streets. More unpredictable are the heavily Muslim, immigrant neighbourhoods, where drugs and gangs create a toxic mix. On grounds of security, as well as secularism, the French may well go ahead and ban the burqa, the face-covering Islamic garment, in public places.

Fifty years after France first granted its African colonies independence, Mr Sarkozy will celebrate "Africa Year", convening a grand France-Africa summit in Sharm el-Sheikh. But he will all the same shrink France's military presence in sub-Saharan Africa, and reorient it towards the Horn of Africa and the Gulf. More generally, Mr Sarkozy will veer between Atlanticism and more Gaullist reflexes, as France marks the 70th anniversary of de Gaulle's London appeal for wartime resistance. He will push his ideas on financial regulation, climate change, Iran and the Middle East. But relations with America will be pricklier than expected, partly because his pretensions to big-power status irk Washington.

By the end of the year the chameleon-like Mr Sarkozy will face hard questions. His promises to get the French to work more, and the state to do less, have gone untested during the recession. The more the economy recovers, the fewer excuses Mr Sarkozy will have for not adopting the reformist agenda that got him elected. ∎

2010 IN BRIEF
France introduces a **tax on carbon**, at €17 a tonne.

Sophie Pedder: Paris bureau chief, *The Economist*

INVESTORS ♥ TURKEY ♥ INVESTORS

Over 21,000 international companies have already invested in Turkey. How about you?

AREVA | BNP PARIBAS | DHL EXPRESS | FABER-CASTELL | GE Healthcare | Groupama | HYUNDAI

Indesit Company | MANGO | Microsoft | ORACLE | TOYOTA | UNITED COLORS OF BENETTON

INVEST IN TURKEY

- A population of 72 million people with an average age of 28,5
- 61% of the population is below 34 years of age
- Approximately 450,000 graduates per year from 143 universities
- Over 24 million young, well-educated and motivated labor force
- Highly competitive investment conditions
- A country that offers 100% and more tax deductions on R&D expenditures

- Access to Europe, Caucasus, Central Asia, the Middle East and North Africa
- 15th largest economy of the world and the 6th largest economy as compared to the 27 EU countries in 2008 (IMF-WEO)
- 15th most attractive FDI destination for 2008-2010 (UNCTAD World Investment Prospects Survey)
- Average annual real GDP growth of 6% for the last 5 years

REPUBLIC OF TURKEY PRIME MINISTRY INVESTMENT SUPPORT AND PROMOTION AGENCY

YOUR ONE-STOP-SHOP IN TURKEY

invest.gov.tr

Beyond the crisis

José Manuel Barroso, president of the European Commission, sets out Europe's policy priorities

We live in a time of transformation. People are worried about the future. The European Union's robust and co-ordinated response to the financial and economic crisis has contributed to pulling the economy back from the brink. But the crisis is not over. The challenge for 2010 is clear: it must be the year in which we set the course for a sustainable recovery.

The crisis has shown how difficult events are to predict. But I will stick my neck out and make a prediction for 2010. I believe that we can come out of the present crisis stronger than ever. There are two reasons for my confidence.

The first is that the EU knows where it wants to go. We have defined our priorities: we want to reinvigorate our inclusive social market economies; we know we must become a low-carbon economy. Second, the solidarity and sense of urgency created by the response to the crisis have actually given us momentum to work jointly towards our goals.

The enlarged EU has been the driving force behind global co-operation through the G20. The combined assets and efforts of 27 member states and the European Commission provide us with the critical mass needed to offer co-leadership in building a new global economy. European ideas have thoroughly informed the solutions agreed upon.

Sustained recovery now requires effective—and global—reform of financial markets. Only a more ethical and responsible financial sector can properly serve the needs of the economy. What is more, effective regulation is in the interests of financial institutions. Prudent institutions must no longer be at the mercy of reckless behaviour by their competitors. Such behaviour destroyed trillions of euros of value and brought the whole system to the point of collapse.

The commission has put forward detailed proposals for a new European and global supervisory architecture to be in place in 2010. This would have been unthinkable two years ago. Now we have a unanimous endorsement from the heads of state and government. We will not let this opportunity slip.

In 2010, more than ever, policymakers must think ahead. No one yet knows when the right moment will come to insist that the banking sector once again stands on its own two feet. It is not yet clear when we should end the current fiscal stimulus.

Our responsibility is to define the right exit strategy and to implement it at the right moment. The current fiscal stimulus cannot go on indefinitely. Too much stimulus over too long a period would saddle future generations with unsustainable debt. It would create a risk of an inflationary bubble. That in turn could lead to a new crisis.

This means that, in 2010, we must already start developing new sources of growth which can take over when the stimulus is eventually withdrawn. We must act strategically.

My main concern is jobs. The crisis will bring about further permanent changes in our labour markets. We must ensure a smooth process of restructuring and help people to move into the jobs of tomorrow. Examples of those include smart, green technologies, but also the health and care sectors. We must also develop a more intelligent, common approach to economic migration to bridge the gaps in our workforce.

Now, about those missing links

We are approaching the 20th anniversary of the 1992 deadline for the "completion" of the EU single market. It is a huge asset. But it is still not working for us as well as it should. We must identify the missing links.

Networks of the future are a top priority. We need access to high-speed broadband for all Europeans. We must develop smart grids which allow us to integrate renewable energies into supply. A secure energy supply requires better inter-connections.

Research is critical. We have started to overcome the fragmentation of national research efforts through joint programming and pooling resources to finance the kind of infrastructure, such as world-class laboratories and top-of-the-range telescopes, that no member state can afford on its own. Europe must become the "continent of choice" for talented researchers from around the globe.

Our innovation policies also need an overhaul. In particular, it is time to harness the power of government procurement to promote innovation. Europe needs a new intellectual-property strategy.

Capitalising on all this requires open markets at the global level. We are committed to the Doha round, but we will also pursue bilateral trade agreements. Non-tariff barriers are a major obstacle for EU exporters, so we will push for greater regulatory co-operation too.

And the race is on to meet our 2020 targets to combat climate change and mitigate its impact. The challenges are huge. The commission will do everything in its power to ensure that, in 2010, we get off to a good start. ■

I believe that we can come out of the present crisis stronger than ever

The eternal leader?

John Hooper ROME

An Italian phenomenon

Italy has become an anomaly in the Western world—a nation led by a populist and a society doggedly resistant to liberalisation. How much of an anomaly Italy remains in 2010 will depend in large part on whether its leader, Silvio Berlusconi, stays in office.

The disclosure of the 73-year-old Mr Berlusconi's still unexplained relationship with a teenage girl, his nights spent with women allegedly paid to give him sex, and above all his treatment of his now estranged wife, Veronica Lario, have shrunk his stature in the eyes of many erstwhile admirers (though not as many as non-Italians might imagine). A large part of the Italian elite is exasperated by his Nero-like behaviour: Roman Catholic bishops, with whom his pet editor picked a row over their newspaper's criticism of Mr Berlusconi's private life; bankers, diplomats and intelligence officials, more aware than their compatriots of the damage being done to Italy's international standing; and a growing number of businesspeople, dismayed by how seriously the scandals have diverted the government's attention from the economy and robbed it of its early reforming zeal.

All that said, no forecaster has yet benefited from predicting the irrepressible media tycoon's demise. Come December 2010, his jester's features could be grinning out from under an even thicker layer of make-up at the government's year-end press conference. He enjoys widespread, though diminished, popular sup-

2010 IN BRIEF

Biofuels, according to a European Union directive, take a 5.75% share of the fuel used for transport in the EU.

John Hooper: Italy correspondent, *The Economist*

Coolissimo

Beppe Severgnini MILAN

The must-haves for 2010

Do you remember back in 1980 when we all rushed to buy a tape recorder that couldn't record? They called it a Walkman. Today, you might be able to pick one up at a charity shop. Thirty years on, what will be the new icons? Here's a view from Milan.

Black cars. Silver cars dominated the European roadscape during the 1990s and for most of the 2000s. Black was for government ministers, archbishops, film stars and Russian oligarchs. Brighter hues were for Germans. All of a sudden, from Paris to Palermo, it's back to black (only Amy Winehouse saw that coming).

White wines. From Australia to California and France itself, white wines will have a boom year. Italy's best *bianchi* come from Friuli, Trentino-Alto Adige and Sardinia. Veneto's prosecco is proving a formidable competitor in the bubbly stakes. Cheaper than champagne but stylish, easy to drink and prettily named.

Standard mobile-phone charger. At last, micro USB connectors for all! The European Commission has convinced ten mobile-phone manufacturers representing 90% of the EU market to commit themselves to standardised chargers. Today, there are over 30 different models, and 50m chargers are thrown out every year because they don't fit the owner's new phone.

Rear-view cameras. These are common nowadays on SUVs and luxury cars, mostly as part of expensive option packages. Expect them to appear on cheaper cars. They're smart, simple and children love them. When you hear "Mum's on camera!", remember to stop.

Washing-up liquid on tap. Just fill up. Why bother with those bulky plastic bottles that are so difficult to dispose of?

Glass lifts. Once seen only on top of hotels or in buildings designed by trendy architects, glass lifts are set to become standard fittings, wherever possible. They're not just cool but uplifting (obviously).

Birkin bag. This was designed for an actress, Jane Birkin, who complained she couldn't find anything in her handbag. The Hermès number will spread and the designer-fakes industry will cater for those who can't afford the $5,000 price tag. Why include an ultra-expensive bag among the icons for 2010? Because it shows a trend. A few people will buy a classic item that will, or should, last a lifetime while most will go for cheap chic from Zara, H&M and the rest. The $250 shirt is no more. Why pay that much for a label?

Prince of Wales check. Designed by Edward VII when he was Prince of Wales for his shooting expeditions on Deeside, it has never been entirely out of fashion. It will be back big time in 2010 as a business-attire option. Bankers blew the cred of pin-stripes and chalk-stripes in the financial crisis of 2008-09.

Bicycles. Chinese city-dwellers may have traded up to cars but bicycles will increasingly be perceived as the only solution for urban-traffic problems. Amsterdam and Berlin are way ahead. But in the run-up to World Expo 2015, Milan too is getting serious about bikes. And if we Italians can give up our cars, anyone can. Trust me.

Fiat 500 and **Ferrari California**. Italy produces both of these automotive jewels, at opposite ends of the price spectrum. Both are perfect, sleek-styled classics. Fiat's takeover of Chrysler will open the doors of America to them.

Kindle. More wireless connectivity means more Kindle. Two years after its release, Amazon's reading device is on the verge of cult status. Unless of course someone else comes up with a newer, smarter toy that will let you read the newspapers, including *The Economist*.

Shorter menus. Remember when you used to end a morning's work by going to a restaurant and poring over a 15-page menu? *Finito*. Restaurateurs have worked out that it just doesn't make sense: too much stuff to buy and store. In 2010 expect short menus and a *piatto del giorno*. Or *plat du jour*, as they used to say when France was blazing the gastronomic trail. ■

Beppe Severgnini: columnist, *Corriere della Sera*

Europe

> No forecaster has yet benefited from predicting the irrepressible media tycoon's demise

port. The right is beholden to his media power, which could be trained mercilessly on any prospective successor. And the most astute of those, the former neo-fascist Gianfranco Fini, has moved so far to the centre that many on the right view him as a traitor.

The opposition is weak and set for further trials. Before the start of the year, the biggest centre-left party, the Democratic Party (PD), will have ditched its stopgap leader, Dario Franceschini, and embraced a tough, capable former communist, Pierluigi Bersani. He will be a lively challenge to Mr Berlusconi, but his election will cause some in the PD to leave and perhaps join Pier Ferdinando Casini's Union of Christian and Centre Democrats. Regional elections expected in March will be an important test.

Italy will recover from the recession. But what remains uncertain—and politically significant—is how quickly. Mr Berlusconi and his finance minister, Giulio Tremonti, tackled the crisis with a show of unshakeable optimism. There were two reasons for this. With global trade slumping, Italy, highly dependent on selling abroad, could not count on exports to get it out of trouble. So maintaining internal demand was vital. The other reason was that the government just could not afford a costly stimulus package: Italy's public debt was bigger than its annual GDP. By minimising the challenge, Mr Berlusconi successfully dampened public expectations of action to tackle it. His claim that Italy would suffer less than other economies proved hollow: in the 12 months to end-June 2009, Italy's GDP fell by more than that of any other G7 member state except Japan.

Weak growth in 2010 could bear out the fear of Italy's retail association, that by 2011 the country's GDP at constant prices might be little greater than ten years earlier, when Mr Berlusconi returned to power, irate that *The Economist* had branded him "Unfit to lead Italy". ■

2010 IN BRIEF

Berlin's international **film festival** celebrates its 60th anniversary—and gives Cannes a run for its money.

Brooke Unger: Germany correspondent, *The Economist*

Still in fashion

Changing the colours

Brooke Unger BERLIN

Germany's new coalition will proceed with caution

If you let me govern with the liberals, promised the chancellor, Angela Merkel, Germany will recover faster from recession. Voters granted her wish. In federal elections in September they dissolved the four-year-old "grand coalition" between her Christian Democratic Union (CDU) and the Social Democratic Party (SPD). The CDU now governs with a new partner, the liberal Free Democratic Party (FDP). In 2010 the main tasks of this "black-yellow" tandem will be to redeem Ms Merkel's pledge and to launch a programme for Germany that is distinctive but still unthreatening to an electorate wary of radical reform.

This will not be easy. The recession formally ended in the second quarter of 2009 but 2010 is the year when Germany will feel it. The economy will grow a bit—after shrinking by 5% in 2009—but unemployment will jump. So far, it has risen modestly thanks to government subsidies for shorter working hours and firms' reluctance to dismiss highly qualified staff. But the number of jobless workers will leap from an average of 3.5m in 2009 to 4.1m in 2010, forecasts the IAB, the research arm of the Federal Employment Agency. Though far less than earlier feared, this is still a painful rise.

The black-yellow balm promised by Ms Merkel will take the form of tax cuts. Under the new coalition agreement the government will provide €24 billion ($36 billion) a year of relief to families and businesses, starting with bigger tax deductions for children and a lower value-added tax for hotels and restaurants in 2010. Later on it plans to simplify income taxes, one of the FDP's main demands. The idea is that rewarding work and enterprise will not only alleviate the crisis but boost growth in the long run.

> Merkel's black-yellow balm will take the form of tax cuts

Less was said about how this will be paid for. The federal budget deficit is likely to hit a record in 2010. By law the government must cut its structural deficit (ie, adjusted for the business cycle) to 0.35% of GDP by 2016. The new finance minister, Wolfgang Schäuble, is a fiscal hawk but does not plan to cut spending while the economy is fragile. The bill will come later, perhaps along with more ambitious reforms hinted at in the coalition agreement. The new government promises to redesign the financing of health care, for example, but leaves it to a commission to say how.

Ms Merkel's new government will court controversy in two areas. To restore the banking system to health it must reform the nine public *Landesbanken*, which hold a large portion of Germany's toxic assets. Germany needs only one to manage cash and settlements for its savings banks but the state premiers have resisted pressure for mergers. The new government must overcome that. To cut energy costs and carbon emissions the CDU ▶

A scent of history

Frederick Studemann BITTERFELD

Eastern Germany has a fresh allure

Bitterfeld used to be known by its smell. The town, in the heart of communist East Germany's "chemical triangle", was notorious for the acrid stench from its local factories—some of which occasionally exploded in deadly accidents.

Now, as the 20th anniversary of German unification approaches (the Germanies formally came together on October 3rd 1990), the town that was once a potent symbol of the economic failures and environmental horrors bequeathed by 40 years of communism has cleaned up its act. Plants that once produced film have given way to ones making solar panels; heavily polluted soil and rivers have been replaced by parks and lakes. "The skies above Bitterfeld are now as clear as elsewhere," says Monika Maron, author of a book on Bitterfeld's renaissance.

For some this remarkable physical transformation—mirrored across the east in renovated town centres and top-notch infrastructure—is evidence that the "blooming landscapes" promised by former chancellor Helmut Kohl on the eve of monetary union in July 1990 are, at last, becoming visible. After years of job losses, industrial collapse and mass emigration, economists now enthuse about improved productivity, better growth and the emergence of a *Mittelstand* (small and medium-sized enterprises) in a region once dominated by monolithic "combines".

None of this comes cheaply. The east will continue to receive transfers amounting to roughly 4% of German GDP, adding to the €1.6 trillion ($2.4 trillion) or so estimated to have been pumped into the region since 1990. Unemployment in the east is double that in the west; most of those in work still earn less than their western cousins.

But although there is still a lot of catching up to do, in some respects the east will increasingly lead the way in coming years. In politics and sport, literally so: the recently re-elected easterner, Angela Merkel, heads Germany's government; another *Ossi*, Michael Ballack, will lead the national football team at the FIFA World Cup in South Africa.

Management and workforces schooled in tough times are more flexible than those in the west. This will have an increasing effect in the west, says Karl-Heinz Paqué, a western economics professor working in the east. Western firms are pushing through wage-cutting deals that recently would have been "unthinkable".

Easterners are psychologically better equipped for a global slowdown, says Ms Maron, because unification has given them 20 years of "crisis management" training. Meanwhile, as the east ages faster than the rest of Germany, so it will have to find solutions earlier.

The German cultural world brims with prize-winning easterners. The east's pulling power is clearest in Berlin, the centre-stage of unification, where all the buzz—from edgy bars to bohemian gentrification—will remain in the east.

Yet for all the progress since unification, divisions remain. Easterners tell pollsters of their nostalgia for the old days and vote in large numbers for the successors to the East German communists. Westerners are often uninterested in the east. "It's amazing how little exchange there is," says Alexander Osang, an eastern writer and journalist.

Ten years ago, on his way to work in New York, Mr Osang predicted the imminent disappearance of the east; now back in (east) Berlin, he is no longer so sure. Ms Maron concurs. "The Americans haven't forgotten their civil war and that was 150 years ago." ■

Frederick Studemann: analysis editor, *Financial Times*

---

and the FDP want to let nuclear-power plants operate beyond 2022, the deadline set by an earlier government for shutting down all such plants. That will provoke street protests in 2010.

Guido Westerwelle, the head of the FDP, has replaced the SPD's Frank-Walter Steinmeier as foreign minister but foreign policy is unlikely to change much. Germany ought to feel more comfortable in a world in which the United States is pursuing better relations with Russia and Iran.

But America will be more demanding. Germany will face pressure to increase its contribution to the war in Afghanistan and to help tighten sanctions against Iran if Iran does not co-operate with nuclear-weapons inspections. With the elections over, the government will be a bit more flexible; it may send more troops to Afghanistan and step up aid to Pakistan. But another election looms that will temper its ambitions, at least until mid-2010. A CDU-FDP coalition in North Rhine-Westphalia, the most populous state, faces a challenge from the wounded SPD in May. Only after that will black-yellow reveal its true colours. ■

A still darker Russia

Arkady Ostrovsky MOSCOW

Once more into the unknown

After ten years of Vladimir Putin's rule, first as president and now as prime minister, predicting Russia's future should have been easier. Mr Putin takes the credit for making Russia more stable than it was in the chaotic 1990s. In the name of this "stability" he took control over Russia's television, its parliament, chunks of its economy and almost all of its politics. He anointed his loyal subordinate, Dmitry Medvedev, as president and himself assumed the role of all-powerful prime minister. As Mr Putin let it be known in September, the next presidential election in 2012 will be decided in similar fashion by him and Mr Medvedev.

Yet Russia's future is as uncertain as ever. This is partly because decisions in Russia depend on Mr Putin's will and on the barely decipherable relationships within the Kremlin, rather than on institutions such as parliament or the courts. And partly because whatever decisions he makes do not always translate into actions: many of them get bogged down in a corrupt and inefficient bureaucracy.

By all accounts, in the past few years corruption has become worse, the economy has become more dependent on oil and the Soviet-era infrastructure is cracking. Most worryingly, the violence in the North Caucasus has spread from Chechnya to the rest of the region. Reports of killings and explosions come daily from Ingushetia and Dagestan, as well as from Chechnya itself.

In an article published in September 2009, Mr Medvedev wrote about the ineffective economy, the half-Soviet social system, weak democracy, negative demographic trends and an unstable Caucasus. But in the same article he cautioned against rushing through political changes. Like many of Russia's technocrats, he seems to believe that a knowledge-based and innovative economy can develop in a political system that is neither free nor just.

Opinion is divided on what awaits Russia in the next year or so. One view is that Russia faces a choice between becoming more authoritarian, nationalist and aggressive towards its neighbours, or opening up its politics to competition and modernising its economy. Another view is that Russia will keep sliding slowly into stagnation. Which view prevails may largely depend on the oil price: a higher oil price would point to stagnation, a big drop would force Russia to make tough choices.

Trial and error

At home, the best test of Russia's direction in 2010 may be the outcome of the second trial of Mikhail Khodorkovsky, a jailed former tycoon. His trial has become a showpiece of political interference and repression. The first case against Mr Khodorkovsky and his former business partner, Platon Lebedev, was a sham. The second one is absurd: not only has it ignored the principle of double jeopardy, it has also alleged that the very existence of Yukos, once Russia's largest oil company, was illegal. Every day the trial makes a mockery of justice.

Mr Khodorkovsky will almost certainly not be freed. He could get another 22 years in addition to the six he has already served. Or he could get a symbolic one or two years on top of his current sentence, which runs out in 2011.

In foreign policy, Russia's new year will begin with the presidential election in Ukraine on January 17th. Five years ago Mr Putin backed Viktor Yanukovich, the Russia-leaning prime minister, who was brushed aside by the Orange revolution that installed Viktor Yushchenko as president. This was one of Mr Putin's most obvious failures and it left a bitter feeling in the Kremlin. Ever since, Russia and Ukraine have quarrelled bitterly over gas supplies, which in 2009 left large parts of Europe freezing. Another gas row can be safely expected in 2010 and the warning shots have already been fired.

In August 2009 Mr Medvedev sent an insulting letter to Mr Yushchenko accusing him of anti-Russian policies. The letter was publicised in Mr Medvedev's videoblog, which showed him ominously dressed in black and overlooking the Black Sea coast patrolled by two Russian warships. The purpose was twofold: to spite Mr Yushchenko, who is almost certain to lose the election anyway, and to send a signal to his successor. In the eyes of the Kremlin, Ukraine is a failed state. After its war in Georgia in 2008, Russia feels it is time to establish its rightful influence in Ukraine. A new law introduced by Mr Medvedev simplifies Russia's use of its armed forces abroad and indicates that nothing has been ruled out.

On May 9th Russia will celebrate the 65th anniversary of its victory in the second world war. Mr Putin has argued that, after the treacherous Munich treaty of 1938, Stalin had no choice but to sign a secret pact with Nazi Germany that divided Poland. Russia may choose to celebrate the anniversary as a common victory over fascism. Or it may use it to justify Stalinism. ■

1945 and all that

> A higher oil price would point to stagnation, a big drop would force Russia to make tough choices

Arkady Ostrovsky: Moscow correspondent, *The Economist*

Cities that consume 30% less energy?

As a leading producer of energy-efficient solutions, ABB helps deliver major power savings, without compromising performance. Our lighting control systems can deliver power savings of up to 50 percent, and our building automation up to 60 percent. While everyone else is talking about energy prices, power shortages and climate change, ABB is doing something about it, right here, right now. **www.abb.com/betterworld**

Certainly.

Power and productivity
for a better world™

ABB

New twists in an old saga

Edward Lucas

Europe struggles to free itself from dependence on Russian energy

Russian gas had a bad year in 2009. Its share of the European market shrank: with demand weak, customers were able to switch to cheaper suppliers. But the Kremlin will once again be on the front foot in 2010. Its top priority will be to get work started on the Nord Stream pipeline, which will link Russia to Germany along the Baltic seabed, bypassing troublesome transit countries such as Ukraine and Poland. Russia's debt-ridden gas giant, Gazprom, lacks the money to build this, so it needs help from the European Union and Germany.

Russia's heavy-handed energy diplomacy is often counterproductive. But it is lobbying hard for Nord Stream and will probably be successful. In 2010 it will increase pressure on Sweden and Finland, both of which have raised environmental concerns. It will also call on support from its most powerful European ally, Germany.

Germany's re-elected chancellor, the canny Angela Merkel, privately dislikes the project. But she knows she cannot block it outright: Germany's energy-thirsty industry is desperate to have a reliable supply of gas from the east. Instead, she will push for a compromise. Germany will get Nord Stream built—if necessary with money from the European Union. But it will also push hard for work to start on another pipeline, Nabucco. This would connect the gas-rich Caspian region with central Europe, via Turkey and the Balkans. Russia's alternative pipeline across the Black Sea, South Stream, will get nowhere. It is too expensive.

Tying up the loose ends on Nabucco will be the main energy story in southern Europe in 2010. Turkey needs to be brought fully on board. That will mean its agreeing to take some Russian gas from Blue Stream, the underused pipeline across the Black Sea. Putting Russian gas in Nabucco dilutes its importance as a counterweight to Russia's monopoly on east-west gas supplies. But it is better than nothing. It will allow gas from Kurdistan (in Iraq), Azerbaijan and other sources to reach Europe directly, for the first time. The EU is determined to get Nabucco built, even if the deal behind it is imperfect.

> The weakest link in the West will be Britain

Russia has another pipeline to play with: OPAL. This would connect Nord Stream to the centre of Germany. In 2010 it will be clear that the Czech government has signed up to this too: so long as the pipeline route crosses a small bit of Czech territory, en route to southern Germany, the government in Prague will not object. That leaves Slovakia and Ukraine, literally, out in the cold. Russia will be able to drive a much harder bargain with these transit states once its supply route to powerful Western countries is assured.

It will be a similar story for oil. By the end of 2010 Russia will be able to close down the ill-named Druzhba ("Friendship") pipeline, built to carry Soviet oil to the western half of the Kremlin's empire. Instead, Russian crude oil will be carried by tankers, from a new port

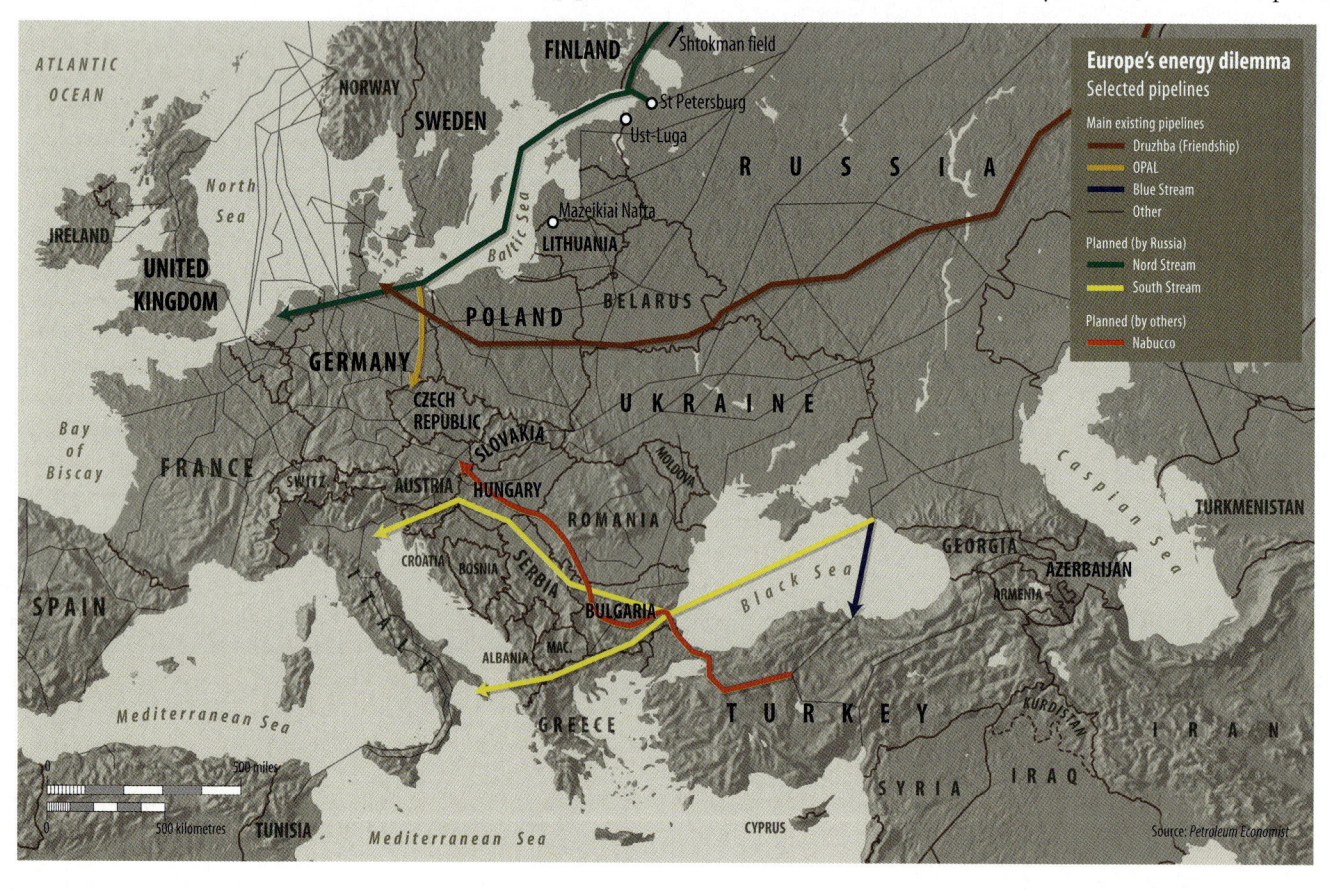

2010 IN BRIEF

Russians get a taste for **high-speed rail** travel, with a winter-proof service between St Petersburg and Moscow.

Istanbul... the most inspiring city in the world.

Istanbul 2010 European Capital of Culture will further inspire you with its contemporary art and urban culture.

Be a part of this unique experience.

istanbul inspirations

ISTANBUL 2010
EUROPEAN CAPITAL OF CULTURE
AVRUPA KÜLTÜR BAŞKENTİ

www.istanbul2010.org

Equity Partner | **TURKISH AIRLINES** | A STAR ALLIANCE MEMBER

No need to weigh the past

Jan Piotrowski WARSAW

Poland is once again ready to look ahead

For Poles 2009 abounded in jubilees. First they feted the series of events that led to the formation of the first non-communist government in September 1989, then bemoaned the Nazi and Soviet invasions of 50 years earlier. Despite an economic slowdown caused by the global crisis many politicians' minds were focused firmly on grievances of yore.

Thankfully, in 2010 no similar celebrations beckon (notwithstanding the politically innocuous 600th anniversary of the rout of the Teutonic Knights at the Battle of Grunwald). The prime event of the political calendar is the presidential election scheduled for the autumn. A rematch of the 2005 contest, it will pit Lech Kaczynski, the unpopular conservative incumbent, against Donald Tusk, the affable prime minister and leader of the centre-right Civic Platform, the senior partner in the ruling coalition.

This time round Mr Tusk should be a shoo-in. Opinion polls consistently give the prime minister at least a two-to-one lead over Mr Kaczynski. He could even secure an outright majority in the first round, dispensing with the need for a run-off. Among other touted candidates only Jolanta Kwasniewska, a savoir-vivre guru and wife of Aleksander Kwasniewski, whom Mr Kaczynski succeeded as president, appears to pose any threat to Mr Tusk, but she has explicitly ruled out entering the fray, to the dismay of the country's left, which lacks viable alternatives.

Some find it puzzling that Mr Tusk is willing to trade in the prime ministership for the presidency, which the constitution vests with little real power. Despite his being chosen by popular vote, the president's only real power is the right to veto legislation. And this, as many see it, is a power that Mr Kaczynski has exercised indiscriminately, just to make life miserable for Mr Tusk, against whom he has held a grudge ever since the Civic Platform ousted the president's twin brother, Jaroslaw, and his Law and Justice party from power in 2007.

The president's penchant for his veto pen has given the Civic Platform a pretext to put off reforms. Though in 2010 Poland will continue to weather the global downturn rather well—its economy will expand by as much as 2%, having been the only European Union country to post growth for 2009—the picture is not all rosy. Unemployment will reach at least 12%, well above the European average.

The public finances will remain a mess, with the central budget deficit doubling to 3.8% of GDP and bringing total public debt perilously close to 55% of GDP, whereupon the government is legally bound to balance its books through an inopportune bout of austerity. To prevent this, Mr Tusk will forge ahead with privatisation, including the sale of several large energy utilities and the stock exchange. This will be grist to the mill of the privatisation-averse president, who, though unable to block it, will make "selling the family silver" the leitmotif of his re-election campaign.

Fearful of a public backlash, the government will procrastinate on other reforms. But once Mr Tusk is sworn in as president, there will be no more excuses. ■

Jan Piotrowski: freelance contributor, The Economist

---

being built at Ust-Luga, near St Petersburg. That is bad and expensive news for countries such as Hungary, with oil refineries dependent on the Druzhba pipeline.

With friends like these

But the Kremlin will not have it all its own way. Russia's gas production, crippled by corruption and bad management, is falling. As domestic and export demand recovers, it will be painfully clear that Russia does not have enough gas to satisfy all its customers. This will result in rapid price rises for countries with no alternative to Russian supplies, and more embarrassing announcements about delays to prestige projects such as the underwater Shtokman field off Russia's north-western coast. Russia's clumsy use of energy blackmail in past years has spurred many European countries to diversify, albeit belatedly. Refineries that once took only Russian oil, such as Lithuania's Mazeikiai Nafta, will start experimenting with supplies from other countries. It may be expensive and technologically more difficult. But it increases these customers' bargaining power.

The weakest link in the West will be Britain, which has left it too late to build new nuclear power stations before its existing ones are decommissioned. Unease, or even panic, will spread in 2010 as consumers digest the prospect of much higher energy bills, blackouts, or both. The likely outcome is a "dash for gas": such power stations are quick and relatively cheap to build. But where will the gas come from? The gasmen in the Kremlin are licking their lips. ■

2010 IN BRIEF

The **Meissen factory**, near Dresden, exhibits its best porcelain to mark its 300th year.

Russia's role in turbulent times

Over the past few years the growing ambitions of "resurgent Russia" became one of the most actively debated topics in the international arena—and often the reason for concern and even alarm. Lately, as economic concerns globally proved to be a priority, the importance of this topic appears to abate. The crisis brings the opportunity to sensibly and rationally evaluate one's own international strategies and the risks emerging from the actions of other states.

In Russia, our priority is to ensure the resumption of economic growth, and this growth should be sustainable, and based on a more balanced structure of the economy. In the course of 2010 we will continue our efforts to modernise the economy, encouraging innovation and diversification.

Globally, Russia will continue to be a reliable source of energy and other raw materials. As such, we will remain dependent on the economic well-being of our customers and countries that provide transit services for Russia's exports. This is why Russia will continue its efforts to promote a legally binding agreement on international energy co-operation. Simultaneously, the task of modernisation of the national economy requires that we remain large importers of new equipment, technology and services. In other words, Russia sees itself as part of the global trade system, and wants to build stronger, more friendly and comfortable relations with all our partners. WTO accession remains on our agenda: we hope to conclude talks in 2010.

I expect 2010 to be a turbulent year, financially and economically, both for Russia and the world: the depth of the current crisis, and the complexity of the problems that it has revealed, mean a protracted period of stabilisation and recovery. The green-shoots talk will be heard now and again, with many countries becoming the unexpected leaders of economic growth. Yet it is the quality of recovery that matters, not the pace.

In 2010 the efforts of governments will focus increasingly on post-crisis development. The foundations of a new economy will start to emerge, and I expect that a reassessment of values will precede this process. The issues of security and environmental protection, reduction in consumption of energy and other natural resources, accessibility of information, health, greater mobility—all of these will become increasingly pressing and urgent. Reflecting these challenges, government spending on research will remain a priority.

Russia will be no exception. We have already intensified our efforts to promote science and research in those fields that will be supportive of long-term sustainable development. We are also ready to invest in energy-saving technologies, research and development in the fields of nuclear power and alternative energy, further exploration of outer space, information technology, new medical technologies and medicines. It will create additional opportunities for global co-operation, and I am confident that Russia's contribution will be in demand worldwide.

Needless to say we must rely on political and diplomatic, rather than military, tools in resolving conflicts. The role of regional co-operation will increase. The policies of the leading world powers will be more and more focused on strengthening global security, rather than securing the dominance of any particular nation. We welcome in this respect the evident willingness of the current US administration to follow this route.

It's good to talk

Finally, a few words on the issue of global forums. Many have been saying lately that the new G20 format is replacing G8, making the latter redundant. Indeed, the G20 summits were some of the most important global events in 2009. In my opinion, there is little sense in comparing the influence of the G8 summit in Italy with the decisions of the London and Pittsburgh G20 summits. The interdependence of countries and regions means that new formats of dialogue will appear. G20 proved to be an effective format for discussion of global economic issues. However, G8 for the time being can remain the main forum for issues of international politics and security. Russia will continue to contribute to the work of both summits. Maintaining some specific summit format is not as important as creating favourable conditions for dialogue.

The experience of the past year has shown the importance of maintaining dialogue at the international level, and while it may not bring immediate results, it helps to reduce tensions and increase trust. This spirit of global co-operation must be carried into 2010. As the economic crisis in the largest economies becomes less acute, it is necessary to turn attention to tackling the global issues whose priority could have slipped over the past 18 months. We can be confident that the world has learnt from the crisis only if the work to reduce global inequality continues, if not intensifies. ∎

Dmitry Medvedev, president of Russia, urges world leaders to carry the spirit of international co-operation into 2010

WTO accession remains on our agenda: we hope to conclude talks in 2010

Investec
Specialist Bank

A world of difference

Where expertise and experience count. We apply fresh thinking to market challenges and create new financial possibilities for our clients. Focusing our talents on providing a specialist product range that includes private banking, capital markets, investment banking, property investments and asset management.

For more information, call **+44 (0)20 7597 4000** or visit **www.investec.com**

Out of the Ordinary™

Private Banking • Capital Markets • Investment Banking • Property Investments • Asset Management
Australia Botswana Canada Hong Kong Ireland Mauritius Namibia South Africa Switzerland Taiwan United Kingdom & Channel Islands United States

Investec Bank plc (Reg. no. 489604) and Investec Asset Management Limited (Reg. no. 2036094) are authorised and regulated by the Financial Services Authority and are members of the London Stock Exchange. Registered at 2 Gresham Street, London EC2V 7QP.

United States

Also in this section:
The economy recovers, weakly 62
The Fed's next battle 63
California's new constitution 64
The 2010 census 66
Three rising stars 68
Michael Kinsley: Can newspapers survive? 70

Mr Obama's unpromising year

Peter David WASHINGTON, DC

Americans will blame bad times on the president

When they voted to send a black man to the White House at the end of 2008, Americans performed one of the most remarkable acts of rebranding in the history of their remarkable nation. The coming year, however, will be a miserable one for Barack Obama. This is not only because of the iron law of waning novelty. His second year as president will expose the underlying weakness of the political coalition that elected him, the scale of the difficulties he inherited, the stubborn resistance of Americans to sudden change, and their enduring attachment to the dream of small government and individual opportunity.

Note first that the novelty of Mr Obama's colour and style did not last all that long even during his first year. The approval ratings of 70% or thereabouts that he enjoyed at the beginning of 2009 fell by the end of the summer to around 50%, pretty much the average (if anything a bit lower) for presidents after their first eight months. That this happened so soon after he performed some decisive economic firefighting—the fiscal stimulus, the restructuring of Detroit's carmakers—suggests that voters in 2010 will not be inclined to thank him for averting a depression that did not come.

They are more likely to blame him for the recession that did. And most Americans will not feel good about their prospects. Jobs will continue to be scarce; taxes will rise in spite of Mr Obama's rash promise not to raise them for the middle classes; and the deficit will still be rocketing heavenwards on an unsustainable trajectory.

By 2010, moreover, Mr Obama will no longer be able to fall back on the excuse that all of this was beyond his control. Given the scale of the crisis he inherited, he could have decided to focus the whole of his first term single-mindedly on economic recovery. Instead he made a bold—and some will say reckless—decision to reach for more.

It is true that large constituencies supported Mr Obama's call for comprehensive health-care reform and legislation to tackle global warming. But in 2010 many of these true believers, who wanted and expected audacious change, will be feeling let down by the weak legislation that will squeak out of Capitol Hill. Others will say that it was a mistake all along to embark on expensive reform at a time of acute economic distress. Beyond this, an underlying problem for Mr Obama is that in 2010 most voters will be feeling the short-term costs of changes in health care and energy and not yet any of the long-term benefits.

The politics of change

This points to another vulnerability. The coalition Mr Obama marshalled in 2008 around the alluring but ambiguous banner of "change" will splinter. The most ideological members of that coalition are already dismayed by "betrayals" such as the president's inaction on causes such as gay marriage, and by policy calls such as the continuing detention of suspected terrorists with-

2010 IN BRIEF
The ground-breaking ceremony takes place for the **George W. Bush Presidential Centre**.

Peter David: Washington bureau chief, *The Economist*

out trial. Disappointed expectations will keep some of them at home in the mid-term congressional elections in November. Other stay-at-homes will include many of those first-time voters, mainly the black and the young, who in 2008 were electrified by his person rather than his policies. Many are likely to take the view that they did enough when they sent Mr Obama to the White House. Unexcited by the ins and outs of cap-and-trade and health-care legislation, and by an election in which Mr Obama's own job is not up for grabs, why should they turn out again?

> A good number of Americans in the middle of politics are furious

Since the complaint of the left is that Mr Obama is governing from the centre, you might expect the self-described independent voters who backed Mr Obama in 2008 to stay with the Democrats in the mid-terms.

Think again. A number of independents will feel no less betrayed by Mr Obama than the left already does. The Republican message that Mr Obama has presided over the biggest expansion of government for decades, and that he has done nothing to rein in the Democratic Party's worst partisans and protectionists on Capitol Hill, will gain traction. A good number of Americans in the middle of politics are furious at the spectacle of Wall Street being bailed out while so many ordinary Joes are losing their jobs, homes and pensions. Hard times in 2010 will ensure that their anger is not going to subside quickly.

Mr Obama will find no consolation on the world stage. Whatever his long-term decisions on Afghanistan and Iraq, American forces will still be suffering casualties in both countries in 2010. In his second year it will become increasingly clear to people at home that America risks losing its status as the world's sole superpower and undisputed top nation as its relative economic power wanes. This trend may be inexorable with the rise of new powers in Asia, but that will not stop voters from blaming the fellow in the White House.

Losing his House?

Above all, the result of November's mid-term elections will reflect the fact that even an economic crisis of extraordinary proportions cannot make most Americans ditch their ingrained belief in a free-market system and embrace bigger government. The perception that Mr Obama is tilting too far left will cost the Democrats a host of seats. Although the Senate will remain out of the Republicans' reach, they might take control of the House of Representatives. No fewer than 84 of the Democrats' seats in the House represent districts that were won by George Bush in 2004 or Senator John McCain in 2008; they could turn Republican again.

It is worth remembering that a miserable 2010 does not mean that Mr Obama will necessarily fail to win re-election in 2012, or that his presidency is destined to be remembered as a failure. Other presidents, including Ronald Reagan and Bill Clinton, managed to bounce back from wretched second years and setbacks in the mid-terms. But the coming year will be a trying one for America's no-longer-so-fresh new president. ■

2010 IN BRIEF
Tina Brown stirs controversy with her new book, "The Clinton Chronicles".

Square-root reversal

Greg Ip WASHINGTON, DC

America will recover, but too weakly for comfort

The American economy in 2010 will be torn between two opposing forces. The first is that deep recessions usually lead to strong recoveries. The other is that financial crises usually produce weak recoveries. The interplay of these two forces will produce a cycle that resembles not a V, U or W, but a reverse-square-root symbol: an expansion that begins surprisingly briskly, then gives way to a long period of weak growth.

Recessions interrupt the economy's natural inclination to grow. They create pent-up demand for homes and other goods, and prompt businesses to slash production, payrolls and investment to levels well below what normal sales require. Ordinarily, the deeper the downturn, the more powerful the reversal of those effects. Based on experience, the American economy, which shrank by some 4% over the course of the 2007-09 recession, ought to grow by as much as 8% in its first year of recovery. The unemployment rate, around 10% in late 2009, should drop to about 8%.

Ground down to zero
Hourly wages, fourth quarter, % change on year earlier
Sources: US Bureau of Labour Statistics; Goldman Sachs
2009 estimate, 2010 forecast

That won't happen. But growth could still beat the consensus forecast of 2.5% in 2010. Business inventories are deeply depressed and even a modest swing to restocking will bring a rapid rebound in factory production. New-home construction is at its lowest proportion of GDP since 1960, and the inventory of unsold new homes the slimmest in 17 years. A sizeable upturn is in store. Capital spending is at its lowest relative to GDP in 40 years and is due to rise. The Obama administration's $787 billion fiscal-stimulus package has been criticised for dribbling money into the economy too slowly, but for that reason it will support growth well into 2010.

Greg Ip: United States economics editor, *The Economist*

None of these factors, however, can sustain strong ▶

The Fed's next battle

Greg Ip WASHINGTON, DC

This time, with politicians

In the 1930s the Federal Reserve stood by as the economy sank into Depression. Retribution followed as Franklin Roosevelt concentrated more of its governance in Washington, DC. Today's Fed, under its chairman, Ben Bernanke, has been hyperactive in preventing another Depression, yet again faces political peril. In 2010 critics in Congress will seek to rein in its independence even as its defenders in the Obama administration push to expand its regulatory powers.

Though its battle against the financial crisis and recession was heroic, the Fed is blamed for two previous blunders. First, its easy monetary policy in 2003-04 arguably inflated a housing bubble. Second, and less debatable, the Fed was at best an intermittent, at worst a negligent, regulator: it did too little to restrain reckless mortgage lending and allowed financial giants such as Citigroup to acquire nearly fatal levels of poorly understood risk.

No one has a coherent solution for preventing bubbles with monetary policy. But, on the second point, many in Congress would like to strip the Fed of oversight of banks. Timothy Geithner, the treasury secretary and a former Fed official, won't let that happen. But nor will he succeed in extending the Fed's reach beyond banks to any big, risky firm, unless it shares that power with other regulators.

Meanwhile Ron Paul, a Texas Republican and strident critic of the Fed, will succeed in opening the Fed's lending and monetary-policy decisions to congressional oversight. But he will compromise on the details so that the Fed's effectiveness won't be hurt much. Some would like to go further by changing Fed governance, in particular reducing the relative independence of its 12 reserve banks. This is so politically explosive (one must hope, and assume) that it will not happen. ■

How tight is Bernanke's grip?

---

growth past 2010 without a self-sustaining cycle of private spending and income growth. Several obstacles stand in the way of that transition. Through to mid-2009 households had lost $12 trillion, or 19% of their wealth, because of the collapse in house and stock prices. That saps their purchasing power and pushes them to save more, especially those nearing retirement. Though they'll boost their saving only gradually, that still means consumer spending (about 70% of GDP) will grow more slowly than income, after two decades in which it usually grew more quickly. High unemployment will hold back wage gains (see chart on previous page); wage cuts are already commonplace. Leaving aside swings in energy prices, inflation, now about 1.5%, will slip to zero and may turn to deflation in late 2010. Deflation drives up real debt burdens, further sapping consumer spending.

High interest rates caused most previous recessions, and low rates ended them. Not this one. When it began, the Fed's short-term rate at 5.25% was not particularly high. The Fed cut it in effect to zero and aggressively expanded its balance-sheet by making loans and buying long-term bonds. In spite of that, bank loans to business and consumers are falling, as are loans packaged into private, asset-backed securities. Only the government-backed mortgage agencies, Fannie Mae, Freddie Mac and Ginnie Mae, continue to expand credit.

This reflects not just a lack of willing borrowers, but the lasting damage to the financial infrastructure that matches savers with investors. The International Monetary Fund studied 88 banking crises in the past four decades and found they led to sustained losses of output. Swathes of America's "shadow banking system" of finance companies, investment banks and hedge funds have been vaporised. The government won't let any more big banks fail, but the survivors are neither inclined nor able to expand their lending much. Residential- and commercial-property values fell by $8 trillion, or almost 20%, through to mid-2009, impairing existing loans and eroding the collateral for new ones. Regulators are also proposing to raise capital requirements, which will further encourage bankers to turn down borrowers.

Other crisis-racked countries, such as Sweden in the early 1990s and South Korea in the late 1990s, rode devalued currencies and booming exports back to health. That won't work for America: the rest of the world isn't big or healthy enough, and a steeply falling dollar would inflict deflationary harm on others.

Fiscal and monetary policies were admirably aggressive in 2009, but a withdrawal of either would threaten growth beyond 2010. The scheduled expiration of Mr Obama's stimulus will subtract up to 2% from GDP in 2011. But Mr Obama will not want to push for significantly more stimulus since voters are already worried about big government and the deficit, and Republicans will exploit that sentiment as they seek to pick up seats in the 2010 congressional elections. The Fed, under fire for its meddling in the markets and expanded balance-sheet, may be tempted to raise interest rates early in 2010 if growth is surprisingly good; it will resist.

The list of roadblocks is depressing, but America will not slip back into recession or a lost decade akin to Japan's in the 1990s. It did not enter its crisis with as much overinvestment as others, Japan in particular; its population is still growing (Japan's is shrinking). It took two years to tackle its banks' problems; Japan took seven. Boom times will be back. Just not very soon. ■

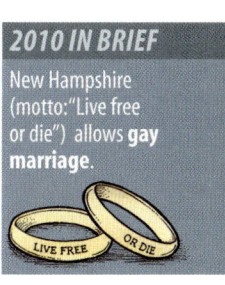

> America will not slip back into recession or a lost decade akin to Japan's

---

2010 IN BRIEF

New Hampshire (motto: "Live free or die") allows **gay marriage**.

Found(er)ing Fathers

Andreas Kluth LOS ANGELES

Californians will discover that voting for a new constitution is easier than drafting one

In November 2010 Californians will vote in a pair of ballot measures to call a constitutional convention. If polls are right, their approval of these measures is all but assured. Californians are fed up with the dysfunctional governance that periodically turns their state into a laughing stock. They want a new constitution.

Their disdain for the existing one is well deserved. It is among the most convoluted such texts in the world, ranking with Alabama's and India's as one of the longest. It contrasts starkly with the minimalist elegance of America's constitution, adopted in 1787, or Alaska's, ratified in 1956.

California's first constitutional convention took place in 1849, before California was even admitted to the Union. A second convention in 1879 tried to right every possible wrong and produced a tome. To this was added, during the Progressive era of the early 20th century, direct democracy—with referendums, recalls and voter initiatives. Such initiatives have since produced more than 500 constitutional amendments. America's constitution, a century older, has been amended 27 times.

Among the quirks in California's current document are: 1) a requirement, from 1933, for two-thirds majorities in both houses of the legislature to pass a budget; and 2) the same two-thirds requirement, added by voters in the infamous Proposition 13 of 1978, to increase any tax. Two other states (Rhode Island and Arkansas) have this requirement for budgets and several others have it for raising taxes, but only California has it for both.

If California's legislature contained moderates, normal fiscal management might still be imaginable. But the moderates have left. Californian elections, as Governor Arnold Schwarzenegger has frequently complained, are won or lost in the party primaries of gerrymandered districts that encourage extremism. Democrats may be in the majority, but nay-saying Republicans can block any budget and habitually do.

The element of direct democracy exacerbates the situation by ensuring that the inmates—ie, the voters—run much of the asylum. Voters pass, for example, "tough on crime" sentencing laws with nary a thought about paying for more prisons. When their elected representatives subsequently cannot muster two-thirds to raise taxes or cut another part of the budget, voters then profess shock at their incompetence.

> The inmates—ie, the voters—run much of the asylum

Thus the state lurches from one fiscal crisis to the next. Last summer, California even had to issue IOUs in lieu of cheques to its creditors. The appeal of starting afresh, with a clean constitution, is obvious.

The idea immediately brings to mind Philadelphia in 1787, where 55 of the most august minds ever assembled shuttled between Independence Hall and the City Tavern for four muggy months of secret deliberations. Despite daunting conflicts—who today owns slaves?—they produced the most robust constitution in history. Surely, air-conditioned California can have a go.

Missing Madisons

And yet, who would be California's "Founding Fathers"? Thomas Jefferson, absent from Philadelphia as minister to France, called the 55 delegates chosen by the states "demi-gods". These were men such as James Madison, deeply versed in Aristotle, Cicero, Locke and Montesquieu, who preferred the word "republic" to "democracy" for fear that the latter might evoke the chaos of ancient Athens.

If California has intellects of this stature, it certainly has none with Madison's nonpartisan credibility. Instead, there is a fear that the state's entrenched interests, from the prison-guards union to party bureaucracies or "Prop 13" fanatics, will take over the process and make it a microcosm of the state's dystopia.

Hoping to meet these concerns, the organisation behind the ballot measures, Repair California, proposes a random, jury-like draft of ordinary citizens as delegates. "Average Californians are the only ones who can lead our state out of the quagmire of special interests and partisanship," argues one adviser.

But can lay people be expected to assume the responsibilities of a Madison? As jurors, citizens deliberate on binary questions of guilt after hearing evidence under the guidance of a judge. In a constitutional convention, the questions will be complex and large. Who would present the evidence, if not the same loonies who cannot agree in the legislature?

The irony that California is preparing to reinforce its populist instincts with yet more direct democracy would surely be too much to bear for Madison, the "republican" founding father. ∎

The constitution stymies even the Terminator

2010 IN BRIEF

The Colorado River Bridge completes the central part of the **Hoover Dam Bypass,** improving traffic between Arizona, Nevada and Utah.

Andreas Kluth: Western correspondent, *The Economist*

ADVERTISEMENT

Top 20 Taiwan Global Brands 2009

In a year when many marquee names have lost their shine, Taiwanese brands have continued to improve their image to consumers through better R&D focus and smarter marketing. While many established leaders have reduced their geographic footprint, Taiwanese companies are reaching even the most inaccessible global locations. And while some of their largest rivals were forced to stay out of the spotlight, Taiwan's best have maintained their brand-building efforts, anchored on quality, innovation and value.

Meet the front-runners of Brand Taiwan, as ranked by Interbrand, the world's largest brand consultancy.

Rank 2009	Company Name and Logo	2009 Brand Value (US$ millions)	Description
1	Acer	1,241	With its new Aspire One laptop and other thin-and-light models, **Acer** beat competitors in market-share gains and is poised to becoming a global household IT brand.
2	TrendMicro	1,235	A global brand in Internet security, **TrendMicro** has navigated the downturn in corporate sales by growing its consumer segment and leading in cloud-client technology.
3	ASUS	1,226	With its innovative, stylish, and eco-friendly products, **ASUS** has won numerous awards and is a media darling at international consumer-electronics fairs.
4	HTC	1,203	An innovation and design contender, **HTC** was first to launch a mobile phone based on the Android platform and sold 2m units of HTC Diamond within six months of launch.
5	MasterKong	916	Popular in China and backed by a Forbes 50 Best Companies in Asia, **MasterKong**'s brand of noodles, drinks and baked goods is out to capture global market share.
6	Want-Want	421	The world's largest maker of rice-cracker snacks, **Want-Want** has gained branding popularity in China and elsewhere with its recognizable logos and TV ad sign-offs.
7	Maxxis	345	Now the world's 10th largest tire maker, **Maxxis** is positioning itself for China's auto boom and growing replacement demand in emerging markets.
8	Giant	262	With a sizable share of the highly fragmented global bicycle market, **Giant** lives up to its "Inspiring Adventure" motto by reaching even the most inaccessible locations.
9	Synnex	255	An integrated logistics brand with global distribution services, **Synnex** firmed up its market share during the downturn by offering working-capital flexibility to clients.
10	ZyXEL	222	**Zyxel**, which markets its internet-access devices such as routers and modems globally, is placing focus on emerging markets such as Asia by offering integrated solutions.
11	Transcend	212	**Transcend** is taking advantage of the consolidating computer peripherals sector by cultivating its brand through its own retail stores and superior customer service.
12	Advantech	204	The world's second-largest industrial PC supplier caters to small and medium-sized businesses, providing it with sizeable and steady amidst the global recession.
13	D-Link	190	With market presence in 64 countries, **D-Link** is well positioned for the global networking-infrastructure boom by enhancing its application and service offerings.
14	Uni-President	173	Known for its noodles, yogurt and tea drinks, Taiwan's largest food empire has received a brand boost by sponsoring the 2008 Olympics and owning a baseball team.
15	Johnson	159	The world's fifth-largest fitness-equipment company catering to homes and health clubs has introduced a range of massage chairs to raise its market positioning.
16	Merida	152	**Merida** has moved into the high-end market for bicycles with its "made by bikers for bikers" designs and by sponsoring the famous Multivan Merida Biking team.
17	CyberLink	93	A provider of media software solutions, **Cyberlink** launched a DVD-player software that immediately garnered 50% of the market last year.
18	Genius	69	Recognised for its computer mouse and other peripherals, **Genius** is strong in Eastern Europe, the Middle East and Latin America with immense potential for further growth.
19	Depo	49	With market share in North America and Europe, **Depo** is expected to maintain its leadership in high-quality auto lamps thanks to its dedicated R&D capabilities.
20	MSI	47	An acknowledged innovator in netbook screen technology, dimension and battery life, **MSI** also caters to the lower-end and thin-and-light segment of the market.

http://www.brandingtaiwan.org

TAITRA

Winners and losers
States likely to gain or lose seats in the House of Representatives after the 2010 census

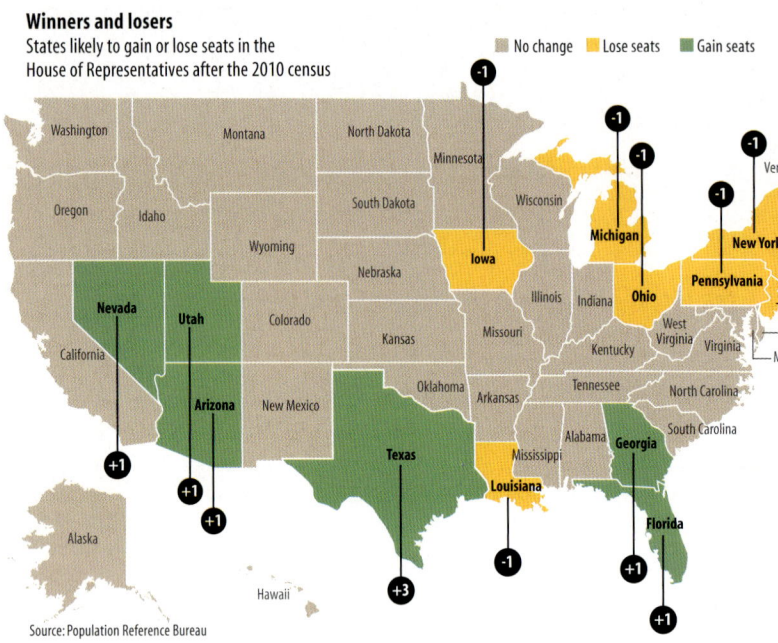

No change | Lose seats | Gain seats

Source: Population Reference Bureau

Counting heads

John Grimond

America's census will make for political mischief

Every ten years since 1790, the United States has held a census. In that respect 2010 will be no different from any other year ending with a zero. Indeed it would be a breach of the constitution to let it pass without a count of everyone living in the country, whether legally resident or not. This census will be relatively modest in ambit. Instead of asking more than 50 questions, as before, the 2010 form will pose only ten, and will, it is hoped, take no more than ten minutes to complete. For the first time, too, some questionnaires—13m out of the total of over 120m—will be distributed in both English and Spanish. Chinese, Korean, Russian and Vietnamese versions will be available on request.

The longer form used to be sent to only a selection of households, from which general conclusions were inferred. The details about income, housing, education, commuting and employment that it elicited are now gathered by an annual survey of a small proportion of the population. Hence the new, shorter form, which will merely count people and provide basic information about their names, ages, sex, ethnicity and so on.

Boring? In countries like Sweden censuses are dull affairs that excite only statisticians and trend-spotters, not trend-setters. In countries like Nigeria they precipitate coups or tribal warfare. Reactions in America fall between these extremes, but the norm is controversy.

The first disagreements were among the Founding Fathers, who could not agree on what constituted a person. The infamous compromise that found its way into the constitution counted slaves as just three-fifths of a "free" person. That may today seem like a concession to the wicked slave-owners. In fact, the slave-holding states wanted their captives to count as full persons, whereas the saintly states that held no slaves wanted them to count for nothing, like native Americans. The reason was that the census was to be used as the basis for representation in Congress and also in the Electoral College, which chooses the president, so all states wanted to maximise their populations, or diminish others'.

The census was also used in the early days for calculating direct taxation, as it had been in the days of Caesar Augustus. In America, the taxation provision was overtaken by the 16th amendment and today the census is used for what might be called reverse taxation: the distribution of about $400 billion in federal funds to local, state and tribal governments each year. But it is also used to apportion seats in the House of Representatives and draw boundaries for state legislatures and school boards. Since these tasks are carried out by partisan politicians, the census in America is seldom uncontroversial.

The most difficult people to count are the poor, the homeless, the itinerant and those in overcrowded buildings. Such people, if they vote, are more likely to vote Democratic, so Democrats tend to favour an overcount and Republicans an undercount. The 1990 census apparently overlooked about 5m people, mostly from minorities, while double-counting several million whites. The 2000 census was said to have produced a net overcount, but still missed about 4m people, 1m of them Latinos.

It was to correct such undercounting that Robert Groves, a Census Bureau official, suggested that statistical sampling be used in addition to the conventional enumeration. The idea produced charges of political tampering. Now Mr Groves is director of the bureau. Both he and the administration have forsworn the redrawing of boundaries, but some Republicans remain mistrustful.

> Gerrymandering is now elaborated by computers, not pens

Quirks in the law can have curious results. Though servicemen abroad are assigned to the states where they were most recently living, soldiers of God similarly deployed are granted no domestic abode. This gave North Carolina, with 18,000 troops and diplomats overseas, an extra House seat after the 2000 census, to the chagrin of Utah, deemed to have 856 fewer inhabitants despite its thousands of Mormon missionaries abroad.

Most of the injustices, though, occur within states in the post-census redrawing of legislative boundaries to take account of population changes. The redistricting in Illinois after the 2000 census produced a 17th congressional district so artfully redesigned that it looks like nothing so much as a jigsaw puzzle attacked by flesh-eating bacteria. Born of Governor Elbridge Gerry's salamander-like redistricting in 1812 in Massachusetts, gerrymandering is now elaborated by computers, not pens, but the guidance still comes from shameless politicians.

The count will begin in the Inupiat Eskimo village of Noorvik in Alaska in January, though census day for most Americans is April 1st. It will end with the news that the resident population stands at 311,349,543 at year-end, give or take a few hundred thousand. ■

2010 IN BRIEF

The **Burning Man festival** for cultural radicals and ageing hippies marks its 20th year in Nevada's Black Rock Desert.

John Grimond: writer at large, The Economist

How can we deliver cleaner energy today?

Scan QR-Code with your mobile and learn more about our environmental portfolio.

With an efficient energy conversion chain from Siemens and the world's most efficient combined cycle gas turbine, saving up to 40,000 tons of CO_2.

Delivering environmentally friendly energy means: generating and transmitting power more efficiently while enabling a reliable distribution. Being the only company worldwide that offers solutions covering the entire energy conversion chain, we develop innovative ways to reduce emissions: for instance our newest gas turbine which will enable the combined cycle plant in Irsching, Germany to save up to 40,000 tons of CO_2 per year while powering a city of 3 million people.

siemens.com/answers

SIEMENS

All the news that's fit to pay for

*To survive, America's newspapers need to experiment like mad, argues **Michael Kinsley**, a columnist and editor-in-chief of a new website to be launched in 2010 by the* Atlantic

In 2010 the only thing harder to sell than a newspaper will be a newspaper company. Already, in 2009, the *Seattle Post-Intelligencer* and Denver's *Rocky Mountain News*, among other historic names, couldn't find buyers and simply stopped printing. The *New York Times*, which paid $1.1 billion for the *Boston Globe* in 1993, spent most of the past year hungrily eyeing bids of under $100m.

After years of Micawberism, many newspaper publishers now accept that no amount of cost-cutting and laying off of journalists can keep up with plummeting revenues. Newspapers missed the brief moment when the government was an easy touch for bail-outs of one "vital" industry or another. It has dawned on those who placed their hopes in *noblesse oblige*—a new generation of rich families that might regard running a newspaper as a civic responsibility—that the old *noblesse oblige* had operated in an environment of 20% profits, not permanent losses. As readers migrate from paper to online, their determination not to pay for news in electronic form seems firmer than ever.

And yet a revival of hopes that the odd penny might yet be squeezed from loyal readers is under way. Barely two years after abandoning the experiment of putting their most popular columnists behind a pay wall, executives of the *New York Times* have talked openly of trying again some different way: perhaps "metering" how long people spend on the site and charging a fee to those who stay beyond their free welcome. Or perhaps some version of a "membership", like the ones in public broadcasting, where voluntary payments are extracted through a powerful combination of imposing guilt and offering tote bags. In either case, the idea is to charge those who really love you and let everyone else in free.

Most of America's top newspapers are now available for a fee on Amazon's Kindle reading device. At a conference on the future of newspapers at the Aspen Institute in August (just one of many, newspapers having replaced NATO in the "future of" conference business), William Dean Singleton, owner of 54 papers including the *Denver Post* and the *Detroit News*, announced his intention to start charging for content on all his properties from the beginning of 2010.

When Rupert Murdoch wildly overpaid for the *Wall Street Journal* in 2007, it was the only American newspaper that had enjoyed reasonable success charging for access online. At that time Mr Murdoch strongly hinted that he would tear down the pay wall and let everyone in free. But in 2009 he said he would not only maintain the *Journal*'s pay wall but build one around all his other properties.

A final straw in the wind: Steven Brill, America's most indefatigable serial hit-and-miss entrepreneur, having just shut down his scheme to sell access to premium security lines at airports, announced that his next project would be a company dedicated to helping media of all sorts to charge for content. Mr Brill characteristically denounces newspaper publishers—his potential customers—as wimps for giving away their content until now. And many observers share Mr Brill's analysis that the big mistake was allowing readers to grow used to getting it free in the first place. But it is not psychology that is at work here. It is the iron laws of economics.

Why has the internet turned into a disaster for newspapers? Mainly because it destroyed the monopoly that most American newspapers enjoyed in their home towns. Sure, you can now get the *Pittsburgh Post-Gazette* in London or New York. But, more important, you can get the *New York Times* or the *Guardian* in Pittsburgh. Every English-language paper published anywhere in the world is now in competition with every other. Competition is what has driven the price down to zero and kept it there. Newspapers' other big revenue source—advertising—has suffered mightily in the recession. That was beyond their control. Losing the classifieds to Craigslist wasn't.

If at first you don't succeed

The big trend for 2010 goes by the name "hyper-localism". Getting the latest from Afghanistan in the *New York Times* is nice, but a site that will tell you about the sale on paint at the hardware store around the corner is even nicer. There is irony in this discovery of ever-smaller local communities. One point of the internet is that it permits the creation of communities without respect to geography: the 130 people around the world who collect glass bowls from the 1830s. But the salvation of newspapers (online, of course—forget about paper) may turn out to be supplying the news for ever-smaller geographical areas.

Or maybe it will be something else. The key is to experiment. The best advice for newspapers is from Clay Shirky, a blogger who wrote that we are in the middle of a revolution like Gutenberg's. In such a time, "Nothing will work, but everything might." Try it all. ■

The big trend for 2010 goes by the name "hyper-localism"

The Americas

Also in this section:
Latin America celebrates 200 years of independence 72
Canada's northern goal 73
Arctic oil off Greenland 74
Shakira: Teaching the poor 75

After Lula

John Prideaux SÃO PAULO

Whoever wins, Brazil should remain in capable hands after its presidential election

Latin America's largest economy is enjoying its best moment for a long time. One of the last countries to enter the global downturn started by the financial sector in 2007, Brazil was also one of the first to come out of it. For the first time in its history it has found a combination of economic growth, low inflation and full democracy—and the good fortune looks set to continue.

Much is due to Brazil's president since 2002, Luiz Inácio Lula da Silva, a charismatic former metal worker, with hair so curly that he was nicknamed "squid" (*lula*). The presidential election in October will be the first one that he has not contested since the country reintroduced direct elections in 1990. At the end of his second term he is so popular that it is hard to imagine that he was once a serial loser. He will leave a hole that nobody vying to be his successor will quite be able to fill.

The two best-placed are José Serra, the governor of São Paulo, and Dilma Rousseff, the head of the *casa civil*, an office analogous to presidential chief-of-staff.

Mr Serra has a head start. His approval ratings in the country's most populous state are high. He was a good health minister in the government of Fernando Henrique Cardoso, and ran for president against Lula in 2002. As Lula proved, losing elections is no barrier to future success in Brazil.

Ms Rousseff's chances depend on whether Lula will be able to transfer his popularity to his anointed successor. Much will also hang on whether her appeal is hurt by other candidates on the left, not least Marina Silva, a senator, former minister and long-time star of the environmental movement.

The vote will split the country geographically, particularly if Mr Serra picks a running-mate who is also from the south-east of Brazil. This would line up the poorer north and north-east against the wealthier, more populous south and south-east. That would suit Mr Serra but would exacerbate the contrast between the two nations within Brazil.

The winner in October will inherit a country with a higher international profile and a more successful economy than when Lula came to power. But there will also be problems, despite a golden period in which tax revenue grew faster than GDP. In response to the global crisis, Lula's government both cut taxes and boosted spending, the kind of policy response that only mature countries can manage without terrifying their creditors.

Rather than the extra spending going on infrastructure, it has been lavished on increases to public-sector wages and benefits. These entitlements will be hard to cut. Revenue from the recently discovered oilfields off Brazil's coast will not come in quickly enough to rescue the new president from this inherited problem.

The rules about how oil money is spent—crucial for the country's development—will be pushed through Congress just as the presidential campaign is getting going. This means that there is a big risk that the debate about the country's future will be swamped by private dealmaking, preventing Brazil from making the most of its "present from God", as Lula has described the oil.

Both main candidates are well-suited to the tasks they will face. Mr Serra's time in the federal government is best remembered for his decision to break the patent on efavirenz, an AIDS drug manufactured by Merck, which has helped Brazil to keep the disease under control. But some fear that Mr Serra, with an economics doctorate from Cornell University, would disturb the institutions of economic policymaking that have contributed towards Brazil's recent success.

Ms Rousseff is also an economist by training, though not such a distinguished one. She is credited with getting Lula's presidency functioning again after the *mensalão* scandal in 2005, when it was revealed that the government had been managing its business in Congress by paying bribes.

The really remarkable thing, from Brazil's point of view, is that it has two technocrats competing for the top job. The country's hard-won political and economic stability is set to continue, whoever wins. ■

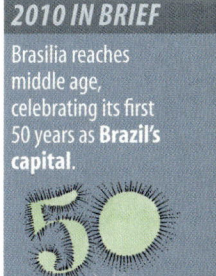

The squid's farewell

> The debate about the country's future will be swamped by private dealmaking

2010 IN BRIEF
Brasilia reaches middle age, celebrating its first 50 years as **Brazil's capital**.

John Prideaux: São Paulo bureau chief, *The Economist*

Bolívar's continent

Michael Reid

Latin America takes stock of 200 years of solitude

The people of Latin America will be invited to look back during 2010, as many of their governments mark two centuries of independence from Spanish colonial rule. There will be much bombast: Hugo Chávez, Venezuela's leftist president, will proclaim a "second independence", this time from alleged domination by the United States. Other leaders may use the occasion to look to the future, and to measure what their countries still need to do to achieve developed status.

That question is all the more pressing since the region will find it hard to reach the 5.5% annual average growth enjoyed from mid-2003 to mid-2008, before the world recession intervened. After a contraction of some 3% in 2009, a lacklustre recovery means that growth for the region as a whole is unlikely to be much more than 3% in 2010. To do better, Latin Americans will have to raise their productivity after years in which sky-high commodity prices mattered more than sound policy. This shift means that pragmatic centrism will be in the ascendant as the region's leftist tide begins to ebb.

Independence will be celebrated early and often. It was a protracted affair—the last Spanish army on the mainland was not defeated until 1825. Brazil broke away from Portugal in 1822. But rebellion started in many places with the proclamation in 1810 of local juntas nominally loyal to the Spanish monarch (who had been imprisoned by Napoleon) but in practice bent on running their own affairs. Bolivia and Ecuador jumped the gun with short-lived uprisings in 1809.

But it is Venezuela that will kick off the big commemorations. On April 19th 1810 a local junta overthrew the Spanish governor in Caracas. Mr Chávez will use every opportunity to identify his own regime with his hero, Simón Bolívar, the great Venezuelan-born Liberator—even though the ideas of the two men differ radically. Similar events will take place in Argentina on May 25th, in Colombia on July 20th and in Chile on September 18th. Mexico will mark its war of independence on September 16th, and weeks later it will commemorate the centenary of the start of its revolution of 1910-17.

Potted future

Celebration may be curbed by austerity. **Mexico** will be looking anxiously over the border for an American economic recovery. For **Venezuela**, the year is a crucial one. Mr Chávez risks losing omnipotence at a legislative election due in December. If the opposition can unite—a big if—it stands a good chance of winning a majority, as recession, inflation and mismanagement erode public support for the president's "21st century socialism". In **Chile** Sebastián Piñera will try to lead the Chilean right to its first victory in a presidential election in half a century. He will almost certainly face a tight run-off ballot in January against Eduardo Frei, a Christian Democrat former president.

Colombia's presidential election in May will turn on an earlier decision: whether the Constitutional Court gives the green light for a referendum changing the constitution to allow a president a third consecutive term—and whether Álvaro Uribe, president since 2002, will risk looking like a Chávez-style autocrat by standing. If he is a candidate, Mr Uribe will win, though more narrowly than in the past. If not, Juan Manuel Santos, a former defence minister, is the best-placed of his would-be heirs. Sergio Fajardo, an independent ex-mayor of Medellín and an engaging former maths professor, will mount a strong challenge, especially if he can find parties to back him. In **Costa Rica** Ottón Solís, a dissident social democrat, may come from behind to win a presidential election in February against Laura Chinchilla, the candidate of the ruling social-democratic party of Óscar Arias, the outgoing president.

With money scarcer, those governments that do not spend it well will find themselves subject to popular protests. If the oil price surges again, Mr Chávez may gain new allies. Otherwise, expect his "Bolivarian" alliance of leftist-nationalists to lose ground, in Venezuela and beyond. Indeed, 2010 may be the year in which Mr Chávez faces a choice of either losing power or keeping it by snuffing out the last trappings of democracy in Venezuela. ■

> Pragmatic centrism will be in the ascendant as the region's leftist tide begins to ebb

2010 IN BRIEF
Cubans get **broadband internet** for the first time, thanks to a new fibre-optic cable linking the island to Venezuela.

Michael Reid: Americas editor, *The Economist*

Canada's northern goal

Jeffrey Simpson OTTAWA

The Arctic is no longer the forgotten frontier

Canada is a northern nation. "O Canada", the national anthem, speaks of "true north, strong and free". But for most Canadians, 80% of whom live within 200km (124 miles) of the United States border, the Far North (Yukon, Northwest Territories and Nunavut) is a vast area never visited, largely unknown, usually forgotten and populated only by aboriginal peoples with quaint customs. All that will start to change in 2010.

Pangnirtung, population 1,300, on the east coast of Baffin Island, a settlement mostly known for Inuit art and a nearby national park, will see construction start on a C$42m ($40.5m) harbour for the small Inuit fishing fleet. At Gjoa Haven, the only settlement on King William Island, cabins used by polar-bear researchers will be upgraded. At Eureka, on Ellesmere Island, an atmospheric laboratory will be overhauled. At Iqaluit, capital of the Nunavut territory, tens of millions of dollars will be spent on badly needed housing, a research institute and a research vessel.

Add to that oil and gas exploration in the Beaufort Sea; C$100m for social housing; the same sum for geology research; another C$90m for economic-development projects; C$85m to improve Arctic research stations. The result is activity such as the Far North, from Alaska in the west to Baffin Bay in the east, has never before seen. And still to come—delayed by debilitating squabbles among Canada's shipbuilders and the usual cost overruns of military projects—are three Arctic patrol ships and a polar icebreaker, plus the publication of plans for a deep-water port at Nanisivik, on the north coast of Baffin Island. Later in the year, if all goes according to plan, the federal government will select a community that will get a High Arctic Research Station.

During the cold war, Canada and the United States constructed a Distant Early-Warning detection system against any attack by Soviet bombers. Apart from this DEW line, Canada paid little heed militarily to the Far North. Soviet and American submarines roamed under the Arctic ice without Canada having any ability to monitor them. The Canadian government outfitted a few Inuit with baseball hats and rifles, called them Rangers, and forgot about the region.

Now, the rush is on to discover the Far North, quite literally in the sense of research into atmosphere, ice and animals; and more urgently to get ready for the widening of sea lanes caused by global warming. Higher temperatures mean less sea ice and more scope for mineral and fossil-fuel exploration, more foreign ships traversing the north, and potential conflicts with other Arctic states over the seabed, sea lanes, and sea and land borders.

The Arctic is full of unresolved border delineations. Canada and the United States disagree over the maritime boundary between Alaska and Yukon. Canada and Denmark have both planted flags on tiny Hans Island. Canada will continue working in 2010 to prepare its claim under a United Nations convention for underwater rights extending as far as the North Pole, a claim that will surely conflict with one already filed by Russia.

No country agrees with Canada's contention that the Northwest Passage (there are actually two or three possible routes) belongs to Canada. The United States, Russia and the European Union all believe the passage constitutes an international strait. The trickiest decision for Canada is whether to consider the United States as friend or rival in the Far North, a decision that has to come soon. Do the two countries co-operate in managing the sea lanes? Do they sort out their maritime border dispute? Do they support each other against Russia, or go their own ways?

Canada's belated interest in its Far North is somewhat ironic given that climate change has hit the Far North harder than any other part of the Earth, and yet Canada's

Jeffrey Simpson: national-affairs columnist, the Globe and Mail

> The trickiest decision for Canada is whether to consider the United States as friend or rival

A new hub for the world

Greenland, the new bonanza

Adam Roberts NUUK

Hoping to become Arctic oil barons

Greenlanders are assuming more powers of self-government from Denmark, after the Danes ceded control in 2009. In 2010, and beyond, the government of the ice-clad island will take control of domestic affairs. Yet full independence remains elusive. That depends on being weaned off generous Danish subsidies worth over $11,000 a year for each of the 57,000 or so Greenlanders.

The government in Nuuk, the capital, is bursting with ideas of how to get the economy running. One scheme is hydropower. The huge Greenland ice cap, some 3km (nearly 2 miles) deep in places, may threaten the rest of the world as it melts and so raises the sea level, but for locals it offers a bonanza: torrents of melt-water to spin turbines. The government wants hydro to supply 80% or more of Greenland's power. Cheap and clean energy, plus a cool climate, could then lure investors. Alcoa is considering whether to put an aluminium smelter in southern Greenland. Google, or other internet firms running hot and energy-hungry servers, may be attracted to the big cool rock in the north Atlantic.

As Greenland's ice retreats, other economic activity will flourish. Miners are prospecting newly revealed rock for gold, rubies, diamonds and more.

A bigger economic prize would be if long-promised deposits of oil and gas were found offshore. Disappearing sea ice is making that task easier. Expectations are high—oil has long been known to seep onshore. In 2007 the United States Geological Survey concluded that at least a few billion barrels of oil, as well as trillions of cubic feet of gas, are probably waiting to be found off Greenland's east and west coasts.

The government is encouraging exploration: 13 licences have been issued so far to large companies, such as ExxonMobil, that are scouring over 137,000 square kilometres (53,000 square miles) of the sea for the sweetest spot to drill. In 2008 the firms produced "very positive" seismic data from Baffin Bay, says the government, and exploration drills will be sunk in the coming year or so. The civil servant in charge of hydrocarbons in Nuuk is confident that one will succeed. To make a discovery more likely soon, another round of licensing will take place in 2010.

Striking a big deposit would cheer Greenlanders and it could be helpful for the geopolitics of Europe. Europe's increasing dependence on Russia for energy makes it harder for politicians to stand up to threatening behaviour from the east. It would not hurt if an alternative supply of hydrocarbons were available from a friendly, democratic country to the west.

As for ties with Denmark, here is a longer-term prediction: a declaration of full independence for Greenland in 2021—the 300th anniversary of the date that is generally accepted to mark the beginning of Danish colonial rule. Oil riches, naturally, would lubricate the process. ■

Adam Roberts: online news editor, *The Economist*

---

record in curbing greenhouse-gas emissions is the worst in the G8. In the Kyoto climate-change protocol, Canada pledged to reduce emissions by 6% from 1990 levels by 2008-12; instead, emissions have risen by 27% and will rise again in 2010, especially if development intensifies in the tar sands of Alberta.

No matter who governs Canada in 2010—the country's fractured political system has thrown up a series of unstable governments—all parties agree that the rush to research, develop and protect the Far North has become a national priority. The Conservative prime minister, Stephen Harper, made the Far North one of his signature issues after being elected in 2006. That the other parties now agree with this priority, without giving him any credit of course, means that the days of benign neglect of the Far North are over. ■

Sí, se puede

Experience of teaching the poor in Colombia has lessons for the wider world, says **Shakira**, founder of the Barefoot Foundation

No child dreams of becoming a militant or drug trafficker

Nine years ago, at the Millennium Summit at the United Nations headquarters in New York, heads of state from around the world agreed on the Millennium Development Goals to reduce global poverty. One of the key goals was to ensure that by 2015 every child, boys and girls alike, would be able to complete primary school. This means that all those finishing primary school in 2015 will be entering school in 2010. It's a daunting challenge, but if the G8, the G20 and other nations join together to establish a Global Fund for Education, we can make real progress towards this deadline.

Barack Obama promised America's support for creating this $2 billion new fund just over a year ago. A similar model already exists. The fund will be an independent and innovative institution similar to the Global Fund to Fight AIDS, Tuberculosis and Malaria. It will include representatives of civil society and developing countries as equal partners alongside donor nations in its governance structure. It will link funding to results—ensuring accountability in the way that funds are spent.

A lot is at stake. In the past two years over 600 schools in Afghanistan have been bombed, burned or shut down by extremists. Eighty percent of these have been schools for girls. Why? Because the education of a child is the most powerful form of national security—and that's why it is such a threat to militants everywhere.

This isn't theoretical to me. Growing up in Colombia after decades of conflict I saw that the people who are born poor, die poor. With rare exceptions, they never have the chance to improve their lives.

These people have difficulties finding decent jobs and making a decent life—and they often end up involved in doing things they never imagined. No child dreams of becoming a militant or a drug trafficker. But in developing countries sometimes life doesn't give you any other option.

Education, education, education
Education is the only way to break this cycle. But in today's world there are still 72m children who are denied the opportunity to go to school and 226m adolescents who don't attend secondary school.

My foundation in Colombia, Pies Descalzos ("Barefoot"), has proved that the poorest children can be educated. For less than $2 a day per child, our schools provide food, education and counselling services to thousands of students. Our schools help underprivileged children grow in sustainable ways and provide them with the tools they need to break out of the cycle of poverty.

Many people don't realise that Colombia has one of the largest internally displaced populations in the world. Over 3m people in the country (out of a population of 49m) have fled their homes because of conflict. For this reason we decided that our programmes in Colombia should specifically focus on serving displaced children.

Our work in Colombia combines high-quality academic instruction with recreation, health care and psychological support. We operate six schools in three diverse regions of Colombia: Barranquilla, Quibdó and Altos de Cazucá. Over 5,000 students are directly served in our schools—but approximately 30,000 people benefit from our programmes. For example, in working to combat malnutrition we not only provide students with nourishing meals and evaluate their nutritional status, but we also provide their parents with critical information on health and nutrition.

In addition to physical-health services, the foundation's programmes support emotional health through counselling and exposure to the arts as well as through advice for families and parenting classes.

We also support the broader community. On any given day our school buildings are hubs of activity—providing a range of services, including adult-literacy classes, youth-leadership development, access to libraries and computer training. Perhaps most importantly, we have also begun to form parent co-operatives focused on teaching parents and on income-generating activities aimed at ensuring that families are financially secure.

We are now in the process of taking this success story to other parts of the world through our non-profit Barefoot Foundation, based in the United States.

If our foundation can bring quality education to some of the poorest children in the world there is no reason why governments can't do the same thing. Our schools in Colombia are proving each and every day that no matter where a child is from, no matter how poor children are, they can thrive if given the chance.

I refuse to believe that it isn't possible to educate every child. By establishing a Global Fund for Education in 2010 we will invest in these children's future—and help to secure our own. ■

Conversations for a Smarter Planet.

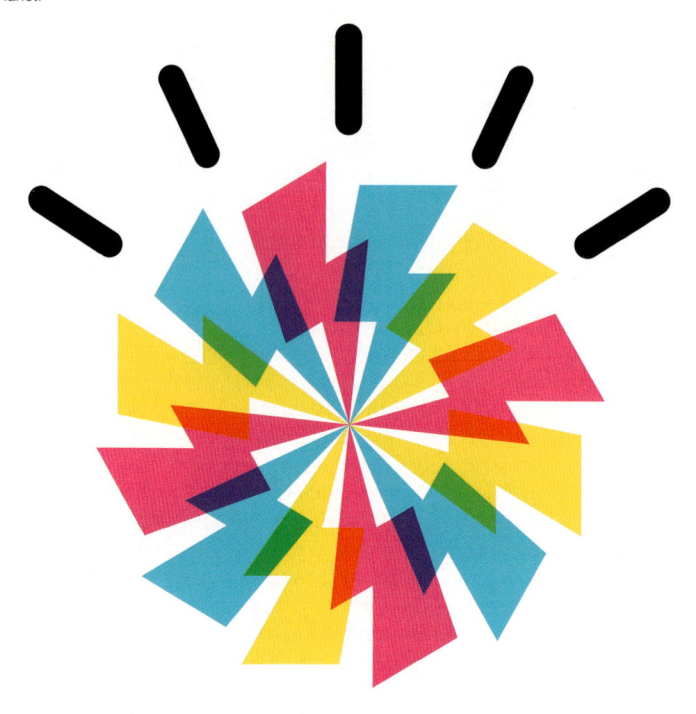

Smarter energy for a smarter planet.

For most of the last century, our electrical grids were a symbol of progress. The inexpensive, abundant power they brought changed the way the world worked – filling homes, streets, businesses, towns and cities with energy.

But today's electrical grids reflect a time when energy was cheap, their impact on the natural environment wasn't a priority and consumers weren't even part of the equation. Back then, the power system could be centralised, closely managed and supplied by a relatively small number of large power plants. It was designed to distribute power in one direction only – not to manage a dynamic global network of energy supply and demand.

As a result of inefficiencies in this system, the world's creation and distribution of electric power is now wasteful. With little or no intelligence to balance loads or monitor power flows, enough electricity is lost annually to power India, Germany and Canada for an entire year. In the UK, Government projections show that without new capacity generation, supply will not meet demand by 2016, whilst at the same time billions of pounds are wasted on energy that never reaches a single light bulb.

Fortunately, our energy can be made smart. It can be managed like the complex global system it is.

We can now instrument everything from the meter in the home to the turbines in the plants to the network itself. In fact, the intelligent utility system actually looks a lot more like the Internet than like a traditional grid. It can be linked to thousands of power sources – including climate-friendly ones, such as wind and tidal.

All of this instrumentation then generates new data, which advanced analytics can turn into insight, so that better decisions can be made in real time. Decisions by individuals and businesses on how they can consume more efficiently. Decisions by utility companies on how they can better manage delivery and balance loads. Decisions by governments and societies on how to preserve our environment. The whole system can become more efficient, reliable, adaptive... smart.

Smart grid projects are already helping consumers save 10% on their bills and are reducing peak demand by 15%. Imagine the potential savings when this is scaled to include enterprise, government departments and universities. And imagine the economic stimulus that an investment in smarter grids could provide in our current crisis.

In fact, there's no need for mere imagination. A recent report by the London School of Economics calculates that an investment of £5 billion in the development of a smart power grid in the UK could create or retain almost a quarter of a million jobs in energy and related industries. It could enable new forms of industrial innovation by creating exportable skills, resources and technology.

IBM scientists and industry experts are working on smart energy solutions around the world. We're working with utility companies globally to accelerate the adoption of smart grids to help make them more reliable and give customers better usage information. We're working on seven of the world's ten largest automated meter management projects. We're even exploring how to harness intermittent wind power by turning millions of future electric vehicles into a distributed storage system.

Our electrical grids can be a symbol of progress again – if we imbue the entire system with intelligence. And we can. Let's build a smarter planet. Join us and see what others are thinking, at **ibm.com/think/uk**

THINK

IBM, the IBM logo, ibm.com and the globe design are trademarks of International Business Machines Corporation, registered in many jurisdictions worldwide. A current list of IBM trademarks is available on the Web at 'Copyright and trademark information' at www.ibm.com/legal/copytrade.shtml

Asia

Also in this section:

Football and the two Koreas 78
Uncertain times for China 79
Chinese workers get scarcer 80
China's economic boom 81
Manufacturing overtakes agriculture in India 82
Fragile Pakistan 83
NATO's woes in Afghanistan 83
Australia set fair 84
Susilo Bambang Yudhoyono: Islam and the West 85

Bring on the new generation

Henry Tricks TOKYO

It will take more than a new government to get Japan out of its fiscal black hole

Japan is a top-down society. As in books, where the characters flow from top to bottom, so life is run vertically, with seniority often synonymous with age. In politics, age is no disqualification for high office: the new cabinet is, on average, over 60. In business, the seniority system is entrenched. Even in the home, hierarchy starts young: there is an honorific for little brothers to address their bossy big sisters.

How galling then, for those down the pecking order, that the numbers of people at the top are rising so fast. In 2010, there will be as many middle-aged people of 45 and over in Japan as there will be people under 45. That not only means more people to bow to. It means more layers to fight through before promotion, and more pensioners to support (by 2010 4m baby-boomers will have retired since 2007—roughly the number of inhabitants of Yokohama, Japan's second-largest city).

This retiring *bebi bumu* generation has reasons to feel proud of its achievements. Over its lifetime, industrialisation has transformed Japan and the elderly have accumulated savings that many can live off comfortably. But do they merit all the deference they receive? In 2010 there will be several alarming statistics that suggest not.

For one, the economy, the world's second-largest since the 1960s, has lurched so treacherously that it will fall behind China's in size in 2010 (see "The dragon still roars" in this section). That will make it even more difficult to persuade the world that Japan matters.

The legacy of not one but two lost decades has saddled Japan's future generations with a debt whose relative size is unprecedented in the OECD. That organisation reckons gross borrowings will exceed 200% of GDP in 2010. The borrowing may be underpinned by high savings, but it has not brought security for Japan's growing number of jobless and poor people. After a collapse in the economy in 2009, the fiscal deficit is expected by the OECD to rise to nearly 10% in 2010. Yet social spending remains low and, the more people age, the more it is likely to increase. Sooner or later the Japanese will realise that a country growing old so rapidly cannot live so absurdly beyond its means.

Let's not have another lost decade

That is why the government of Yukio Hatoyama, which swept to power in 2009, ending more than half a century of almost unbroken rule by the Liberal Democratic Party (LDP), has a devilishly hard task in its first year in office. It was elected because the Japanese were sick of the LDP's crony capitalism, in which government, bureaucrats and favoured industries carved up the spoils of the budget. But as it seeks to rebalance the economy, by redirecting privileges away from the export and construction industries towards domestic firms, it will need to break some labour-market and wage rigidities. It risks temporarily pushing unemployment higher.

That would be unpalatable unless there were a stronger welfare system and retraining subsidies. But the

> The seniority system is entrenched

2010 IN BRIEF

Myanmar holds a "free and fair" election.

Henry Tricks: Tokyo bureau chief, *The Economist*

Political football

Charles Lee SEOUL

Not just a game for North and South Korea

Ever since their division at the end of the second world war, the two Koreas have been locked in fierce rivalry. In 2010, however, their most direct competition will be on football pitches in South Africa. For the first time, South and North Korea have simultaneously qualified for the FIFA World Cup finals.

Koreans on both sides of the demilitarised zone are mad about football. They take enormous pride in their teams' achievements in previous World Cups. The North defeated Italy to reach the quarterfinals of the 1966 tournament in England. The South advanced all the way to the semifinals of the 2002 World Cup that it co-hosted with Japan. In South Africa, each Korean side will try to outshine the other, regardless of whether they end up playing head-to-head.

Off the football pitch, relations between the two Koreas will remain far tenser. Though destitute, North Korea is ploughing ahead with its nuclear-weapons programme. Its dictatorial leader, Kim Jong Il, who is believed to turn 69 in February, may be slowly dying of multiple illnesses. He has reportedly chosen his 20-something third son, Jong Un, as his heir. But if the dynastic succession goes awry, uncertainty over the fate of the North's reclusive regime—and the stability of the entire Korean peninsula—will grow.

North Korea's hot-and-cold relationship with the outside world will not change. Soon after its second atom-bomb test in mid-2009 it hurled insults at foreign critics, even mocking the looks of the American secretary of state, Hillary Clinton ("a pensioner going shopping"). But just two weeks later Mr Kim wined and dined her husband and former American president, Bill Clinton, in Pyongyang when he went to rescue two American journalists held captive there. Managing the North's hissy fits will, as usual, be a high-maintenance chore for the South and other regional powers.

South Korea, for its part, will work overtime to accentuate the differences with its northern rival. It has a golden chance to do so when it hosts a G20 summit of the world's leading economies in November 2010. As the first Asian country since the onset of the global financial crisis to take up the group's rotating chair, the South will be eager to show how it and others in the region are helping to drive global growth.

South Korea is also keen to serve as an honest broker between rich and developing countries on global economic issues. It believes that its own successful transition from poverty to wealth gives it credibility. Of course, should the North decide to embark on a path of nuclear-weapons-free reform, the South will happily lend it a guiding hand.

But many Koreans will feel a deeper sense of solidarity in watching the World Cup. They will want to see the teams of both North and South do well. And they will be united in cheering for whichever country is playing against Japan—the Koreas' *bête noire* of history and their shared rival in Asian football. ■

Charles Lee: freelance contributor, *The Economist*

Better on the field than off

2010 IN BRIEF
Tonga reforms its parliamentary system, with **King Siaosi Tupou V** giving up many of his political powers.

---

money for that must compete with government promises of support for families to encourage them to have more children, and pension support for the old. It is not clear whether, in its 2010 budget, the government will be able to cut enough waste to pay for such largesse.

What Japan needs is tax reform so that revenues rise. But that is a non-starter in 2010. The highlight of the political calendar is an upper-house election in the summer in which Mr Hatoyama's Democratic Party of Japan hopes for a majority so that it can pass legislation in both houses without coalition partners. To achieve that, the danger is that the new government will err on the side of timidity and squander its political capital.

If the government cannot right the ship, can business? Its flair for innovation and design is legendary (in 2010 Nissan will bring the all-electric Leaf to the streets of Japan and America, and it will warn pedestrians of its approach with a futuristic sound reminiscent of the flying cars in "Blade Runner"). There may even be a chance for fresh thinking in the monolithic *Keidanren* business chamber, after the election of a new leader in June.

But business, too, is often a slow-moving gerontocracy, hidebound by a reluctance to let creative individuals make quick decisions. It ought to pile into China and South Korea in 2010, given the decline of the American consumer market. But it is likely that the government will make the greater inroads. Mr Hatoyama has reached out to both countries, and on the 100th anniversary of Japan's occupation of Korea in 1910 there is even an invitation for Emperor Akihito to visit Seoul.

What Japan really needs in 2010 is the sort of once-in-a-generation change in business management that came to politics in 2009; that is, the realisation that those who make mistakes, however senior, can be kicked out and replaced by fresh thinkers. It is too much to hope it will happen in a year. But it had better start soon. ■

The cautious leap forward

James Miles BEIJING

China prepares a new plan for uncertain times

In the year ahead China's leaders will revel in the growth their country enjoys and the envy this arouses elsewhere, especially the West. The World Expo, which begins in Shanghai in May, will help to display the brash, futuristic face of a country determined to prove that China is the exception to global malaise. But President Hu Jintao will still be worrying. China's economy remains troubled and the worst ethnic unrest in many years is proving hard to tame.

China's economic growth may be stronger than many other countries', but it is weaker than before the crisis began. Rebalancing the economy to depend less on the battered export sector and more on domestic consumption will take years. Massive stimulus spending cannot be sustained indefinitely. As Mr Hu prepares to step down as Communist Party chief in 2012 and president in 2013, China faces a far more unsettled economic environment than it did when he assumed those roles a decade earlier.

Such concerns will not be evident at the World Expo, which China describes as an "economic Olympics". As it did in the Olympic games in Beijing in 2008, China sees this event as a huge milestone on its journey to great-power status: it casts its eye back to the first such event in London in 1851 (the Great Exhibition as it was called) with its purpose-built Crystal Palace, and to the one in Paris for which the Eiffel Tower was built in 1889.

Planning the inheritance

Comparisons with the glory days of the West's industrial rise will be well received by the many Chinese who see the Western world's current economic distress as an opportunity to shift the balance of global power towards China. But China's leaders will refrain from over-egging the significance of the country's rise. A stable relationship with America remains of vital importance to Mr Hu (notwithstanding his continuing eagerness to build up China's military strength: 2010 could be the year when China's first aircraft carrier is unveiled). The coming year will see his government trying at least to appear to be working with America to address the world's problems, from economic distress to climate change.

China will commit itself to few if any sacrifices to curb its greenhouse-gas emissions. But it will not want to be seen as a pariah following the international climate-change talks in Copenhagen in December 2009. It will talk of reducing its carbon intensity (the amount of carbon emitted per unit of GDP) and of a date (well beyond Mr Hu's political horizon) when it aims, not promises, to reach a peak in its carbon emissions. It will make bigger commitments to boost the share of renewable sources in its energy consumption. Its talk will be calibrated to give President Barack Obama the political cover needed to push his climate-change agenda at home. But anything more will require American money and technology. Chinese government frustration will grow if these are not forthcoming. Talk of co-operation could give way to bickering.

In 2010 the government will formulate a new five-year economic plan to take effect in the following year. When the Communist Party meets in the autumn to give its views (or, to be more precise, issue instructions) on this, much attention will be focused on what it decrees for China's environment. Officials have suggested that carbon-intensity targets should be written into the plan. This would be a first for China. But the plan will, as always, give priority to GDP growth.

Mr Hu does not have to worry about meeting the current plan's targets. It called for GDP to reach 26.1 trillion yuan ($3.8 trillion) by 2010. That level was surpassed in 2008. Another goal was to double GDP per head from its level in 2000. This happened within the plan's first couple of years. A revision of China's per-head data, however, could well be required after a national census on November 1st 2010, the country's first in ten years. The likelihood is that China's population is several tens of millions bigger than officials have been estimating.

The census operation will be supervised by Li Keqiang, a deputy prime minister who is widely expected to be appointed the country's next prime minister (replacing Wen Jiabao) in 2013. Vice-President Xi Jinping looks on course to take over from Mr Hu as party

> Mr Hu will worry about his legacy

2010 IN BRIEF
Private developers promise to greet visitors to Shanghai's World Expo with a replica on a nearby island of **Michael Jackson's Neverland Ranch**.

James Miles: Beijing bureau chief, *The Economist*

Some will get there faster than others

chief and president. But although Mr Hu enjoyed the smoothest succession in communist China's history, there is no guarantee his luck will be repeated.

Mr Hu will worry about his legacy. Despite rapid economic growth in the ethnic-minority regions of Tibet and Xinjiang, these areas have been roiled by unrest since a flare-up of rioting in the Tibetan capital, Lhasa, in 2008. Security deployments and widespread arrests have maintained control, but in July 2009 far bloodier rioting erupted in Xinjiang's capital, Urumqi. The authorities fear that a relaxation of security measures could end in more violence. October 2010 will mark the 60th anniversary of China's invasion of Tibet. Mr Hu will not be able to let down his guard. ■

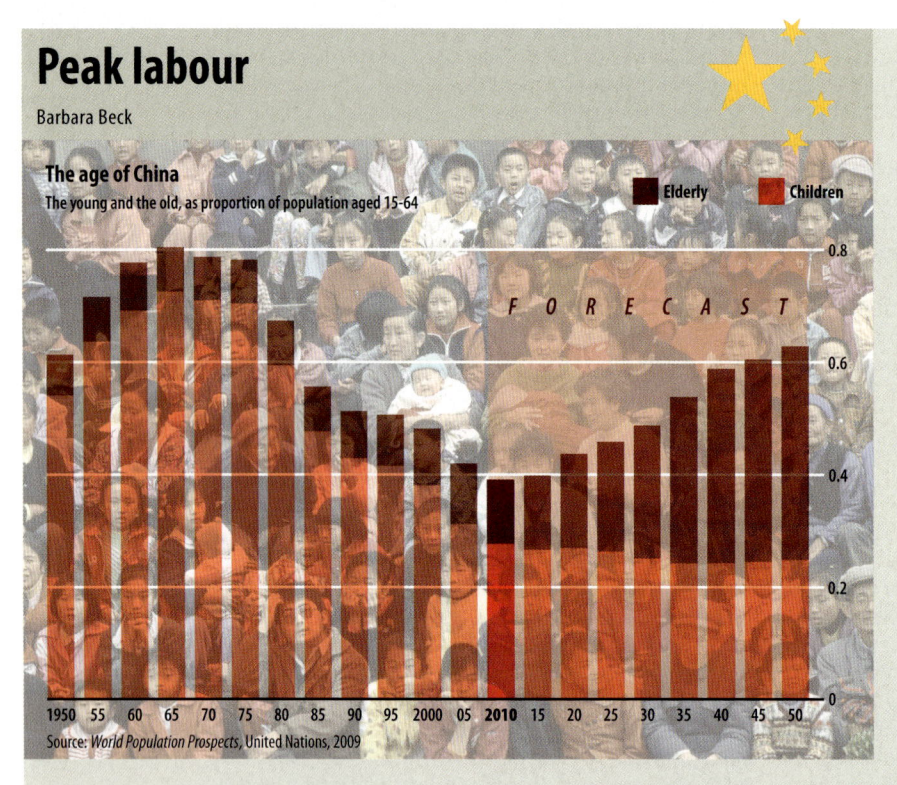

Peak labour

Barbara Beck

The age of China
The young and the old, as proportion of population aged 15-64

Source: World Population Prospects, United Nations, 2009

Chinese workers will become scarcer

Demographers in China will celebrate 2010 as a golden year: the moment when the "demographic dividend" of the past couple of decades will reach its peak. Since the 1970s China's birth rate, and therefore the number of dependent children, has been plummeting, whereas the number of elderly people has been rising only gradually. The result has been a low "dependency ratio"—the proportion of dependants to people at work. Now at around 0.4, that ratio has helped to fuel China's prodigious growth.

From 2010 it will start to change. The number of dependent children will remain low because China's one-child policy of the late 1970s is still broadly in place. However, as life expectancy goes up (at 74, it is already half as long again as it was 50 years ago), the number of older people will grow, and the dependency ratio will rise with it, to above 0.6 by 2050.

Dependency ratios are beginning to rise all over the rich world, especially in Asia's "tiger" countries—Hong Kong, South Korea, Singapore and Taiwan. By contrast, dependency ratios in most developing countries will fall until at least 2030. China is unique in getting old before it has got rich. That matters, because a higher dependency ratio means a lower growth potential. Nor is the government in a position to provide the pension, health-care and other benefits that a vastly increased number of older people will need.

When most of China's industry was state-owned, the "iron rice bowl" provided cradle-to-grave social security for its workers. But that system was dismantled 20 years ago, and now pension and health-care provision is patchy at best.

China is running out of children to look after the elderly, a state of affairs often summed up by the formula "4-2-1": four grandparents, two parents, one child. The country has about 20 years to get its act together. Although its workforce will start shrinking from 2010 relative to the population, in absolute terms both its number of workers and its population as a whole will grow until about 2030, when the population will peak at around 1.46 billion. After that it will begin to decline gently.

The government is well aware of the problem, and has drawn up detailed plans to beef up the pension and health-care systems. But given the numbers involved even basic provision will not come cheap. China officially became an "old" country in 2000 when its share of over-60s reached 10% of the population, or 130m. That has already risen to 166m and is forecast to grow to a daunting 342m by 2030—a body of pensioners larger than the current population of the United States.

Having a large rural population to draw on, China will not immediately run short of labour. But the supply is not inexhaustible. The young migrants who have made the labour force so flexible will become thinner on the ground, and more expensive. That will drive jobs to countries with lower labour costs, such as Vietnam or Indonesia.

The Chinese government finds itself in a dilemma. It has been spectacularly successful with what it calls its "family policy"—in effect, forcibly limiting the number of children couples are allowed to have. The one-child policy has done what it was meant to do: since the early 1990s it has pushed the fertility rate below replacement levels. The average number of children per woman is now around 1.8.

> China is unique in getting old before it has got rich

If the government really wants to rejuvenate the population, it will need to loosen its policy. More children would increase the dependency ratio until they were old enough to join the labour force. But if it were done soon, some of those children would reach working age just before the crunch time of 2030, easing the labour shortage from then on.

Most officials are adamant that the policy remains in place. But in Shanghai, where the birth rate is well below the national average, the city government is now encouraging couples entitled to more than one child to take full advantage. Where it leads, others may follow. ■

Barbara Beck: special reports editor, *The Economist*

The dragon still roars

Pam Woodall HONG KONG

How sustainable is China's economic boom?

China will reach two economic milestones in 2010. It will overtake Japan to become the world's second-largest economy (at market exchange rates). And its exports will reach 10% of world trade—matching Japan's share at its peak in 1986. But China's economy also resembles Japan in the 1980s in more worrying ways. Will its boom turn to bust as it did in Japan?

China has rebounded faster from the global downturn than any other big economy, thanks to massive monetary and fiscal easing. China's slowdown in late 2008 was only partly caused by the slump in American demand. It was also self-inflicted by tight credit controls, so the economy responded quickly when the government turned the credit tap back on full and launched huge infrastructure spending. This stimulus will stretch into 2010; private consumption will remain strong, and a rebound in home sales will boost construction. As a result, China's GDP should grow by around 9%.

But for how long can China sustain such growth? Its GDP has increased by an average of almost 10% a year for the past 30 years. Even assuming a slowdown in the pace of expansion, many economists expect China's economy to overtake America's within 20 years. But the same was predicted of Japan in the 1980s before its bubble burst, resulting in a lost decade of sluggish growth. The gap between Japan and America has instead widened.

Some analysts claim that China today looks ominously like Japan in the late 1980s: chronic overinvestment, they say, has resulted in excess capacity and falling returns; a tidal wave of bank lending threatens a future surge in bad loans; and stock and property markets look dangerously bubbly. Banks' non-performing loans will surely rise in 2010, and unless the government tightens monetary policy it will store up future problems which could harm economic growth.

Luckily there are some important differences between China today and Japan during its bubble era, which make it less likely that China's boom will end in a prolonged economic bust. China's GDP per head is less than one-tenth of that of Japan or America. Its economy is still in the early stages of development, with ample room to play catch-up with rich countries by adding to its capital stock and lifting productivity. A successful developing economy should have a higher rate of investment because it starts with much less capital than advanced economies. China's capital stock is barely half as big as Japan's in relation to output; capital per person is only 5% of that in Japan. In addition, with almost half of its labour force still in agriculture, China still has plenty of scope to lift productivity by moving surplus labour into industry and services. This is very different from Japan in the 1980s.

China does have excess capacity in a few sectors, most notably steel. But concerns about overinvestment are exaggerated. During 2009, new investment in industries with overcapacity was relatively modest; most money went into infrastructure. And unlike Japan, which built roads to nowhere to prop up its economy, China still needs more public infrastructure. In general, investment in roads, railways and the power grid will help China to sustain future rapid growth.

Over the next decade, China's annual growth will slow from the 10%-plus pace of the past few years to perhaps 7%—still one of the fastest rates in the world. But future growth will be less dependent on exports. As China's share of world exports hits 10% in 2010, up from 4% in 2000, Japan's experience will be instructive. It suggests that there are limits to a country's global market share: after reaching 10%, its share of world markets fell as the yen strengthened. Likewise, China will be under foreign pressure to allow the yuan to resume its climb against the dollar in 2010.

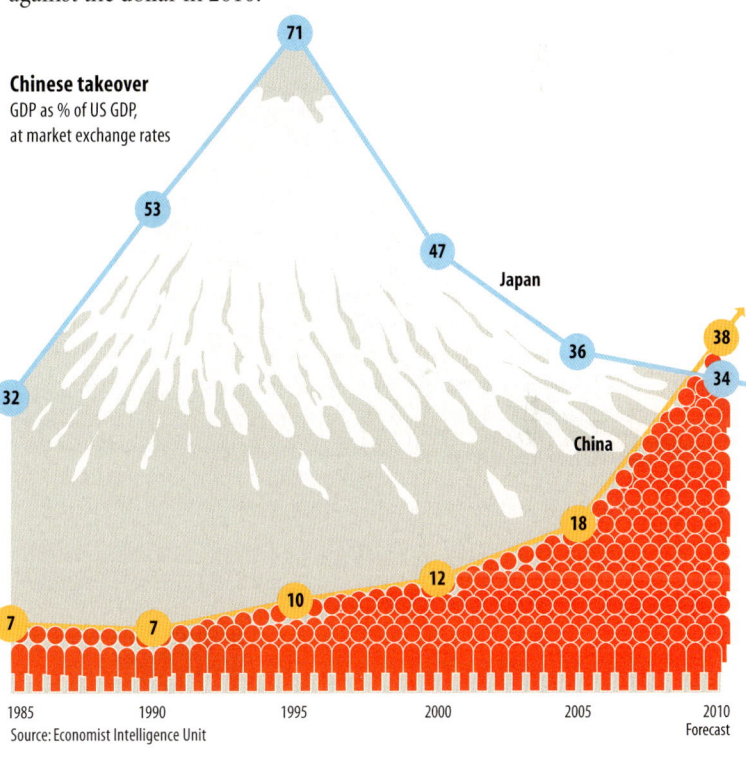

More of China's growth will therefore need to come from consumption. Infrastructure investment was the best way to boost domestic demand quickly, but in the longer term the government needs to lift consumer spending by shifting income from firms to households and by improving welfare support and health care. Slower export growth and stronger domestic spending will cause China's current-account surplus to shrink below 5% of GDP in 2010, less than half its peak in 2007.

Slower future growth, based on more domestic spending and a smaller trade surplus, would direct China to a more sustainable path. Over the past 20 years, China has made an unprecedented leap from being the world's tenth-biggest economy to becoming number two. At some point, before it leapfrogs America, China may well suffer a nasty slump—but not in 2010. ∎

> Some analysts claim that China today looks ominously like Japan in the late 1980s

2010 IN BRIEF

Work begins on a 29km (18-mile) **bridge** linking Hong Kong with Macau and Zhuhai in China.

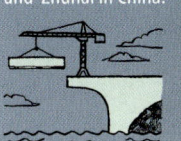

Chinese takeover
GDP as % of US GDP, at market exchange rates

Japan: 32 (1985), 53, 71, 47, 36, 38
China: 7, 7, 10, 12, 18, 34

1985 – 2010 Forecast

Source: Economist Intelligence Unit

Pam Woodall: Asia economics editor, *The Economist*

An imperfect storm

Simon Cox DELHI

Thanks partly to the monsoon, manufacturing will overtake agriculture for the first time in India

From the village of Vijay Pura in the Indian state of Rajasthan, the global financial crisis seems remote. The downturn is something people here read about in the newspapers, according to Dhanna Singh, a member of the Mazdoor Kisan Shakti Sangathan (MKSS), a union of activists and farmers. The villages have welcomed back migrant workers from neighbouring states, where people no longer find work twisting steel in Mumbai or polishing diamonds in Surat. But, by and large, India's rural poor were protected from the crisis by the same things that make them poor. If you never had secure employment or many financial assets, you cannot lose them to the crisis.

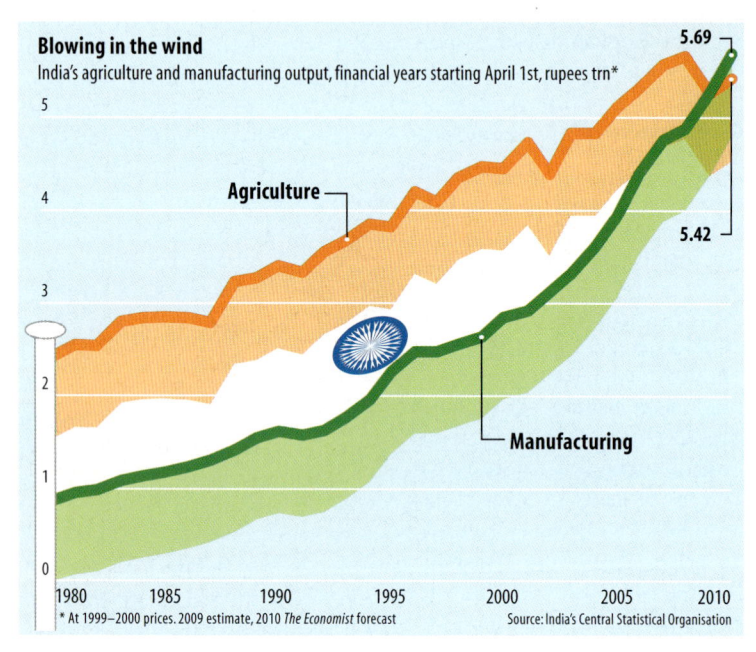

In Rajasthan, this resilience is also the result of government policy. The National Rural Employment Guarantee Act (NREGA), extended to every rural district in April 2008, is supposed to offer 100 days of work a year, at the minimum wage, to every rural household that needs it. Rajasthan, a parched state with a long history of drought-relief works, comes closer to fulfilling that promise than anywhere else, providing 68 days of work on average in the year to March 2008, according to a survey published in *Frontline*, an Indian newsweekly. Vijay Pura is cross-hatched with hard-packed roads built by people on the act's payroll. Thanks to the roll-out of the NREGA and a hike in the minimum wage, "People here are feeling a sense of security for the first time," says Shankar Singh of the MKSS.

The strength of rural demand is one reason why India escaped from the crisis so lightly. Sales of many "fast-moving" consumer goods, such as shampoo and toothpaste, are now growing faster in the villages than in the cities. Rural India's purchases of *chyawanprash*, an ayurvedic paste that eases digestion and bolsters the immune system, outpaced urban India's by over six percentage points in the second quarter. And Maruti Suzuki, India's biggest carmaker, more than doubled its sales in rural areas in the year to March 2009.

But, having weathered the financial crisis, rural India must now weather the weather. The monsoon rains, which feed India's unirrigated farmland, have been fickle, inflicting drought on almost half of India's districts, followed by floods in some areas as the monsoon departed. In a worst-case scenario, India's agricultural output could shrink by up to 7% in the fiscal year ending in March 2010, according to Citigroup. That would drag India's GDP growth down to 5.2%, slower than in the thick of the financial crisis.

The drought will raise food prices, adding to inflation. India is already the only big economy where consumer prices are rising faster now than they were before the crisis. The price of pulses rose by 20% in the year to August 28th; the price of sugar by 35%. That will force the Reserve Bank of India to tighten monetary policy. Goldman Sachs expects it to raise rates by as much as three percentage points in 2010. Spending on drought relief will also add to the government's yawning fiscal deficit, which will exceed 10% of GDP this fiscal year, if the budget gaps of the state governments are included.

The monsoon once decided India's economic fate. Now it only influences it. Agriculture's share of India's national output has dropped from 40% 30 years ago to 17% in 2009. Indeed, India's economy is now on the cusp of an historic transition. In 2010 agriculture will account for a smaller share of GDP than manufacturing: India's output of widgets will exceed its output of wheat, rice, cotton and the other fruits of the land. The factory will surpass the farm.

Return to the glory days

That is not just because agriculture is poised to shrink. Manufacturing, which stagnated during the crisis, should recover smartly in 2010. It was already growing by over 7% in July 2009, according to the index of industrial production. Investment in new plant and machinery will get a boost from the return of foreign capital inflows, some $44.1 billion in the year to March 2010 and $52.1 billion the following year, according to Rohini Malkani of Citigroup. About 35-40% of those flows will be foreign direct investment.

India's historians often hark back to the glory days of manufacturing in the 18th century, when Indian artisans produced calicoes and other fabrics of such appeal that Britain's spinners, weavers and printers clamoured (successfully) for import bans to protect their livelihoods. During Britain's industrial revolution, however, Indian weavers were "thrown back on the soil". India's first prime minister, Jawaharlal Nehru, wrote that India's industrial destiny had been thwarted by imperial economics. In 2010, thanks to a failure of the monsoon and a recovery of the world economy, India's agriculture will at last give way to its manufacturing prowess. ∎

> India's economy is now on the cusp of an historic transition

---

2010 IN BRIEF
Contemporary art takes pride of place at the **Biennale in Gwangju**, where 30 years ago South Korean students rose up against the military regime.

Blowing in the wind
India's agriculture and manufacturing output, financial years starting April 1st, rupees trn*

Agriculture: 5.69
Manufacturing: 5.42

* At 1999–2000 prices. 2009 estimate, 2010 The Economist forecast
Source: India's Central Statistical Organisation

Simon Cox: South Asia business correspondent, *The Economist*

Worryingly fragile

James Astill ISLAMABAD

Pakistan has a chance to become more stable. Don't bet on it

By its recent chaotic standards, Pakistan had quite a good 2009. Admittedly, more than 2m people were displaced by fighting between the army and Taliban militants. The economy was in the doldrums. And a threat of political crisis, pitting President Asif Zardari against his main rival, Nawaz Sharif, loomed. Yet his government, a coalition led by the Pakistan People's Party (PPP), looked stable. An injection of IMF cash—and a promise from America of an extra $1.5 billion a year—kept its creditors at bay. And the army, despite much suffering, won the biggest victories of a floundering eight-year campaign on its north-west frontier. Without catastrophic violence—an important assassination or a terrorist attack in India—Pakistan will be messy, but stable after this fashion, in 2010.

Peace be upon you?

> Of all the threats, another terrorist strike in India would be the most dangerous

The army will also make a bit more progress against the militants. Goaded into action in early 2009, after the Taliban seized areas of North-West Frontier Province alarmingly close to Islamabad, it pushed them back ruthlessly. Compounding the Taliban's troubles, their supreme leader, Baitullah Mehsud, who was responsible for a two-year suicide-bomb spree (and allegedly for the 2007 murder of Mr Zardari's wife, Benazir Bhutto), was killed by an American missile last August. And in October the army launched an assault on his former fief, in South Waziristan. Alas, it has shown no interest in pursuing members of the other Taliban, Afghanistan's former rulers, who have found refuge in Pakistan.

America's effort in 2009 to redefine Afghanistan and Pakistan as a single theatre ("Af-Pak") was partly to deal with this. The strategy recognised that neither country can be stable while the other is not—and that an unstable Pakistan, with over 180m people, nuclear bombs and a history of war with India, is of particular concern.

James Astill: South Asia correspondent, *The Economist*

A grim prospect

James Astill KABUL

NATO may lose in Afghanistan

In August 2009 General Stanley McChrystal, America's (and NATO's) top commander in Afghanistan, said that the international effort there was at grave risk of failing. He reckoned he had a year to start turning things around, or risk losing American support. If that is right, while professing support for General McChrystal's efforts, America and its European allies in Afghanistan will in 2010 start looking for ways to leave.

Most Afghans still seem to back their efforts to stabilise the place. But that is no substitute for an effective counter-insurgency strategy or a functioning state. In the absence of either, the Taliban have recaptured much of the south and east, levying taxes and dispensing justice.

For a better strategy, General McChrystal has ordered great changes to the way foreign troops conduct themselves, especially to make them more respectful of local people and mores. This shift, he concedes, will probably lead to an increased number of Western casualties. He has also requested an extra 60,000 troops, to be added to his current 100,000-strong forces. But with public opinion in Western countries turning against the war, governments there, most importantly America's, are reluctant to accept either outcome. As 2010 loomed, it was unclear whether Barack Obama would agree to send more American troops.

With an edge of desperation, the Europeans would rather discuss plans to "reintegrate"—or make peace with—the Taliban. Sooner or later, most Afghans and foreigners agree, this is inevitable. Yet there will be little progress on the task in 2010, and little agreement on how it should be attempted: the Americans want to win over low-level militants, the UN and some European governments advocate top-level peace talks. Nor is there much sign of reciprocal interest from the militants themselves.

Strengthening the Afghan state will be even harder—especially after the country's disastrous 2009 presidential election, rigged in favour of President Hamid Karzai and to the obvious disadvantage of his nearest challenger, Abdullah Abdullah. The ensuing furore will further discredit the international effort in the eyes of Afghans and foreigners alike. It will also worsen Afghanistan's main ethnic division between Pushtuns, Mr Karzai's group, and a powerful Tajik minority who voted mostly for Dr Abdullah.

It is a grim prospect. Indeed, it is hard to be optimistic about Afghanistan in 2010. ■

KING'S College LONDON
University of London

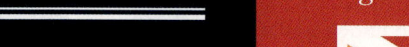

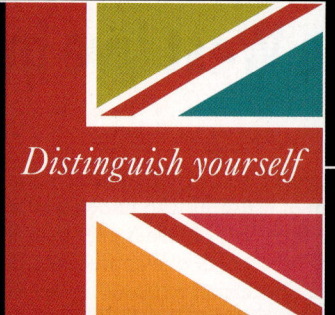

Distinguish yourself

King's is ranked in the top 25 universities worldwide* and based in the heart of London. With nine Schools and six Medical Research Council centres, King's offers world-class teaching and research. Our extensive range of subjects includes science and technology, arts and humanities, law, health, biomedical, social and management sciences.

*Times Higher-QS World University Rankings, 2009

www.kcl.ac.uk

Empower your future.

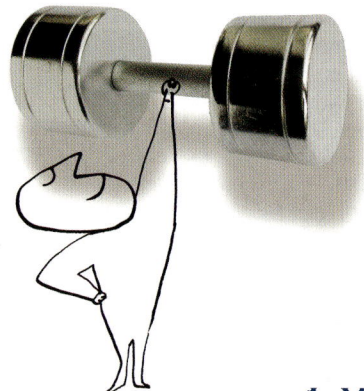

There comes a time when you recognise your own true value. This is the time to move ahead and shift into top gear with an MBA at SDA Bocconi, Italy's number one School of Management.

The experience you will have in Milano, a city where Italian culture and creativity meet the world, will empower your future and remain with you for the rest of your life.

SDA Bocconi. Knowledge and imagination.

1-YEAR FULL-TIME MBA
GLOBAL EXECUTIVE MBA
Milano, Italy

More info at www.sdabocconi.it/mbakit

Bocconi School of Management

SDA Bocconi

Middle East and Africa

Also in this section:
Struggle and strife in Iran 88
Iraqis rule Iraq 89
The year of African football 90
The worst country on Earth 91
Jacob Zuma: Africa and the World Cup 92

Mission not quite impossible

David Landau JERUSALEM

Israel is not alone in confronting Iran

Israelis enter 2010 with one issue uppermost in their minds: the Iranian bomb. Concern over Iran's nuclear ambitions has been a chronic condition in the Jewish state in recent years. In 2010 it will become acute. "All options are on the table" is the vague but menacing formula favoured by Israeli and Western politicians when they grope for a policy on Iran. In 2010, they will actually have to choose their option—as will Iran.

Israel's incessant warnings have converged with a new atmosphere of urgency around the world. Suddenly, the prospect of serious sanctions against Iran appears real. Russia and even China admonished Tehran in late September 2009, after the three Western permanent members of the UN Security Council disclosed evidence of a secret uranium-enrichment facility buried deep beneath a mountain near the holy city of Qom. Iran had long contended that its enrichment plant at Natanz was intended for peaceful purposes and was open to international inspection. It never divulged the existence of this second one.

The policy of engagement with Iran launched by the Obama administration now took on a stern aspect. In words, at least, the world's leaders seemed united as never before: if there was not full compliance and disclosure, the Security Council would impose tough new sanctions, blocking Iran's export of oil and import of refined petroleum products. France's President Nicolas Sarkozy set the start of 2010 as the deadline.

From Jerusalem, this is what successive Israeli prime ministers have long urged, none louder than the present leader, Binyamin Netanyahu, who has made Iran the focus of his rhetoric for more than a dozen years.

Ariel Sharon (2001-06) and Ehud Olmert (2006-09) favoured quiet diplomacy with the Western powers and Russia, and also with Sunni Arab states fearful of Iran's Shiite zealotry and hegemonic pretensions. Iran, they held, was a world problem, not just an Israeli one—this despite President Mahmoud Ahmadinejad's persistent Holocaust denial and his challenge to the very right to existence of the Jewish state. They encouraged secret efforts to set back Iran's research and production schedules.

Mr Netanyahu embraces all this, but wants much more—and a much higher profile for what he sees as Israel's historic confrontation with a tinpot Hitler. Under him, the Israeli air force conducts bombing exercises over far-off targets and seems gratified when they are disclosed. At home, a civil-defence drill is bruited as preparation for a rocket response from Iran's local proxies, Hizbullah and Hamas, in the event of an Israeli attack on Iran's nuclear plants.

The looming showdown in 2010 between Iran and the world holds out promise for Israel, but it makes Israel's own moment of decision nearer and starker. If sanctions are not applied after all, or are applied but fail, Mr Netanyahu may feel he can wait no longer.

To some of his critics, Mr Netanyahu's melodramatics are rooted in cynicism. Iran, they suspect, is his pretext for putting off peacemaking with the Palestinians, while he haggles with America over "natural growth" in Jewish settlements in the occupied West Bank.

A prime minister with Iran on his mind

2010 IN BRIEF
Geopolitics permitting, Iran's first **nuclear-power plant**, built with Russian help at Bushehr, goes onstream.

David Landau: Israel correspondent, *The Economist*

Struggle and strife

Xan Smiley

Iran's threat is from within and without

The two big questions for Iran in 2010 are, first, whether the Islamic Republic will reassert its authority over the Iranian people and, second, whether Israel or the United States will bomb Iran's nuclear sites in an effort to stop—or at least delay—its regime from producing a nuclear weapon.

On the first count, it is unlikely that the clerical authorities will regain the unchallenged control they enjoyed in the previous several decades. On the second, the chances are narrowly in favour of Iran continuing to escape the full military fury of either the Americans or the Israelis. But if anyone were to attack it, Israel is the likelier.

It is uncertain whether street demonstrations or unrest in the universities will resume and challenge the ruling establishment as they did in the weeks after the disputed presidential election of June 2009, when the incumbent, Mahmoud Ahmadinejad, was declared the winner. Mir Hosein Mousavi, who claimed to have won the 2009 election, will keep up his opposition to Mr Ahmadinejad, backed by a lesser candidate on the reformist side, Mehdi Karroubi. Supporters of both thwarted candidates will use the web and other electronic means to undermine the authorities, whose legitimacy will steadily drain away. The real power struggle will shift from the street and the campus to the inner circle of the ruling clergy.

Two former presidents, Akbar Hashemi Rafsanjani and Muhammad Khatami, will go on seeking to unseat President Ahmadinejad. The supreme leader, Ayatollah Ali Khamenei, will vacillate but continue, on balance, to back the president. By so doing, Mr Khamenei will lose popular esteem and legitimacy across the land. Several of the president's and the supreme leader's senior opponents, such as Mr Mousavi, may be put in prison. But, as the regime's unpopularity grows, they could yet end up on top.

Almost all Iranians believe Iran should have nuclear power as a matter of national pride. But even within the clerical establishment a bitter debate will ensue over whether or not to co-operate more fully with the International Atomic Energy Agency, the UN's nuclear watchdog, and with Western governments that want to prevent Iran from getting a bomb or acquiring a rapid "break out" capacity.

If economic sanctions fail to deter the regime, Israel will be tempted to bomb Iran's nuclear facilities, even though the United States will forcefully tell it not to. Iran's sites are so widely scattered and so well dug in underground that Israel would have to conduct a series of attacks over several days or even weeks.

Despite the fury of its rhetoric, Israel is unlikely to carry out its threats without an American green light. If it did, Iran would certainly spur its friends and proxies into retaliation against Israeli and American targets in the region and across the world, and would seek to close the Strait of Hormuz, blocking the export of Gulf oil to the West and dramatically raising the world oil price. It is a frightening prospect—but may not come to pass.

With or without a rain of Israeli bombs, the Islamic Republic—or, at least, its rigidly Islamic component—is doomed sooner or later to fizzle, though not necessarily as soon as 2010.

Xan Smiley: Middle East and Africa editor, *The Economist*

V for what?

▶ Others have a different sense of the prime minister's single-mindedness. "He is a man on a mission," says a senior Israeli politician. "His mission, in his own eyes, is to save Israel from the Iranian bomb. The peace process is a distraction; it is not part of that mission."

That could change if 2010 does indeed usher in an era of determination on the part of the major powers to strip Iran of its nuclear-weapons potential. The popular press in Israel calls the linkage between war with Iran and peace with Palestine "Yitzhar for Bushehr" (it rhymes better in Hebrew). The former is a Jewish settlement planted in the heart of the West Bank. The latter is an Iranian nuclear-power plant.

The suggestion has always been that America could wring concessions from Israel on Palestine in return for a "green light" for an Israeli strike on Iran. It was based on the assumption that the Security Council was paralysed and that America had ruled out military action.

Now, Mr Netanyahu's mission may be achieved by a concerted show of international will. In that event, Israel will claim that its own threat of force stiffened that will. President Barack Obama, for his part, will have a moment of opportunity to prise Israel, the Palestinian Authority and moderate Arab states—all potential victims of a rampant Iran—out of their obstinate gridlock and into a swift-moving peace process. ■

Iraqis rule Iraq

Xan Smiley

Hope laced with danger

Nearly seven years after the Americans toppled Saddam Hussein, Iraq is still groping towards normality. If 2009 was its calmest year since the invasion, 2010 may mark the moment when it can claim to have fully recovered its independence.

The first big event of the year will be a general election due by the end of January. The second, if Barack Obama sticks to the timetable he adjusted after winning the presidency, will be the departure of most American troops by the end of August. By the end of 2010 it should become clearer whether Iraq can stand on its own feet both politically and militarily. The odds, just, are that it will do so. But it will be a year of danger and uncertainty as well as hope.

Much will depend on the smooth emergence of a new government and prime minister. Though shenanigans in late 2009 within the dominant Shia establishment cast doubt on the political survivability of Nuri al-Maliki, who became prime minister in 2006, he has a chance of keeping his post for the next few years. But he must decide whether to join an electoral list that embraces most of the main Shia religious parties, which together won the last general election four years ago, or whether he forges alliances with more secular-minded Shias and with Sunni Arabs of various stripes, including former Baathists once loyal to Saddam.

As before, the Kurds, though not as solid a block as they were, may hold the balance. Mr Maliki's relations with Massoud Barzani, Kurdistan's regional president, have been periodically poisonous, but it may be in the interest of both of them to kiss and make up in order to mould a coalition government at the federal centre.

Again as before, a dangerous period of post-election haggling may ensue, perhaps for three or four months, creating a mood of nervous uncertainty. Government may drift, opening a vacuum that violent groups may seek to fill. At this point Mr Maliki may be ousted.

In any event, the insurgency will persist, but at a far lower level than in its bloody heyday in 2005 and 2006, when in some months more than 3,000 civilians were being killed. The monthly average death toll in 2010 is likely to be less than a tenth of that. But that is still high enough to deter foreign investors and dissuade most of Iraq's 2m refugees and 3m internally displaced people from going home.

All American troops must be out by the end of 2011

Several issues, if mishandled, could reignite a bloodier conflict all over again. A bitter dispute over the ownership of the oil-rich Kirkuk area, which the Kurds now dominate and insist on keeping, will probably not be solved; the longer the Kurds hold the upper hand, the harder it will be to dislodge them. Other points along what is known as the "trigger line" between Kurds and Arabs, especially in the Mosul area and its surrounding Nineveh province, are also dangerous. The Americans have proposed "three-way" patrols comprising themselves, Arabs and Kurds to cool the hottest spots. If things go violently wrong, Mr Obama, who has talked of keeping a reserve of not more than 50,000 troops in Iraq mainly as trainers (down from 125,000 or so at the end of 2009), may briefly try to reimpose peace.

But not for long. Under a "status of forces agreement" signed by George Bush, all American troops must be out by the end of 2011. There will be talk of the UN sending peacekeepers, but the world body will probably still deem such an operation too dangerous.

OK girls, it's ours now

Al-Qaeda's shrinking Iraqi branch will carry out the occasional mass-casualty suicide attack but its pool of recruits will continue to dry up—unless Mr Maliki, or whoever emerges as Iraq's leader, fails to bring the Sunni tribes and their vigilante groups, which helped America make its "surge" effective in 2007, into Iraq's security web and give them their due spoils of patronage. Iraqi forces and leading personalities will be the main targets rather than the Americans. If a more harshly sectarian Shia-led government emerges, a wider Sunni insurgency could yet be rekindled.

Oil production and the supply of electricity, medical and other services are likely to improve after years of stagnation. If the central government can strike a deal with the Kurds, production and exports might at last take off in a big way, giving Iraqis a long-awaited dose of prosperity.

If Mr Maliki retains power, he will seek to soften the sectarian political mood that has prevailed since the fall of Saddam. He may also strengthen the central levers of power and tighten his grip on them, reversing the federal trend that his Shia rivals had promoted. He may also chip away at human rights and other freedoms (of the press, for instance). Expect talk of an Iraqi Putin emerging. Many Iraqis, after the traumatic post-Saddam chaos, will view that as their least-bad option. ■

2010 IN BRIEF

Construction begins in Egypt on the Arab world's first **nuclear-power station**.

The year of African football

Jonathan Ledgard NAIROBI

The FIFA World Cup will reveal a continent's talent—and also its flaws

2010 IN BRIEF
Fourteen former colonies in Africa celebrate **50 years of independence** from France.

Africa will host its most spectacular global event in 2010: the football World Cup in South Africa. It will not be Africa's coming-out party. New genetic evidence released in 2010 will show that that party was 60,000 years ago, when a band of *Homo sapiens* made it across the narrows of the Red Sea, and from there to every point on the planet. Still, many of their descendants, together with those of the football-obsessed Africans who stayed behind, will be glued to their televisions from the World Cup's kick-off on June 11th to its final on July 11th. The cumulative audience of some 30 billion will include larger numbers of soccer-resistant Americans, Chinese and Indians than ever before.

The World Cup will be a chance to showcase Africa, but can Africa handle the pressure? Despite high levels of violent crime, unhappy construction workers and a shaky economy, South Africa will prove sceptics wrong. It will do Africa proud, perhaps too proud: for the first time other Africans will see that South Africa is in many ways closer to Australia or Argentina than it is to their ramshackle countries. South Africa is likely to do better than Poland and Ukraine, which will jointly host football's European Championship in 2012; Ukraine's preparations have been singled out as shoddy. Sunshine will help. So will South Africa's sporting culture, and its keenness for acceptance after the long years of the anti-apartheid sporting boycott.

The more pressing question is whether South Africa will benefit from the World Cup. New airports and roads will attract more foreign investment to provincial cities, including Polokwane and Port Elizabeth. But the boost in tourism in poorer country areas will hardly offset the broken promises of investment by the crony-ridden African National Congress. And the newly built stadiums will be filled only occasionally by the national rugby team.

South Africa will prove sceptics wrong

A worry for the Fédération Internationale de Football Association (FIFA) is that the tournament will not be African enough. Of South Africa's domestic football clubs, only Soweto's Kaizer Chiefs and Orlando Pirates draw big crowds. There will not be many fans travelling from qualifying African countries. Many black South Africans will not be able to afford even the subsidised ticket prices for matches; gifts of tickets to nurses and teachers will be needed. Complaints from teams may quieten the rowdier African fans and their *vuvuzelas* (plastic trumpets). So Africa's moment may be uncomfortably white.

Controversy over the crowds will not extend to the pitch. The World Cup will be set alight by African footballers. Indeed, in 2010 Africa will rival Latin America as a football power. For the first time, there will be six African teams represented. No host nation has failed to reach the second round and South Africa's national team, Bafana Bafana, which won the African Nations Cup in 1996, will stumble through on home support. Ghana and Côte d'Ivoire will do better, and could even surprise the world by making a push for the final.

The pull of Europe
This reflects the steady progression of the African footballer, says Steve Bloomfield, author of "Africa United", a portrait of the game on the continent. It was a shock when Cameroon beat Argentina in the 1990 World Cup. Only a handful of Africans then played in Europe, labouring in the lower divisions and suffering racist taunts. An African win over even Italy in 2010 would not be a shock. According to Mr Bloomfield, there are 80 Senegalese footballers playing professionally in France. Côte d'Ivoire boasts Didier Drogba of Chelsea, Emmanuel Eboué of Arsenal, Kolo Touré of Manchester City and his younger brother Yaya Touré of Barcelona. Ghana's Michael Essien remains the most expensive African footballer. His move to Chelsea in 2005 is worth $51m in today's money. With half of all Africans under 18 years old, in 2010 more African raw material—boys with prodigal footballing gifts—will be

Cameroon
Samuel Eto'o to Inter Milan from Barcelona
$29m*
* As part of swap deal

Togo
Emmanuel Adebayor to Manchester City from Arsenal
$40m

Ghana
Michael Essien to Chelsea from Olympique Lyonnais
$51m

Côte d'Ivoire
Didier Drogba to Chelsea from Olympique Marseille
$49m

Jonathan Ledgard: eastern Africa correspondent, *The Economist*

The worst country on Earth

Leo Abruzzese

Piracy, poverty and perdition: Somalia takes our unwanted prize

Fed up with awards for the best? *The World in 2010* asked the analysts at the Economist Intelligence Unit, a sister company of *The Economist*, to identify the world's worst country in the year ahead. Previous winners of this dubious honour have included (pre-2001) Afghanistan and Turkmenistan. This time, the champion is in Africa. Plagued by civil war, grinding poverty and rampant piracy, Somalia will be the world's worst in 2010.

Calling Somalia a country is a stretch. It has a president, prime minister and parliament, but with little influence outside a few strongholds in the capital, Mogadishu. What passes for a government is protected by an African Union peacekeeping force guarding the presidential palace. Most of the country is controlled by two armed, radical Islamist factions, al-Shabab (the Youth) and Hizbul Islam (Party of Islam), which regularly battle forces loyal to the government. Both demand the imposition of strict Islamic law, in what would amount to the Talibanisation of Somalia. Al-Shabab took responsibility for suicide-bombings in Mogadishu in September that killed 17 peacekeepers; America considers the group an al-Qaeda ally.

Just trying to improve

Poor countries are often defined by their weak health, education and income measures, but conditions in Somalia are mostly too wretched to record. What little data can be gleaned are truly awful: according to the UN's World Food Programme, more than 40% of the population need food aid to survive, and one in every five children is acutely malnourished. The constant fighting has internally displaced more than 1.5m people, with a third living in dire, makeshift camps. Aid workers have been able to supply them with less than half the daily water needed.

Somalia would be little noticed were it not for its fastest-growing industry: piracy. Somalia drapes over the tip of east Africa and into the Gulf of Aden, one of the world's busiest shipping lanes. More than 20,000 merchant vessels pass through the Gulf each year, an inviting target for Somali pirates, who have developed a lucrative business seizing and holding ships for ransom. The International Maritime Bureau counted around 40 successful hijackings in 2008 and another 31 in the first half of 2009. Warships from the European Union, the United States and other powers now patrol the waters, but pirates have shifted their attacks farther offshore.

Somalia's future is bleak. What little income it can muster comes from its diaspora, but remittances have slowed with the global slump. International agencies have promised more aid, but lack of security stands in the way. Peacekeepers are too few in number to make a difference. Most disturbing, many young Somalis are becoming increasingly radicalised, leaving little hope that the political situation will stabilise. The world's most failed state, regrettably, threatens to become a bigger problem for the rest of the world. ■

Leo Abruzzese: editorial director, North America, Economist Intelligence Unit

League of degradations

	Mortality rate, under-5 (per 1,000)*	
1	Sierra Leone	262
2	Afghanistan	257
3	Chad	209
4	Equatorial Guinea	206
5	Guinea-Bissau	198
6	Mali	196
7	Burkina Faso	191
8	Nigeria	189
9	Rwanda	181
10	Burundi	180

*Somalia is 19th-worst, with a rate of 142
Source: World Bank, World Development Indicators; 2007 data

	Worst corruption	
1	Somalia	-1.90
2	North Korea	-1.74
3	Myanmar	-1.69
4	Afghanistan	-1.64
5	Equatorial Guinea	-1.62
6	Sudan	-1.49
7	Iraq	-1.48
8	Chad	-1.45
9	Zimbabwe	-1.37
10	Guinea	-1.35

Lower values indicate worse corruption
Source: World Bank, Governance Indicators; 2008 data

	Riskiest business environments†	
1	Iraq	82
2	Guinea	79
3	Myanmar	79
4	Zimbabwe	79
5	Turkmenistan	78
6	Uzbekistan	76
7	Venezuela	76
8	Tajikistan	73
9	Ecuador	72
10	Eritrea	71

100 = Most risk
†Somalia not rated
Source: Economist Intelligence Unit

▶ signed by top clubs. The only restriction on the English clubs will be a British visa regime which requires Africans to play regularly for a national team before they can be considered.

Football will be Africa's success story in 2010, but it will remain shockingly administered at home. The pitches of Africa's national stadiums will remain dusty, pocked and almost unplayable. Domestic leagues will be eclipsed by the English Premier League, still by far the biggest entertainment in Africa. Local administrators will still use football to build a political power base. But imagine their venality restrained by World Cup pressures: if a football federation can be made to clean up its act, perhaps a government can be too. ■

The world's eyes on Africa

*Africa must grab its potential for exponential growth, argues **Jacob Zuma**, president of South Africa*

On Friday June 11th 2010, the first-ever FIFA World Cup held on African soil will get under way in Johannesburg. Watched by soccer fans across the world, it will be a bold statement of the continent's determination to revive its fortunes after decades of marginalisation.

From the flagship stadium in Johannesburg to the new bus rapid-transit systems in major host cities, the 2010 World Cup will showcase the biggest infrastructure investment programme in South Africa's history. At a time of world economic crisis, this programme has helped place the country in a position to take advantage of the global recovery.

The infrastructure programme goes far beyond football. Since the turn of the century, South Africa has embarked on a massive investment programme in road and rail networks, public-transport systems, power generation and telecommunications. New schools and clinics are being built. The infrastructure of our growing cities is being enhanced.

Combined with private-sector investments, this has seen gross fixed capital formation as a percentage of GDP rise from 15% in 2001 to 23% by the middle of 2009. In the three-year period to 2012 our public-sector investment programme will amount to over $100 billion.

All this investment will have benefits well beyond the immediate challenge of sustaining economic activity in a downturn. It will reduce the cost of doing business, accommodate far greater rates of growth and respond to the country's social needs.

Unlike other countries that have had to implement stimulus packages, South Africa's public investment programme predates the economic crisis. Money is not being spent on bailing out banks or badly run private enterprises, but on building roads and schools.

This has been made possible by the sound management of public finances. Moreover, our banks operate within an effective regulatory framework, which has mitigated the impact of the financial crisis.

That is not to say that South Africa has been spared the impact of the global crisis. In 2009, for the first time in the 15 years of democracy, South Africa entered a recession. With revenue declining, the budget has come under pressure, and the country is having to borrow more. But we are doing so in a responsible manner, such that credit-rating agencies have retained their outlook for the country and our international bond issues have generally been over-subscribed.

Nonetheless, there are systemic challenges. Unemployment remains stubbornly high, in part because of our narrow skills base.

It is for this reason that my administration is stressing education in plans for the next five years. We are working hard to get the fundamentals of schooling right, improving access and quality for the poor, and measuring results against international benchmarks.

The other critical challenge is health. While 95% of South Africans now live within 5km of a health facility, life expectancy has declined in the past decade, partly a consequence of the devastating effects of HIV/AIDS. We are improving public health care as a stepping stone towards an affordable and efficient health system that integrates the capacities of the public and private sectors.

These challenges are typical of many developing countries. It remains to be seen whether the economic crisis will undo the benefits of the commodity boom and new investment programmes for many African economies.

It has certainly reduced the availability of credit and slowed investment and trade. Africa cannot be allowed to slide backwards. Global financial institutions need to ensure that African countries will still have access to investment resources and markets for their exports. Rich countries need to remove the trade and other barriers that stifle the development of African agriculture; they need to honour their commitments to increase development assistance to Africa.

Victory begins at home

Ultimately, though, Africa's future rests in the hands of Africans. The economic crisis has demonstrated only too clearly the vulnerability of economies that rely on commodity exports. African economies need to develop their manufacturing capacity, and take advantage of the huge, untapped market that they collectively represent.

Of one thing we are certain: if there is one part of the world that possesses the potential for exponential growth in the coming few decades, it is the African continent. This ranges from the extraction and processing of mineral resources and infrastructure development to the manufacturing of goods and provision of services for a growing employed population and middle class.

The prospects for Africa in 2010 are good. It might even be the year in which, for the first time, an African team holds aloft the FIFA World Cup trophy. ■

Rich countries need to honour their commitments to increase development assistance to Africa

Visit Chopin in Poland

2010 is the Year of Chopin.
Concerts, piano competitions
and lots of other attractions
for culture and music enthusiasts.
Celebrate it with us.

www.poland.gov.pl
www.chopin2010.pl/en

The world has never been so delicious to fly around.

We're proud to fly you to more than 150 destinations aboard our young fleet, offering you more comfortable seats, culinary delights and an exclusive flight experience along our expanded routes.

Enjoy the privileges of exploring the world on Turkish Airlines and connect to over 960 destinations, taking advantage of Star Alliance network.

TURKISH AIRLINES | A STAR ALLIANCE MEMBER

turkishairlines.com | +90 212 444 0 849

THE WORLD IN 2010   95

Also in this section:
Our hits and misses for 2009 96
A busy year for nuclear diplomacy 97
Margaret Chan: The swine-flu pandemic 98
Conflicts over natural resources will grow 99
A World Cup double 99
Young people gather in London to save the planet 100
Will 2010 be a year of social unrest? 101
Mohamed Nasheed: Climate change and the most vulnerable 102

International

A modern guide to G-ology

Gideon Rachman

The clubs that would rule the world

Medieval scholastics are reputed to have enjoyed debating how many angels you can fit on the head of a pin. The equivalent debate for modern diplomats is what number you should place after the letter G.

At present, a number of groups are jostling to be the pre-eminent forum for discussions between world leaders. The G20 ended 2009 by in effect replacing the old G8. But that is not the end of the matter. In 2010 the G20 will face a new challenger—the G2. To confuse matters further, lobbies will emerge advocating the formation of a G13 and a G3. It would be foolish to expect the debate to be resolved definitively. But the likeliest outcome is that the G20 summit of world leaders will further establish its position as the world's most important talking shop. Attempts to divert the real decisions to a G2 made up of just the United States and China will not succeed. The G8, a largely Western grouping, will continue its rapid decline into irrelevance. And the G13 will not get off the ground. (As for the G77—don't even ask.)

The formation of the G20 group of world leaders is likely to be the most lasting institutional consequence of the global financial meltdown of 2008. Long before that drama, it was a commonplace of international diplomacy that the big institutions of international governance, such as the UN Security Council and the G8 (that is, the G7 group of rich countries plus Russia), no longer matched the realities of international power.

However, it took a global economic crisis to force change. The G20 had already been formed for finance ministers in response to the Asian economic crisis of the late 1990s. Crucially, its members included the giant emerging economies—China, India and Brazil—and together accounted for 85% of world output. Because the subject matter for the G20 is exclusively economic, its members can avoid tricky debates about politics.

The success of the G20 since its first summit in Washington, DC, in November 2008 has surprised many sceptics. It is true that some of the group's initial promises—to forswear all further acts of protectionism, for example—were broken. But at the second G20 summit in London the assembled leaders made it clear that they could work together, committing themselves to a global fiscal stimulus and an increase in resources for the IMF. The summit marked a turning-point in investor and business confidence. And at the Pittsburgh summit in September 2009 it was announced that the G20 would replace the G8 as the main body for the discussion and co-ordination of global economic policy; the older group will simply become a

> It currently suits neither America nor China to elevate the status of the G2

2010 IN BRIEF
The United Nations celebrates the snappily named International Year for the **Rapprochement of Cultures**.

Gideon Rachman: chief foreign-affairs columnist, *Financial Times*

2010 IN BRIEF

America, Brazil, China, Indonesia and Japan all carry out a **population census**—but not Russia, cancelling its census on grounds of cost.

caucus within the G20.

Inevitably, however, the G20 also has flaws, which may become more evident at its next meetings, in Canada in June and South Korea in November. The group's virtue—its size—is also its problem. In Pittsburgh, there were in fact 33 leaders around the table, once you included the heads of various international and regional organisations, such as the World Bank and ASEAN.

The battle of the G-spots

Some lament that, as a result, the G20 is threatening to turn into a mini United Nations. Hence the talk of cutting the group down to size again, with a G13: the G8 plus China, India, South Africa, Brazil and Mexico. But any such move would offend some important G20 members, and so probably create as many headaches as it solved. Besides, the G20 has the distinct advantage of actually existing already.

A more radical solution would be to opt for a G2 of China and America. Most of the really big international issues—from climate change to global economic imbalances, currency management and nuclear non-proliferation—will ultimately depend above all on agreement between the world's two largest economies. The institutional framework for this dialogue already exists. In 2009 the regular economic summits between China and America were renamed as a "Strategic and Economic Dialogue"—signalling the formal broadening of the agenda, beyond purely economic issues.

But the G2 is unlikely to become the world's most important international forum in 2010. For different reasons, it currently suits neither America nor China to elevate the status of the G2.

The Chinese have benefited from a relative shift in power, following the global economic crisis. But they know that, in most respects, this is still far from being a dialogue of equals. The United States is a much richer country than China, with a larger and more sophisticated economy and a global military reach. The Americans have their own reasons not to want to elevate the status of the G2. American officials believe that it makes sense economically and politically to include other major democracies, such as the European Union and Japan, in discussions with China. EU officials are already talking hopefully of forming a G3, with China and America. But this idea is premature.

For all these reasons, it will be the G20, rather than the G2 or G3, that wins the battle of the G-spots in 2010. ■

Our greatest hits…

Daniel Franklin

…and misses for 2009

"The only function of economic forecasting", said J.K. Galbraith, a Harvard economist, "is to make astrology look respectable." How did our stars align in *The World in 2009*?

In some respects, surprisingly well. We imagined what would happen if, after years of fuelling the world economy with their spending, Americans suddenly started saving 5% of what they earn. They did, and the result was as predicted: recession. The rich-world recession proved even deeper than we expected, but we rightly believed that actions by governments and central banks would avoid a 1930s-style depression. We gave warning that Britain would lose control over its public finances (its budget deficit has soared) and quickly see unemployment surge to 8% (by July it was 7.9%).

Growth in emerging markets, we thought, would remain relatively robust in many countries. So it has turned out. In the dark days of the slump many people would have been amazed if China's growth in 2009 proved to be as vigorous as the 8% we forecast. Yet it has.

No great skill was required to point to a coming surge in bankruptcies or a shake-up in finance. Better, we identified Goldman Sachs, JPMorgan Chase and Banco Santander as three banks likely to emerge as winners from the crisis. And amid the market gloom a year ago, we suggested that bulls might be ready to charge again in 2009.

In politics, too, several of our main prognostications came true: Barack Obama's difficulties in living up to unrealistic expectations of him, the West's deepening troubles in Afghanistan, big emerging economies seeking a greater say in running the world. We gave notice that talk of abolishing nuclear weapons would grow louder; in Prague in April Mr Obama duly ratcheted up the rhetoric with his call for a nuclear-free world.

Perhaps the most precise prediction was on British politics. We pinpointed June 5th—just after the elections for the European Parliament—as the day of greatest peril for Gordon Brown. The knives were indeed out for the prime minister at that time. But, as we thought he would, he survived, lame but unmovable.

However, where would be the fun in forecasting (or the wit in Galbraith's jibe) if there weren't plenty of misses as well as hits? Sure enough, we had our share in last year's issue.

We were confident that the 2016 Olympics would be awarded to Chicago; Rio de Janeiro triumphantly proved otherwise. We underestimated the strength of the Congress party's election victory in India and of the opposition DPJ's triumph in Japan. Our report on the death of the European Union's Lisbon treaty proved to be greatly exaggerated.

Just as important as the sins of commission are those of omission. Readers of *The World in 2009* had to work hard to find a reference to the increasingly important G20 group of leading economies (though thanks to Kevin Rudd, Australia's prime minister, it wasn't completely ignored). They would have found no mention of a scandal over politicians' expenses in Britain or a bail-out of American carmakers. We failed to flag the post-election unrest in Iran, or the ethnic unrest in China's Xinjiang province. The biggest news story of the year was missing entirely: the death of Michael Jackson.

All this should help readers interpret the predictions they find in the current issue. We hope many of these will prove right. No doubt quite a few will turn out to be wrong. And, inevitably, some of the most important events of the year ahead will be missing altogether. For those really unpredictable things—what Donald Rumsfeld has called the "unknown unknowns"—you might as well look to the zodiac. ■

Daniel Franklin: editor, *The World in 2010*

Nuclear non-proliferation entreaty

From our diplomatic editor

A busy year for nuclear diplomacy

To wags during the cold war, ground zero was a favoured spot: better to be incinerated in the first mushroom cloud, they joshed, than to wake up to a world of radioactive rubble. But "getting to zero" is suddenly a dream, not a nightmare. Everyone from America's Barack Obama to Iran is officially signed up for a world free of nuclear weapons. Yet if by the end of 2010 Iran and North Korea are continuing to defy the world with their nuclear programmes, the nuclear-free dream will look like a passing fantasy.

In the coming year, Russia and America will make deeper cuts in their nuclear arsenals. Mr Obama, reversing George Bush's position, will press for Senate ratification of a global test ban. In May the 189 countries that have signed the Nuclear Non-Proliferation Treaty (NPT) will gather, as they do every five years, to debate strengthening its rules. Just before they meet, America will organise a smaller, 35-nation summit to find new ways of locking down the most dangerous nuclear materials and minimising their use in civilian nuclear programmes. Meanwhile the 65-member UN Conference on Disarmament in Geneva, where the test-ban was first negotiated, will be grappling with a new treaty to end the production of fissile material, meaning highly enriched uranium and plutonium, for bombmaking.

Mr Obama has made "getting to zero" an organising principle of his foreign policy, to global applause. Oddly, Brazil, Egypt, South Africa and other countries that have long claimed leadership of the world's disarmament camp may prove the least helpful to his cause.

First, the nuclear numbers. Overall these will go on tumbling. Yet as Russia and America aim ever lower, to 1,000 or fewer strategic nuclear warheads apiece, pressure will build for the other three recognised nuclear powers—Britain, France and China—to put their smaller arsenals on the negotiating table too. But five-way talks are harder than bilateral ones, and China and France will be unenthusiastic. And what to do about the unofficial weapons caches of Israel, India, Pakistan and (it claims) North Korea?

So beyond a point weapons cuts will slow. That will annoy the disarmament crowd. So will pressure from Mr Obama's opponents in Congress for more modern warheads so as to be sure of America's shrinking stockpile. In cash-strapped Britain, by contrast, pressure will build to cut back or drop entirely plans to modernise Trident,

The world's worst nightmare

its submarine-launched nuclear-weapons system.

As for rewriting nuclear rules, some governments will resist using the NPT conference to strengthen the badly weakened treaty on the ground that the nuclear powers have still not done enough. North Korea, once a member, won't be there this time: it has left the treaty and declared itself a nuclear power. Iran, which denies nuclear ambitions but refuses full co-operation with inspectors, will be—working hard to block progress.

One idea is to require all countries (so far the process has been voluntary) to sign up to enhanced safeguards, known as the Additional Protocol, to replace the more basic ones that came with the 40-year-old NPT. Another is to demand that any country leaving the treaty hand back equipment or materials acquired while a member.

Half-life of a dream

In theory, almost everyone in the treaty except Iran (and Syria, another alleged miscreant) supports the idea of tightening the rules. In practice, Brazil has been holding out against the Additional Protocol on the (improbable) ground that it could put at risk commercial secrets from its uranium-enrichment programme. Egypt says it will accept the protocol only when Israel, not an NPT member, gives up its bombs. All this looks like letting Iran off the hook.

Fuel-making technologies in the wrong hands can be abused for bombmaking. But plans to curb their spread will move ahead only slowly, if at all. Australia, Canada and South Africa, all with deposits of natural uranium, are reluctant to accept limits on their future rights to enrich it for profit. If they don't budge, plans for an international fuel bank of last resort, to help dissuade countries going for nuclear power from thinking they need proliferation-prone uranium-enrichment and plutonium-making capacities too, are likely to fail.

> All this looks like letting Iran off the hook

Even the test ban and a new treaty to cut off production of fissile material—both obvious first steps to a nuclear-free future—will be dogged with difficulty. India, seeing China as its chief nuclear rival, will refuse to swear off nuclear tests and will go on building up its arsenal; and Pakistan won't sign up unless India does. When it comes to a fissile-material ban, foot-dragging roles are reversed, with Pakistan the chief hold-out, saving India the bother. That is because new trade arrangements under a controversial civil nuclear deal with America will allow India to devote more of its scarce domestic uranium to its military programme. Pakistan, with China's help, is determined to keep up.

So there will be lots of disarmament talk in 2010. But not a whole lot will get done. ∎

2010 IN BRIEF

The United Nations begins a "**decade for deserts**", aiming to reduce their spread.

Predicting the path of the swine-flu pandemic

Influenza pandemics are remarkable, recurring events that have historically spread around the globe in two, sometimes three, waves. Caused by a virus that is new as well as contagious, they encounter no "firewall" of protection from pre-existing immunity. It is this almost universal susceptibility to infection that gives pandemics their power to sweep through the world population. And the large numbers infected within a short time make pandemics disruptive, even when the virus itself is not an efficient killer.

The pandemic that began in 2009 is unique in at least one regard. Past pandemics have always announced themselves with a sudden explosion of cases, taking the world by surprise. This time, scientists were ready and waiting, conditioned by a nervous five-year watch over the lethal H5N1 bird-flu virus. For once, the world was alert, prepared and, most likely, more scared than it needs to be.

How will this preparedness serve the world as the pandemic continues to evolve? Predictions are tricky. But the behaviour of past pandemics offers a few ground rules. And because the 2009 pandemic first spread in countries with good surveillance and reporting systems, the year will begin with a reasonable body of knowledge about the H1N1 virus and the pattern of illness it can cause.

The pattern seen during the second half of 2009 will hold. The overwhelming majority of cases will experience mild symptoms followed by rapid and full recovery. The virus will preferentially infect a young age group, with schools and other institutional settings, like military barracks, initially amplifying local transmission, then spreading into the wider community. The frail elderly, who account for 90% of severe and fatal cases during seasonal flu, will be largely spared, at least during the early phase of the second wave.

Severe cases will be exceptional, but pregnant women will be at increased risk, as will people with a number of widespread underlying conditions, like asthma, diabetes and cardiovascular disease. Obesity, and especially morbid obesity, will be observed in a high proportion of severe cases, and scientists will frantically try to discover why. The virus will kill, but in nowhere near the numbers seen during the devastating 1918 pandemic, which claimed an estimated 50m lives worldwide. Projections of deaths and economic losses (as much as $3 trillion) based on the lethal bird-flu virus will look like gross exaggerations.

The pandemic will not affect all parts of the world, or even all parts of a country, at the same time. Disruptions will be abrupt and acute, but mercifully brief, felt especially as schools, offices and public services experience high rates of absenteeism. In a given area, the worst will usually be over in four to six weeks as the virus rushes through a susceptible population, cases peak and infections decline with equal speed. Areas or population sub-groups spared during the first wave will be vulnerable targets when the virus returns.

Winters of discontent

As the pandemic gains ground during the winter seasons, first in the northern hemisphere, later in the south, this largely reassuring picture will be undercut by extremes. With the number of infections growing exponentially, vast differences—in the spectrum of illness, access to vaccines, response capacity and impact—will become strikingly apparent, sometimes tragically so.

Most patients will not need any form of medical care. But a small subset of others will rapidly fall so ill that their lives will depend on highly specialised treatment in intensive-care units. Though the numbers will be small, the burden in terms of staff, equipment, supplies and costly stays in hospital will be enormous—the potential tipping-point for disruptions in overall health services. In many developing countries where health systems are weak, most of these patients will die.

The supply of vaccines will be woefully inadequate. As global manufacturing capacity is not easily augmented, the world will find itself several billion doses short of what is needed. The distribution of vaccines among countries will be extremely uneven, as affluent countries will have reserved most of the year's output well in advance. Many will have enough to cover their entire population. For the rest of the world, vaccine donations totalling 200m doses, secured by the WHO, will barely be sufficient to protect health workers.

Above all, a truly global event like this one will reveal, in a highly visible way, the consequences of decades of failure to invest adequately in basic health services and infrastructures in the developing world. The same virus that causes manageable disruption in affluent countries will have a devastating impact in countries with too few health facilities and staff, no regular supplies of essential medicines, little diagnostic and laboratory capacity, and vast populations with no access to safe water and sanitation. ∎

The first pandemic of the 21st century will expose stark differences between the world's rich and poor, predicts **Margaret Chan**, director-general of the World Health Organisation

The supply of vaccines will be woefully inadequate

The Madagascar model

John Parker

Conflicts over natural resources will grow

In the world's earliest written legal code, dating from 1790BC, Hammurabi, the king of Babylon, laid down rules governing the maintenance of irrigation systems and the amount of water people could take from them. Two generations later, his grandson abandoned this rules-based approach and used the river Tigris as a weapon against rebels in Babylon.

The world is charting a similar course, away from rules governing scarce resources towards conflict over them. For most of the past 50 years, the striking thing about such conflicts is how rare they have been. Treaties between states that use the same rivers have held up. Disputes over oilfields that straddle frontiers have been resolved. Arguments between people using the same water or grassland have been kept within limits.

But in 2010 the world will wake up to a new era of conflict over resources. The era was ushered in by a coup in Madagascar in March 2009. There, South Korea's Daewoo Logistics leased half the island's arable land from the government to grow food: the company would get the land rent-free; existing farmers would not be compensated; all the food would be exported. When news of this seeped out, the reaction gave impetus to a surge of opposition that swept the government from power. The new president's first act was to quash the deal. He sent a chill through Africa and parts of Asia, where dozens of similar land grabs worth billions of dollars have been signed or are under negotiation.

This drama showed the characteristics of conflicts over scarcity. They do not usually involve pitched battles. Rather, they are episodes of friction in which the resource in question adds to tension but is not the sole source of it. Other examples include China's crackdown on the water tower of the world, Tibet (ten of Asia's largest rivers have their source in the Tibetan plateau); Rus-

2010 IN BRIEF

Girl Guides around the world celebrate a centenary year.

John Parker: globalisation correspondent, *The Economist*

A World Cup double

Matthew Glendinning

England for 2018, America for 2022

In December 2010 the 24 members of the executive committee of FIFA, world football's governing body, representing all corners of the soccer world, will take part in an unprecedented series of votes. Unprecedented because the chosen few, including FIFA's Swiss president, Sepp Blatter, will elect not one but two World Cup hosts at the same sitting. After 18 months of lobbying, horse-trading and analysis, the white smoke will emerge and the hosts for the competitions in 2018 and 2022 will be named.

Competition is intense. Australia, England, Indonesia, Japan, Russia and the United States have all bid for both championships, and there are joint bids from Belgium with the Netherlands and Spain with Portugal. Qatar and South Korea have submitted bids for 2022 only.

Having given up the formal rotation between continents that ushered in South Africa and Brazil as hosts for 2010 and 2014 respectively, FIFA faces a big choice. The new voting format should benefit the Europeans, who have nine members on the committee and who believe that one in every three World Cups should be staged on their continent. After Germany in 2006, the Europeans will be eager to get one of their own installed for 2018. With its established stadiums and the leading global brand of Premier League club football (as well as the advantage of a simple,

Mine's a ticket for 2022

single-country bid), England is favourite to take the honour—more than 50 years after it last hosted the event, in 1966.

The 2022 tournament is a tougher call. Australia, now part of the Asian federation, is a stronger continental challenger than either Japan or Korea, the joint hosts in 2002. To the dismay of other sports, notably tennis, soccer's growth has been rapid in Australia, which offers FIFA an attractive new market. The small, gas-rich Gulf state of Qatar has its merits, too, not least in its plan to use innovative cooling technology for a new generation of stadiums in the desert.

But the United States, which played host in 1994, should have the edge, thanks to its size, its impressive array of stadiums and the added glamour of a presidential endorsement. In a letter to FIFA, Barack Obama waxed lyrical: "As a child, I played soccer on a dirt road in Jakarta, and the game brought the children of my neighbourhood together. As a father, I saw that same spirit of unity alive on the fields and sidelines of my own daughters' soccer games in Chicago." More prosaically, FIFA will compare America's market size with Australia's, and follow the money. ■

Matthew Glendinning: sports and business writer

Today London, tomorrow the world

Alexandra Suich NEW YORK

Young people gather to save the planet

The World Economic Forum, famous for bringing together the great and the good in Davos, Switzerland, has for some time run a programme for people it modestly anoints as Young Global Leaders. But in 2010 the Davos lot (maximum age: 40) will be old hat. Truly young would-be leaders, no older than 25, will gather on February 8th-10th in London for a "summit" called One Young World. Their purpose? Solve the world's problems. Why? Their elders seem unable to.

The marketing industry has taken a particularly keen interest in the trendsetting habits of the Facebook generation. So it is perhaps no surprise that the event's co-founders are advertising executives. And no surprise that one of them, David Jones, boss of Euro RSCG, a unit of Havas, is himself one of Davos's Young Global Leaders (class of 2008)—though he is now in his 40s. But the aims of the conference, which is not-for-profit and aspires to become an annual event, are lofty.

Sessions will be streamed online and resolutions drafted in workshops. The 1,500 young people selected to attend the event (whose tag line is "25 today, leading the world tomorrow") will find that they have influential ears listening to their ideas on climate change, human rights and the like. Kofi Annan, a former UN secretary-general, and Archbishop Desmond Tutu from South Africa (neither of them spring chickens) are due to chair sessions.

Proportional representation is meant to ensure that people from the most populous countries, not the richest ones, will make up the bulk of the delegates (China and India will have the most). Those interested in attending are encouraged to download an application on Facebook so their friends can vote for them, and to submit a video on a YouTube channel about why they want to take part.

Despite such techniques, the event will depend on old-fashioned corporate sponsorship for its financing. The founders are looking to business to cover the cost of individuals who come (€3,000, or $4,500, a person) and entire country delegations. They are urging firms to take an interest in building a community of young leaders; sponsors are more likely to want a community of young customers.

Mr Jones insists that the event is about innovation. Marketers use social media and new technology to reach young people and sell products. The founders of One Young World want to use that expertise, he says, and channel it for the good. ■

Alexandra Suich: contributor, *The Economist,* and invited delegate

---

2010 IN BRIEF
The world's airlines submit plans to the UN to halve their **CO₂ emissions** by 2050 from levels in 2005.

...sia and Canada beefing up their presence in the Arctic as the icy waters become navigable; and the conflict between Darfuri tribes, the Sudanese government and others in western Sudan, where rainfall has dropped by up to a third in 40 years.

The thread that connects these disparate places is the fear that basic supplies of land, water and fuel might soon not be available or affordable. John Beddington, Britain's chief scientific adviser, forecasts that over the next 20 years the world's population will rise by up to a third, demand for food and energy will rise by half and demand for fresh water will increase by 30%.

Rising demand alone would not necessarily be cause for alarm, if supplies could rise proportionately. But they might not. There are few swathes of farmland lying fallow and much of the world's available fresh water is already being used. Climate change is making both problems worse, as are misguided policies: one factor behind the 2009 land grabs was the imposition of food-export bans, raising fears among importers that they

> Over the next 20 years, demand for food and energy will rise by half

might one day not be able to get food at any price.

The conflicts of scarcity are not the same as the cataclysms of Malthus. One day, there will be new fuels, improvements in dryland farming and increases in the efficiency with which water is used. But between now and then, problems of scarcity will grow.

They will increase the role of the state. Governments will rush to secure raw materials. There will be politically controversial acquisitions of natural-resource companies, such as China's (failed) attempt to buy part of RTZ, a mining giant, or its bid in late 2009 for one-sixth of Nigeria's oil reserves. Conflicts are likely to arise in the 250-odd river basins shared by more than one country, which contain a fifth of the world's fresh water and two-fifths of its population. Resources-strapped governments will make alliances with resources-rich countries. The result will be contests in target regions such as Central Asia (where rival gas pipelines are being built), the deep-sea oilfields of Asia and the Arctic and on the Himalayan plateau.

In 2009 fear of food shortages caused trouble throughout Africa. In 2010 fear of energy, water and other raw-material shortages will spread these troubles through the rest of the world. ■

Delayed explosion

Laza Kekic

Will 2010 be a year of social unrest?

Over the past year much of the world has experienced falling incomes and sharply rising unemployment. At the height of the global economic crisis in early 2009 a striking warning about the possible political consequences came from America's director of national intelligence, Admiral Dennis Blair, in testimony before the United States Senate. He declared that the risk of global political instability triggered by the economic crisis had become America's "primary near-term security concern". The heads of the IMF and the UN, among others, also issued stark warnings about the danger of social unrest.

So far, however, the feared spread of unrest has not occurred. Voters have not flocked to the far left or the populist right. Most people affected by the crisis have suffered in silence.

Does this mean that all the warnings were misplaced? It's too soon to relax. There are reasons to expect that 2010 could be a year of upheaval. The relative social peace of 2009 may have been only the quiet before the storm.

Indeed, a congruence of calamities could prove politically tempestuous: a sharp rise in unemployment, increased poverty and inequality, weakened middle classes and high food prices in many countries. Austerity is also on the agenda in 2010 following the extreme fiscal relaxation of 2009.

Historically, political reactions to economic distress have tended to come with a lag. The same is true of labour-market developments: even once the recession ends, unemployment continues to rise. According to Economist Intelligence Unit (EIU) estimates, in 2010 there will be 60m more unemployed worldwide than in 2008. The International Labour Organisation reckons some 200m workers are at risk of joining the ranks of people living on less than $2 a day.

Declines in incomes are not always followed by political instability. Vulnerability to unrest depends on a host of factors. These include the degree of income inequality, the state of governance, levels of social provision, ethnic tensions, public trust in institutions, the history of unrest and the type of political system ("intermediate" regimes that are neither consolidated democracies nor autocracies seem the most vulnerable).

The places at risk

Nearly half the countries assessed by the EIU—77 out of 166—are at very high or high risk of social unrest in 2010 (22 are in the very-high-risk category). For 52 countries the risk of instability is rated as medium and for the remaining 37 countries it is low.

Sub-Saharan Africa is, unsurprisingly, well represented in the high-risk categories: it accounts for about one-third of the high-risk group. Almost a quarter of the high-risk countries are in eastern Europe, the region that has been hit hardest by the crisis and which also has many of the underlying characteristics associated with unrest. A fair number of high-risk countries are in Latin America and Asia—including the world's largest and most successful emerging market, China.

But this is not just an issue for poor countries. In Europe, protests have toppled governments in Latvia and Iceland. France is no stranger historically to popular unrest. And in 2010 Britain may be at risk. Around the world, it will be a year for anger management. ■

> In 2010 there will be 60m more unemployed worldwide than in 2008

Laza Kekic: director, country forecasting services, Economist Intelligence Unit

2010 IN BRIEF

To coincide with the Winter Olympics, Vancouver launches a **Culture Olympiad**, ranging from Latin jazz bands to a gay rap opera.

States of combustibility
Risk of social unrest in 2010
- Very high
- High
- Medium
- Low
- Not rated

Source: Economist Intelligence Unit

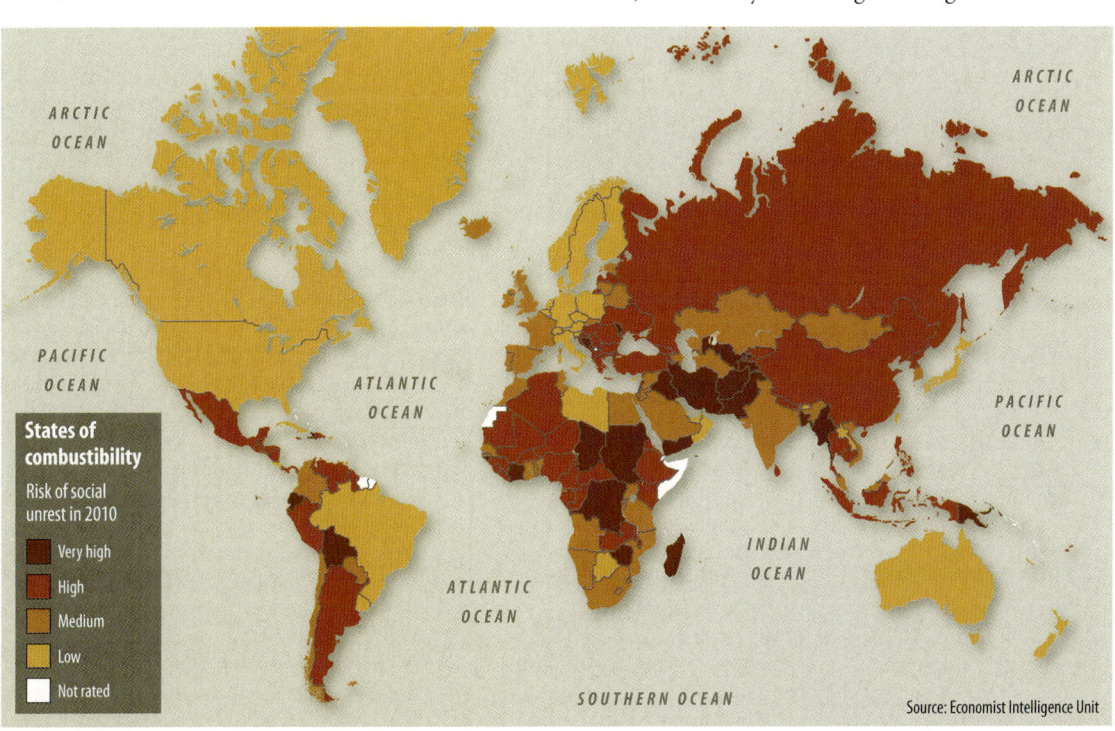

Where survival is at stake

Mohamed Nasheed, president of the Maldives, argues that the rich must help the poor combat climate change—or else all will face disaster

If environmental politics in 2009 were dominated by the build-up to the December Copenhagen climate-change negotiations, in 2010 they will be dominated by post-Copenhagen analysis. That analysis will include the creeping realisation that climate negotiations are not really negotiations between nations at all. Climate change is not a grand bargain between the United States and China; nor the European Union and India. Rather, humanity is negotiating with Mother Nature. And mother appears in no mood to compromise.

Less than one degree Celsius of warming since the pre-industrial age has unleashed frightening and unforeseen change, including glacier-melt and unprecedented coral-reef degradation. A commitment to limit warming to two degrees by 2050, as proposed by the G8 club of rich countries, will not halt climate change. Either humans slash the amount of CO_2 in the atmosphere to near pre-industrial levels or the world will continue to warm, with awful consequences.

In low-lying areas, people will watch the steady retreat of Arctic ice, a precursor to rising sea levels, with increasing apprehension. Health officials will note with alarm the spread of tropical diseases to more temperate climes. And the 1 billion people who rely on the world's coral reefs will await a potential 2010 El Niño, whose hotter temperatures can be devastating for reefs, with trepidation.

Climate change will also be a multiplier of poverty, as increasingly erratic weather induces more drought, flooding, erosion and soil degradation. Aid agencies already fear that this will undo decades of development efforts in poor parts of the world.

More vulnerable nations will be forced to invest large sums of money in adaptation measures. In the Maldives, the government needs to build a $40m seawall around our third-most-populous island, Fuvahmulah, to protect it from coastal erosion. For a country with total government revenue of just $550m a year, this is more than loose change. If the Maldives and other countries at risk are lucky, new finance mechanisms will help poor countries pay for adaptation initiatives. Otherwise, climate-change adaptation will drain the reserves of vulnerable nations.

The aftermath of Copenhagen will affect the international image of the world's nations and their ability to project "soft power". Bogeyman, foot-dragging countries will have been identified at Copenhagen and America is unlikely to be the sole environmental offender. Other countries with hitherto positive images could also find themselves on the uncomfortable receiving end of global ire.

And it is not only soft power that comes into focus. In 2010 there will be a gradual shift from perceiving climate change as a "soft" green issue to seeing it as a "hard" military one. Nowhere will this be more apparent than in America. A 2007 report by CNA Corporation, a Pentagon-funded think-tank, gives a taste of things to come. If greenhouse-gas emissions are not reduced, it concludes, climate change has the potential to "create sustained natural and humanitarian disasters on a scale far beyond those we see today." It adds that "weakened and failing governments…foster the conditions for internal conflicts, extremism and movement toward increased authoritarianism and radical ideologies." Climate change will make the world an increasingly unsafe place and military capabilities will have to respond accordingly.

Green shoots

However, 2010 will not be all doom and gloom. While some fossil-fuel industries pour money into climate-denying lobbying, other nations, companies and entrepreneurs will invest in the green economy of the future.

In the Maldives, the government will continue to implement its ten-year carbon-neutral strategy. Spearheaded by a switch from oil to renewable-power production, the strategy aims to all but eliminate the use of fossil fuels in the Maldivian archipelago by 2020. In 2010 the Maldives will commission renewable-energy projects and advance waste-to-energy initiatives. And new concepts, such as the introduction of biochar, will help improve farming and reduce emissions.

Local Maldivian companies will pioneer technologies to help grow a new green economy. Soneva Fushi, for instance, will become the world's first carbon-neutral tourist resort. It will host a symposium to demonstrate how, through a combination of technical wizardry and commonsense solutions, it has slashed carbon emissions, putting to bed the myth that luxury necessarily equates with environmental degradation.

I have, in the past, talked of buying land elsewhere as an "insurance policy" should our islands disappear under the sea. But our hope is that concerted international action against climate change will mean the policy will never be invoked. ■

More vulnerable nations will be forced to invest large sums of money in adaptation measures

The world in figures: Countries

Europe				Latin America	Middle East and Africa	Morocco 111
Austria 103	Italy 104	Turkey 106	Pakistan 107	Argentina 109	Algeria 110	Nigeria 111
Belgium 103	Latvia 104	Ukraine 106	Philippines 107	Bolivia 109	Angola 110	Saudi Arabia 111
Bulgaria 103	Lithuania 105	United Kingdom 106	Singapore 107	Brazil 109	Cameroon 110	South Africa 111
Croatia 103	Netherlands 105		South Korea 107	Chile 109	Egypt 110	Tanzania 111
Czech Republic 103	Norway 105	Asia	Sri Lanka 108	Colombia 109	Ethiopia 110	United Arab Emirates 111
Denmark 104	Poland 105	Australia 106	Taiwan 108	Cuba 109	Iran 110	Zimbabwe 111
Estonia 104	Portugal 105	China 106	Thailand 108	Ecuador 109	Iraq 110	
Finland 104	Romania 105	Hong Kong 106	Uzbekistan 108	Paraguay 109	Israel 110	
France 104	Russia 105	India 106	Vietnam 108	Peru 109	Jordan 110	
Germany 104	Slovakia 105	Indonesia 107		Uruguay 109	Kenya 110	For an interactive version of these pages, go to: www.economist.com/theworldin
Greece 104	Slovenia 105	Japan 107	North America	Venezuela 109	Lebanon 111	
Hungary 104	Spain 106	Kazakhstan 107	Canada 108		Libya 111	
Ireland 104	Sweden 106	Malaysia 107	Mexico 108			
	Switzerland 106	New Zealand 107	United States 108			

TOP GROWERS

Qatar's economy will grow by nearly a quarter in 2010 as new gas projects come on stream, but no other country will reach double figures. As the global economy emerges from recession, most of the leading performers in 2010 will be minor emerging markets, especially aid-driven countries in sub-Saharan Africa. But energy production, as in the past, also tells part of the story: Congo (Brazzaville) will be boosted by rising oil output, and hydrocarbons production helps to place Turkmenistan among the top dozen.

China performs best among large economies as stimulus spending fills the hole left by the slump in the developed world. India, at ninth, regains some of its pre-crisis momentum as its services sector revives. Post-conflict recovery boosts Iraq to tenth place. Madagascar, at 11th, will enjoy a peace dividend as foreign grants flow in.

Rank	Country	GDP growth,%
1	Qatar	24.5
2	China	8.6
3	Congo (Brazzaville)	8.0
4	Turkmenistan	8.0
5	Ethiopia	7.0
5	Uzbekistan	7.0
7	Djibouti	6.5
8	Sri Lanka	6.3
9	India	6.3
10	Iraq	6.2
11	Madagascar	6.2
12	Vietnam	6.0

2010 forecasts unless otherwise indicated. Inflation: year-on-year annual average. Dollar GDPs calculated using 2010 forecasts for dollar exchange rates (GDP at PPP, or purchasing-power parity, shown in brackets). All figures simplified by rounding.

Source: **Economist Intelligence Unit**
london@eiu.com

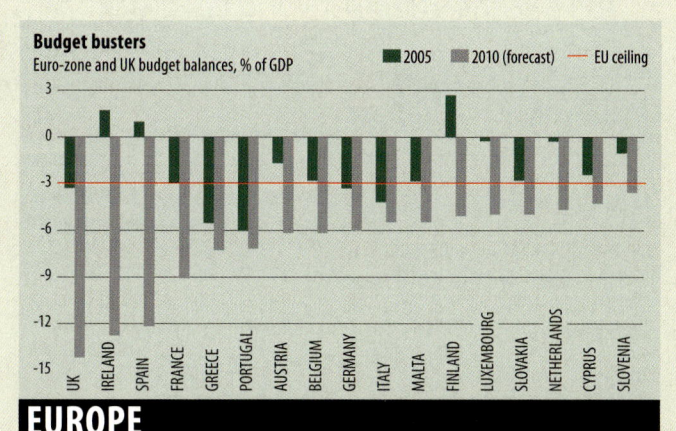

Budget busters
Euro-zone and UK budget balances, % of GDP
■ 2005 ■ 2010 (forecast) — EU ceiling

EUROPE

Main event: UK Conservatives: back from the wilderness **Euro-zone growth**: 0.6%
EU-27 growth: 0.6% **Eastern and central Europe**: 1.0% **Russia and CIS**: 2.3%

AUSTRIA
GDP growth:	0.8%
GDP:	$398bn (PPP: $322bn)
Inflation:	0.8%
Population:	8.4m
GDP per head:	$47,310 (PPP: $38,260)

The grand coalition of the Social Democratic Party and the Austrian People's Party is working well, allowing the government to focus on the weak economy. Budget policy will concentrate on boosting consumer spending, pumping money into R&D, and shoring up the banks. Austria will be flagged for breaching Europe's fiscal-deficit ceiling, but with so many others in the same position it will be let off with a warning.

BELGIUM
GDP growth:	0.8%
GDP:	$455bn (PPP: $386bn)
Inflation:	0.0%
Population:	10.6m
GDP per head:	$42,840 (PPP: $36,300)

An impasse between Flemish and French-speaking parties over the devolution of federal power to regional authorities will divert political attention from the vital task of nursing the economy through the downturn, and may even bring down the coalition government before its official term ends in 2011. The economy will grow by 0.8%, which will feel only marginally less painful than the contraction of 2009 as unemployment continues to rise and living standards stagnate.

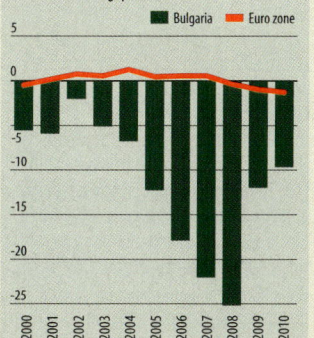

BULGARIA
GDP growth:	1.0%
GDP:	$50bn (PPP: $92bn)
Inflation:	2.3%
Population:	7.4m
GDP per head:	$6,720 (PPP: $12,370)

Off balance
Current-account gap, % of GDP
■ Bulgaria — Euro zone

Boiko Borisov, the prime minister, and his Citizens for European Development of Bulgaria party will build on their July 2009 election victory by cracking down on organised crime and corruption. The government is likely to survive its minority position in parliament, and if a successful attempt to topple it were to force fresh elections, it might well add seats. The economy will grow slowly.

To watch: Help! Bulgaria's heavy external-debt load and large current-account deficit may force the government to join the queue at the IMF's bail-out window.

CROATIA
GDP growth:	0.3%
GDP:	$64bn (PPP: $78bn)
Inflation:	2.6%
Population:	4.5m
GDP per head:	$14,300 (PPP: $17,400)

The coalition government is adjusting to new leadership after the resignation of the prime minister, Ivo Sanader, in 2009. Jadranka Kosor, his replacement, lacks his credentials, and policymaking may drift. The goal of EU membership will give cohesion to the ruling coalition, but disagreements will flare over such issues as financial support for farmers. Rising unemployment and tight credit will hold growth to a mere 0.3%.

CZECH REPUBLIC
GDP growth:	0.9%
GDP:	$194bn (PPP: $260bn)
Inflation:	1.4%
Population:	10.2m
GDP per head:	$19,050 (PPP: $25,480)

The Civic Democratic Party (ODS) is marginally better placed to lead the government after elections to be held by June 2010 than its main rival, the Czech Social Democratic Party, which was blackened after calling a no-confidence vote that plunged the country into turmoil while it held the rotating EU presidency. The long-held aim of adopting the euro would suffer under a government led by the Eurosceptic ODS.

SPAIN

GDP growth:	-0.8%
GDP:	$1,435bn (PPP: $1,394bn)
Inflation:	0.7%
Population:	45.9m
GDP per head:	$31,250 (PPP: $30,360)

Seven seats short of a majority, the centre-left government of the prime minister, José Luis Rodríguez Zapatero, could find itself in trouble if regional parties withdraw their informal support. However, disarray in the main opposition Popular Party lowers the odds. A home-grown property bubble meant Spain was hit early and hard by the credit crunch; consumer confidence will remain fragile, and the housing market, although stabilising, will remain weak. Growth will not return until late in the year at the earliest, and unemployment and the budget deficit will soar.

To watch: AVE Maria. Overheated Madrileños will be able to hit the beach at Alicante in record time when the high-speed AVE train link opens.

SWEDEN

GDP growth:	1.3%
GDP:	$435bn (PPP: $337bn)
Inflation:	1.5%
Population:	9.3m
GDP per head:	$46,730 (PPP: $36,160)

The centre-right coalition government has retained public support despite the economic crisis, but the opposition block is still searching for ways to hold together and present a coherent front. The September election is too close to call, but if a programme of tax cuts and budget spending brings recovery from the 2009 recession into sight, the coalition will start as the favourite.

To watch: Baltic backwash. Two of Sweden's four major banks are heavily exposed to the benighted Baltic economies and may need bailing out if those countries are forced to devalue.

SWITZERLAND

GDP growth:	0.7%
GDP:	$473bn (PPP: $318bn)
Inflation:	0.4%
Population:	7.8m
GDP per head:	$60,690 (PPP: $40,780)

The Swiss People's Party (SVP), the country's largest, is back inside the government tent after spending a year in opposition in 2008. That means Switzerland's consensus-based way of governing will be better equipped to ride out the economic downturn and engineer changes in the financial system, including implementing rules weakening the secrecy laws synonymous with Swiss banking. However, the SVP will continue to oppose its coalition partners' overtures to the EU.

TURKEY

GDP growth:	3.0%
GDP:	$687bn (PPP: $913bn)
Inflation:	7.0%
Population:	73.3m
GDP per head:	$9,370 (PPP: $12,450)

The tussle between the moderately Islamist Justice and Development party government and the staunchly secularist political and military establishment will continue to test the country's institutions. The economy will be equally testing in 2010, and a fresh crisis, including the spectre of debt default, will threaten if the government fails to shore up confidence among foreign investors by reaching a new deal with the IMF. Peace talks over Cyprus, a big factor in Turkey's EU membership bid, will proceed, but bring no deal.

To watch: Cultural earnings. Tourism receipts will be boosted by Istanbul's designation as a European capital of culture, along with Essen in Germany and Pécs in Hungary.

UKRAINE

GDP growth:	1.0%
GDP:	$122bn (PPP: $291bn)
Inflation:	12.2%
Population:	45.5m
GDP per head:	$2,670 (PPP: $6,390)

The year will kick off with a presidential election, marking the next round in the battle for control among the country's post-Soviet factions. Viktor Yanukovich of the opposition Party of Regions, who opposed the revolution, is likely to come out ahead of the prime minister, Yulia Tymoshenko, its champion, and a large field of also-rans. Previously, benign economic conditions meant dysfunctional politics bore little cost, but in the wake of a contraction likely to have approached 17% in 2009 people will be less forgiving and could show their displeasure on the streets.

UNITED KINGDOM

GDP growth:	0.6%
GDP:	$2,255bn (PPP: $2,160bn)
Inflation:	2.3%
Population:	62.2m
GDP per head:	$36,250 (PPP: $34,730)

Economic growth will resume, but damage done by the global economic crisis—to the country's fiscal position, to the reputation of London as a financial centre and to the standing of the governing Labour Party—will take a generation to repair. The political cost will be evident in a probable May election, when voters will vent their fury on politicians as a class, but mainly on Labour. Though there is hardly a groundswell of enthusiasm for the opposition Conservative Party, it will win in the election and achieve an overall parliamentary majority.

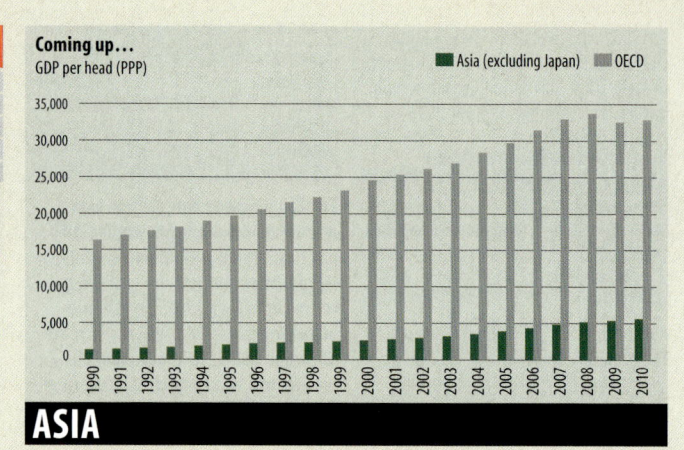

Coming up...
GDP per head (PPP)

[Bar chart showing Asia (excluding Japan) and OECD GDP per head from 1990 to 2010, with OECD ranging from approximately 15,000 to 35,000 and Asia (excluding Japan) ranging from below 5,000 to approximately 5,000]

ASIA

Main event: China becomes the world's second-largest economy
Asia growth (excluding Japan): 5.5% **ASEAN growth**: 3.7%

AUSTRALIA

GDP growth:	1.7%
GDP:	$1,125bn (PPP: $839bn)
Inflation:	2.8%
Population:	21.5m
GDP per head:	$52,290 (PPP: $39,020)

In any other year, opposition attacks on the government's economic management might have hit home. But Australia was among the select few that avoided recession in 2009, thanks in part to successful fiscal and monetary policies, so the thrusts will cause only flesh wounds. Kevin Rudd, who heads the Labor Party government, is here for the duration. Stronger business investment and rising exports to China will help the economy to grow faster in 2010, though at a less-than-full-blooded 1.7%.

CHINA

GDP growth:	8.6%
GDP:	$5,588bn (PPP: $9,845bn)
Inflation:	2.4%
Population:	1,339.2m
GDP per head:	$4,170 (PPP: $7,350)

After selling to consumption-crazed Americans and Europeans during the boom, China is using the proceeds to spend its way through the bust. Indeed, thanks to the global recession, growth will slow to the moderate rate that cautious economists—worried about overheating—have been recommending for years. Even so, the economic stimulus is producing industrial overcapacity and asset-price bubbles in stocks and property. A surge in bank lending, accompanied by weak risk assessment, will bring a worrying rise in bad loans.

HONG KONG

GDP growth:	2.8%
GDP:	$218bn (PPP: $306bn)
Inflation:	1.0%
Population:	7.1m
GDP per head:	$30,720 (PPP: $43,180)

While mainland China forges ahead, this former British outpost will struggle with the economic ills of the developed world, emerging from the 2009 recession to only tepid growth. The mainland's strong performance will help, but the world trade in goods on which Hong Kong's economy depends will remain depressed.

To watch: Ballotproof. The pro-democracy protests held every year could be particularly loud in 2010. The souring economy has undermined support for the chief executive, Donald Tsang, and the mainland-dominated system behind him.

Share croppers
Shanghai composite index, Dec 19th 1990=100

[Line chart showing Shanghai composite index from 2007 to 2009, peaking around 6,000 in late 2007 and declining to around 2,000-3,000 through 2008-2009]

INDIA

GDP growth:	6.3%
GDP:	$1,468bn (PPP: $3,876bn)
Inflation:	8.6%
Population:	1,184.1m
GDP per head:	$1,240 (PPP: $3,270)

A resilient domestic market and low reliance on exports have allowed India to grow through the global downturn, thanks in part to decisive fiscal stimulus and growth in credit. The downside is that the fiscal deficit—which has been a worry for years—is widening sharply. Indebtedness will also grow, and India's home-grown way of measuring non-performing loans will only disguise a growing problem. The Congress party-led coalition government will focus on short-term economic growth, to the detriment of structural reform.

To watch: Track records. The Commonwealth Games, contested by 71 countries that mostly share a common past as part of the British Empire, will take place in India for the first time, security permitting.

INDONESIA
GDP growth:	4.5%
GDP:	$594bn (PPP: $993bn)
Inflation:	5.1%
Population:	243.0m
GDP per head:	$2,440 (PPP: $4,090)

As in India, a strong domestic market and low trade dependency are helping the country weather the global slump, supporting growth rates that advanced economies can only envy. President Susilo Bambang Yudhoyono heads a disparate coalition, but has a strong mandate and will remain in power. Difficult economic conditions will hold up progress on long-promised reforms such as labour-market liberalisation.

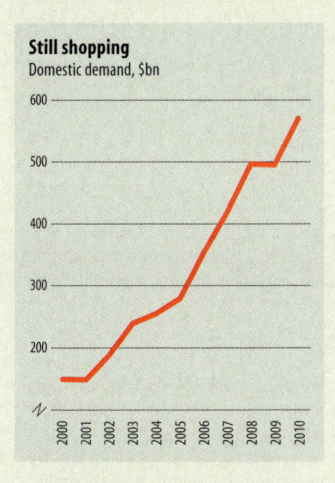

Still shopping
Domestic demand, $bn

To watch: Home-town hero. Relations with the US could get a boost: President Barack Obama, whose stepfather was Indonesian, spent some years in the country as a child.

JAPAN
GDP growth:	1.3%
GDP:	$5,128bn (PPP: $4,228bn)
Inflation:	-0.2%
Population:	126.8m
GDP per head:	$40,440 (PPP: $33,340)

The country will enter the year in uncharted political territory, following the electoral defeat in 2009 of the Liberal Democrat Party (LDP) after 53 years of almost uninterrupted power. In its place, the Democratic Party of Japan (DPJ) will aim to loosen the grip of the civil service and increase pay-outs to the poor. But holding together a loose coalition will be difficult, and the new prime minister, Yukio Hatoyama, must contend with the DPJ's power behind the throne, Ichiro Ozawa. The economy will improve, but hesitant US and European consumers will limit the export recovery Japan needs to sustain a turnaround.

To watch: Sino sign-up. The new government will align foreign relations more closely with China, weakening the bond with the US that was an article of faith for the LDP.

KAZAKHSTAN
GDP growth:	2.2%
GDP:	$116bn (PPP: $183bn)
Inflation:	6.7%
Population:	16.2m
GDP per head:	$7,160 (PPP: $11,320)

Squabbling among the country's rulers has led to cabinet changes and the purging of business leaders, but the government appears stable for now. Although an election is not due until 2012, an early vote could be called if the government thinks the economy will worsen, which it might. The banks remain troubled and the currency could face a speculative attack, but oil-sector projects, higher commodity prices and the positive results of the stimulus package will help the economy to grow.

MALAYSIA
GDP growth:	3.9%
GDP:	$220bn (PPP: $401bn)
Inflation:	0.8%
Population:	28.9m
GDP per head:	$7,630 (PPP: $13,880)

The ruling Barisan Nasional and the combative prime minister, Najib Razak, have a solid power base and will remain in charge, but a fierce contest with the opposition Pakatan Rakyat for the loyalty of individual legislators will keep politics confrontational. Malaysia's worst recession in a decade will turn into a respectable rebound in 2010 as world demand rallies. But an even stronger pick-up in imports will lead to a significant deterioration in the trade balance, and this will exert a drag on GDP growth.

To watch: Legal defence. Supporters of opposition leader Anwar Ibrahim, who is facing a second trial on sodomy charges, could take to the streets if he is convicted.

NEW ZEALAND
GDP growth:	1.9%
GDP:	$133bn (PPP: $120bn)
Inflation:	1.5%
Population:	4.4m
GDP per head:	$30,350 (PPP: $27,360)

A budget that postpones tax cuts planned for April and reduces government spending met with public approval, suggesting voters are realistic about the pressures on the prime minister, John Key, and remain broadly supportive of his government. After years of splurging, New Zealanders will save more, dampening consumer spending. The damaging effects of falling house prices will also persist, putting a further brake on consumption. Modest recession in 2009 will become modest recovery in 2010.

PAKISTAN
GDP growth:	2.4%
GDP:	$170bn (PPP: $461bn)
Inflation:	8.6%
Population:	185.5m
GDP per head:	$910 (PPP: $2,480)

National security will remain the most pressing issue for the president, Asif Ali Zardari. After a lull following the death of Pakistan's Taliban leader, Baitullah Mehsud, in a US drone attack, hostilities in the country's lawless north-west will regain their former intensity, bringing the government's stability into question. American military and development assistance will continue, but the United States will demand greater accountability from Pakistan's authorities. Pakistan's main export industry, textiles, will suffer from weak global demand.

To watch: Don't LOL. Wags sharing jokes at Mr Zardari's expense via electronic media could face 14 years in prison under a new law.

PHILIPPINES
GDP growth:	3.7%
GDP:	$166bn (PPP: $344bn)
Inflation:	3.8%
Population:	99.9m
GDP per head:	$1,660 (PPP: $3,440)

In the post
Workers' remittances, $bn

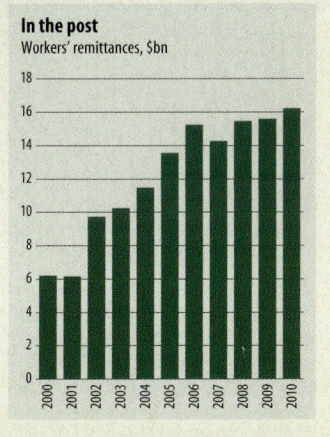

Peace talks with communist insurgents may resume after a four-year hiatus, but a final settlement is unlikely. President Gloria Macapagal Arroyo cannot stand for a third term in the 2010 election, but will try to retain influence by shifting the centre of power to the legislature. Remittances from overseas workers will continue their recovery, helping to push economic growth to 3.7%.

SINGAPORE
GDP growth:	3.8%
GDP:	$178bn (PPP: $199bn)
Inflation:	2.0%
Population:	5.0m
GDP per head:	$35,630 (PPP: $39,720)

Entrepôt to the world, the city-state was battered by the collapse in world trade that accompanied the credit crunch. Plentiful foreign reserves have helped the ever-ruling People's Action Party government to soften the blow, but long-suppressed calls for greater political openness will intensify.

To watch: Cybersoccer. More than 3,000 robots from 40 countries will take to the soccer pitch to compete for the RoboCup in the world's biggest robotics and artificial-intelligence event.

SOUTH KOREA
GDP growth:	2.8%
GDP:	$882bn (PPP: $1,421bn)
Inflation:	2.6%
Population:	49.5m
GDP per head:	$17,810 (PPP: $28,700)

As elsewhere, the authorities will use monetary and fiscal policy to mitigate the economic downturn, at the cost of public indebtedness and a growing budget gap. A modest economic recovery will bring some much-needed respite to the president, Lee Myung-bak, whose uncertain handling of the downturn

---

2010 IN PERSON

Emerging from the sometimes bizarre rule of Saparmurat "Turkmenbashi" Niyazov, Turkmenistan needed a leader of character. **Gurbanguly Berdymukhammedov** has been up to the task, sweeping aside the paraphernalia of his predecessor's personality cult and throwing open the country's shutters. In foreign policy he has broken free of Russia's grip and started to build relationships with the West and China, which have been welcomed. He quickly showed a new leadership style at home after coming to power in 1997—paying overdue public-sector salaries, for example, and exhorting citizens not to celebrate his birthday. With access to Caspian gas reserves likely to matter a lot in 2010, the coming year could see Mr Berdymukhammedov make his mark on the international stage too.

Countries The world in figures

Factory fightback
Industrial production, 2005=100

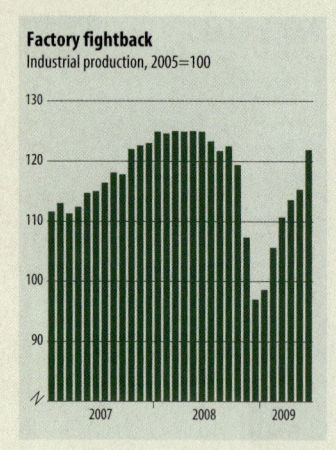

has estranged voters. US ties will get a boost from close co-operation over North Korea, but pending ratification of a free-trade agreement will continue to face opposition in South Korea and the US.

SRI LANKA
GDP growth:	6.3%
GDP:	$49bn (PPP: $104bn)
Inflation:	8.7%
Population:	20.4m
GDP per head:	$2,410 (PPP: $5,070)

Military victory over the Tamil Tigers will deliver a modest peace dividend, with a burst of inward investment driving growth to 6.3%, but underlying ethnic tension and isolated terrorist attacks will persist. President Mahinda Rajapakse and his United People's Freedom Alliance government should do well in parliamentary elections which are due by April but may well come earlier.

TAIWAN
GDP growth:	3.9%
GDP:	$376bn (PPP: $824bn)
Inflation:	1.2%
Population:	22.9m
GDP per head:	$16,430 (PPP: $35,990)

President Ma Ying-jeou and his Kuomintang government have a strong mandate—the ruling party controls both parliament and the presidency—and a rallying economy should reverse a slide in popular support. Growth will reach 3.9%, reversing a slump of similar size in 2009. Improving ties with China will remain a priority, and an economic co-operation agreement with the mainland may be reached in 2010.

THAILAND
GDP growth:	3.3%
GDP:	$274bn (PPP: $555bn)
Inflation:	2.2%
Population:	67.5m
GDP per head:	$4,060 (PPP: $8,230)

The political maelstrom surrounding the prime minister, Abhisit Vejjajiva, reflects the power struggle that has infected Thai politics for the past decade. Under sustained attack from the opposition, Abhisit is also seeing political friends dragged through the courts and coalition allies eyeing the exits; this is likely to be yet another election year. Starting from a weak fiscal position, a three-year stimulus programme that began in 2009 will swell the public debt while delivering modest growth.

UZBEKISTAN
GDP growth:	7.0%
GDP:	$31bn (PPP: $83bn)
Inflation:	8.7%
Population:	28.6m
GDP per head:	$1,100 (PPP: $2,890)

Islam Karimov will once again demonstrate his expertise in staying on the presidential throne—most of his opponents are living in exile—and speculation about the succession will become relevant only if he dies. Stimulus measures and rising public-sector wages will support consumer spending, and improving global markets for the country's commodities exports will drive economic growth to 7%.

VIETNAM
GDP growth:	6.0%
GDP:	$101bn (PPP: $274bn)
Inflation:	8.5%
Population:	87.8m
GDP per head:	$1,150 (PPP: $3,120)

Red territory
Budget balance, % of GDP

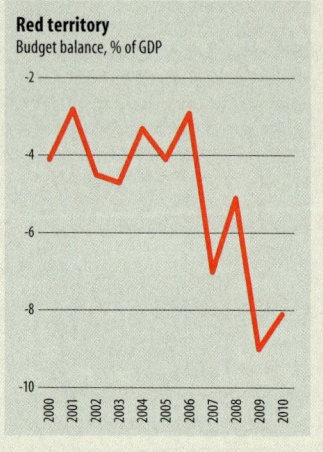

Vietnam was less badly affected by the global recession than its neighbours, but growth still halved between 2007 and 2009. The Communist government, under Nguyen Tan Dung, will lend and spend as necessary to keep the economy growing, storing up imbalances for future years. The government will continue gradually to shift its foreign relations in China's favour—a hotline was set up in 2009. The rebalancing will place some strain on relations with America.

To watch: Prost! It will be steins, schwarzbrot and stollen as Vietnam celebrates German Year (and Germany celebrates Vietnam Year), marking 35 years of diplomatic relations.

Following the leader
GDP growth (bars) and unemployment (lines), %
Canada Mexico US

NORTH AMERICA

Main event: The verdict on Obamanomics in America's November mid-term elections
North American (NAFTA) growth: 2.4%

CANADA
GDP growth:	2.0%
GDP:	$1,478bn (PPP: $1,321bn)
Inflation:	1.4%
Population:	34.0m
GDP per head:	$43,450 (PPP: $38,850)

An election in 2010 is possible as the opposition Liberals manoeuvre to bring down the minority Conservative government, although signs that economic recovery is under way are likely to lift the incumbents. Export demand will increase in 2010 as commodity prices stabilise and economic growth in the US—by far Canada's most important customer—moves back into positive territory. But the recession revealed the dangers of over-dependence on US demand, and trade policy will focus on diversifying export markets to fast-growers such as China. The economy will grow moderately, after 2009's contraction, but high unemployment will prevent a strong recovery.

MEXICO
GDP growth:	3.0%
GDP:	$887bn (PPP: $1,668bn)
Inflation:	3.3%
Population:	112.5m
GDP per head:	$7,890 (PPP: $14,830)

The strong links with the United States that helped the economy early in the decade plunged Mexico into its worst recession since the 1930s in 2009, and the pace of the recovery will be constrained by the performance north of the border. After handing majority control of the legislature to the once-hegemonic Partido Revolucionario Institucional in mid-2009 elections, the ruling Partido Acción Nacional under President Felipe Calderón will be unable to implement structural reforms already long overdue. Should the global recovery fade, Mexico will be ill-prepared to confront a new downturn.

To watch: Double celebration. Mexico celebrates 200 years of independence (September) and the centenary of its revolution (November).

UNITED STATES
GDP growth:	2.4%
GDP:	$14,840bn (PPP: $14,840bn)
Inflation:	1.0%
Population:	309.6m
GDP per head:	$47,920 (PPP: $47,920)

The fiscal surge coursing through the economy—the budget deficit in 2009 was equal to a staggering 12% of GDP, and will be almost as large in 2010—will help to restore growth. So, too, will the unorthodox monetary conditions that have been in place for the past year. But a second dip is a worrying possibility as the stimulus fades and joblessness remains elevated. President Barack Obama will struggle to balance the left-leaning factions of his party with its centrists, but will secure enough support in Congress—where he has majorities—to advance his programmes. Embittered Republicans will give him no quarter, and far-right paranoia will take on disturbing tones. Although Republican obstructionism will not be popular, the Democrats will lose ground in the November mid-terms.

Moving out
Home-ownership rates, % of total homes

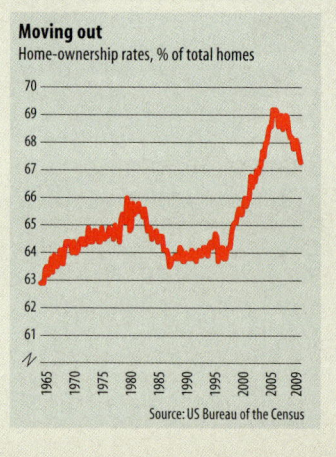

Source: US Bureau of the Census

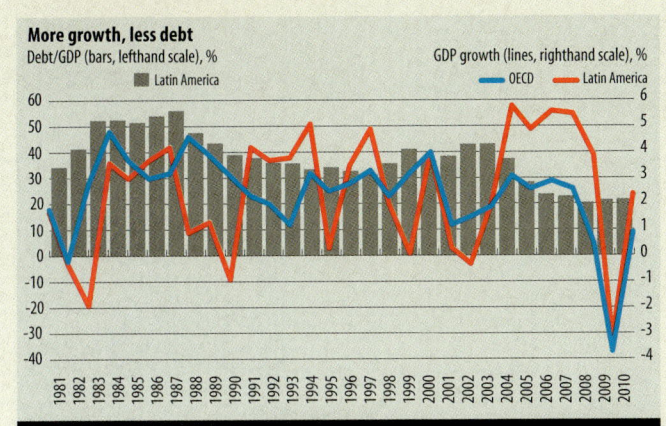

LATIN AMERICA

Main event: Brazil's presidential election in October
Latin American growth: 2.4%

More growth, less debt
Debt/GDP (bars, lefthand scale), %
GDP growth (lines, righthand scale), %

ARGENTINA
GDP growth:	1.4%
GDP:	$293bn (PPP: $593bn)
Inflation:	8.3%
Population:	40.5m
GDP per head:	$7,230 (PPP: $14,630)

Cristina Fernández de Kirchner is a lame-duck president in danger of losing her job before her term ends in 2011. The opposition controls the legislature and loyalty within her own Peronist Party is sagging. Economic policies designed mainly to secure the Kirchners' power base are being exposed by the global recession. There is an outside risk of paralysing political protest and a new, home-grown economic crisis.

To watch: Gaucho gala. The country celebrates 200 years of independence on May 25th.

BOLIVIA
GDP growth:	2.8%
GDP:	$20bn (PPP: $47bn)
Inflation:	4.4%
Population:	10.1m
GDP per head:	$1,940 (PPP: $4,710)

The political divide will remain sharp, with both the leftist president, Evo Morales, and Senate candidates in the eastern opposition heartlands set to do well in the end-2009 elections. With Mr Morales confirmed in office until 2014, his state-led development model will become more entrenched. The hydrocarbons windfall that financed government stimulus spending in 2009 will fade, subduing economic recovery.

BRAZIL
GDP growth:	3.8%
GDP:	$1,669bn (PPP: $2,113bn)
Inflation:	4.0%
Population:	196.8m
GDP per head:	$8,480 (PPP: $10,740)

In contrast to neighbouring Argentina, thrifty economic management has cushioned Brazil against the recession's worst, and growth will resume in 2010. Even so, the ruling Workers' Party is no shoo-in for re-election in October. Voters have not taken to its candidate-in-waiting, Dilma Rousseff, and the opposition candidate, José Serra, who is governor of São Paulo state, will shine as economic hardship persists.

CHILE
GDP growth:	3.9%
GDP:	$170bn (PPP: $257bn)
Inflation:	2.3%
Population:	17.1m
GDP per head:	$9,950 (PPP: $15,010)

The likely victory of Sebastián Piñera of the right-of-centre La Alianza in the December 2009 presidential election will mark the return of the right two decades after a military dictator, Augusto Pinochet, restored civil rule, but will signify little change in the consensus-led, pro-market policies that have characterised the intervening years. The 2009 recession was shallow, and growth will resume.

To watch: Out of Africa. The 32nd Dakar rally will again be held in the Andean highlands between Chile and Argentina in March. The event's African home was deemed too dangerous.

COLOMBIA
GDP growth:	2.4%
GDP:	$250bn (PPP: $418bn)
Inflation:	4.1%
Population:	48.9m
GDP per head:	$5,110 (PPP: $8,540)

The centre-right is likely to retain power in the May election, but the two-term incumbent, Álvaro Uribe, may not be its candidate after his party lost the contest for leadership of Congress in 2009, setting back plans to lift a constitutional ban on third terms. If he isn't, his former defence minister, Juan Manuel Santos, is the favourite, and would continue Mr Uribe's pro-market economic reforms.

CUBA
GDP growth:	3.5%
GDP:	$59bn (PPP: $116bn)
Inflation:	4.7%
Population:	11.2m
GDP per head:	$5,220 (PPP: $10,330)

Handling the domestic backwash from global upheaval is routine for the Castros, and Raúl, who took over as president from Fidel in 2008, will squeeze government spending and discourage imports. More tentative steps will be taken in the long march towards normalised relations with the US.

ECUADOR
GDP growth:	2.3%
GDP:	$56bn (PPP: $110bn)
Inflation:	5.0%
Population:	14.2m
GDP per head:	$3,960 (PPP: $7,770)

President Rafael Correa is beholden to the small parties on the far left that prop up his coalition after his own party, Alianza País, lost majority control of the legislature in 2009; this will ensure that the radical populism driving his policies continues. Default on a portion of the foreign debt in 2008 scared off lenders, but the government may repeat the tactic as external financing needs bite.

To watch: Flight plan. Quito's new airport, which increases capacity tenfold, will open in 2010.

PARAGUAY
GDP growth:	2.5%
GDP:	$14bn (PPP: $29bn)
Inflation:	5.1%
Population:	6.5m
GDP per head:	$2,140 (PPP: $4,510)

After a rough start, the government of the president and former priest, Fernando Lugo, will get a shot in the arm when fees start flowing in for Brazilian use of energy generated on the Paraguayan side of the jointly owned Itaipú hydroelectric complex. The cashflow will restore the budget to surplus, and help raise economic growth. Political capital from the Itaipú deal will strengthen Mr Lugo's grip on power.

PERU
GDP growth:	3.0%
GDP:	$134bn (PPP: $257bn)
Inflation:	2.3%
Population:	29.8m
GDP per head:	$4,520 (PPP: $8,610)

Tensions between indigenous highlanders and a largely coastal elite are returning to the fore and will present a challenge to the administration of Alan García as the 2011 election approaches. Thirty people died in armed clashes in 2009, and Mr García has signalled a harder line still, hinting at violence to come. By contrast, the economy will perform smoothly.

URUGUAY
GDP growth:	2.0%
GDP:	$34bn (PPP: $45bn)
Inflation:	7.1%
Population:	3.3m
GDP per head:	$10,220 (PPP: $13,330)

A new year, a new government term, but probably the same ruling party—José Mujica of the Frente Amplio was favourite ahead of late-2009 elections. If he wins, he will take over from the president, Tabaré Vázquez, in March, though almost certainly at the head of a minority government. With the economy recovering, policy will shift to an emphasis on fiscal rebalancing.

VENEZUELA
GDP growth:	-3.4%
GDP:	$333bn (PPP: $334bn)
Inflation:	31.4%
Population:	28.6m
GDP per head:	$11,660 (PPP: $11,990)

The country will buck the global trend of economic recovery and remain deeply in recession. With so little revenue, there cannot be much more government stimulus. Moves to centralise further government control will deepen social divisions and lead to outbreaks of violent protest. But Hugo Chávez's revolution will roll on, and a divided and harassed opposition will be unable to exploit the opportunity presented by legislative elections in December.

2010 IN PERSON

Long known as the poorest country in the Western hemisphere, Haiti has stumbled from one crisis to another since the Duvalier years. But under its prime minister, **Michèle Pierre-Louis**, the country has an opportunity to make substantial and sustainable gains in both economics and politics. Her domestic achievements are already considerable, holding together a diverse coalition and quelling a determined opposition. Abroad, she has worked well with international leaders and won some influential friends, including Bill Clinton, a former US president. The tenure of Ms Pierre-Louis, whose social-activist brother-in-law was assassinated in 1998, may conceivably mark a turning-point in the country's long battle with extreme poverty, bloody confrontation and deep-rooted social injustice.

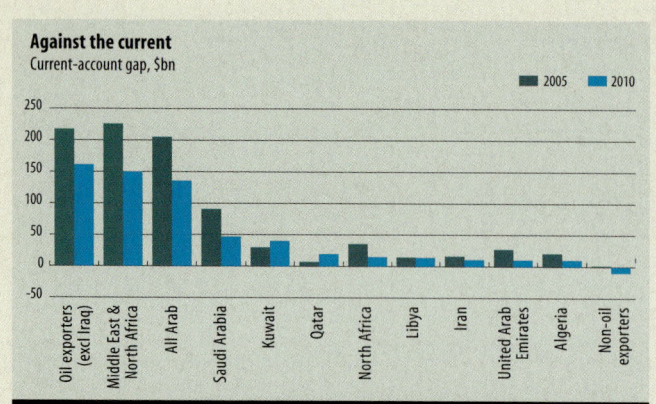

Against the current
Current-account gap, $bn
■ 2005 ■ 2010

MIDDLE EAST AND AFRICA

Main event: Mounting pressures in Iran, both political and economic
Middle East & North Africa growth: 4.4%
Sub-Saharan Africa growth: 3.1%

ALGERIA
GDP growth:	4.6%
GDP:	$182bn (PPP: $301bn)
Inflation:	3.7%
Population:	35.5m
GDP per head:	$5,140 (PPP: $8,470)

The re-election of Abdelaziz Bouteflika to a third successive presidential term in 2009 promises continuity but will also see increased instability as his opponents, both liberals and Islamists, chafe at their lack of influence. Discontent could be limited to street protests, but could extend to attacks on the army or a renewed campaign of terrorist bombings.

ANGOLA
GDP growth:	5.5%
GDP:	$98bn (PPP: $128bn)
Inflation:	11.4%
Population:	19.0m
GDP per head:	$5,160 (PPP: $6,760)

José Eduardo dos Santos, president for the past three decades, will win re-election in a delayed vote likely to take place in 2010, and his Popular Movement for the Liberation of Angola will continue to dominate politics. After a temporary decline in oil exports under OPEC's quota regime in 2009, output will rally, pushing growth to 5.5%.

To watch: Ill wind. Mr dos Santos is rumoured to be ill. If he is forced to drop his re-election bid, the lack of succession candidates may stir up political conflict.

CAMEROON
GDP growth:	1.4%
GDP:	$24bn (PPP: $42bn)
Inflation:	3.2%
Population:	20.0m
GDP per head:	$1,190 (PPP: $2,090)

President Paul Biya has taken flak for too energetic a focus on securing his personal power base—including, unusually, from members of his own Beti ethnic group. Still, his supporters will gather round when needed, and a weakened opposition doesn't pose much threat. Little is likely to happen to damage Mr Biya's overwhelming chances of winning re-election when his term ends in 2011.

To watch: Relieved. Sufferers from prostate troubles will benefit from the removal of a conservation ban on harvesting the Prunus Africana, an indigenous tree whose bark yields compounds beneficial in treating prostate-related conditions.

EGYPT
GDP growth:	4.5%
GDP:	$212bn (PPP: $498bn)
Inflation:	6.2%
Population:	84.8m
GDP per head:	$2,500 (PPP: $5,870)

Despite the regime's clear distaste for public discussion of 81-year-old President Hosni Mubarak's health (four newspaper editors were jailed in 2007 for publishing speculative stories), the succession will dominate political thinking. The ruling party has said it will not choose a presidential candidate until 2011, when elections are due, but the shift to a new leader—presumed to be Mr Mubarak's son, Gamal—will top the agenda in 2010, even if it doesn't happen. In the meantime the government will continue with a budget-busting programme designed to support living standards and quell popular discontent.

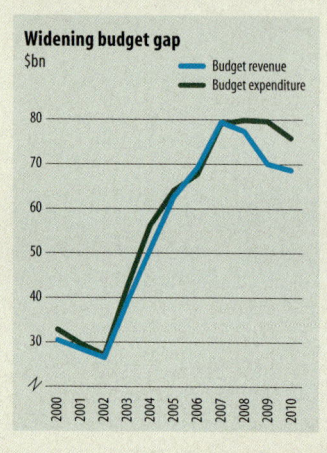

Widening budget gap
$bn — Budget revenue / Budget expenditure

ETHIOPIA
GDP growth:	7.0%
GDP:	$35bn (PPP: $83bn)
Inflation:	12.0%
Population:	75.1m
GDP per head:	$464 (PPP: $1,100)

Political tensions will rise around the May election, but the Ethiopian People's Revolutionary Democratic Front will stay in power. The IMF has rewarded the government's economic management with financial support, and a strong performance in agriculture, the mainstay of the country, will make this one of the world's fastest-growing economies.

IRAN
GDP growth:	2.9%
GDP:	$415bn (PPP: $889bn)
Inflation:	14.0%
Population:	75.1m
GDP per head:	$5,530 (PPP: $11,840)

Mahmoud Ahmadinejad, re-elected in a questionable vote in 2009, will be back firmly in the driving seat after a shaky start to his second term. Critics from within the conservative camp have been largely neutralised by the need to fight off the fury of the opposition and the regime's opponents in the West. The end of the oil boom will expose the weaknesses in Iran's economic model, squeezing domestic financing while foreign investment flows are restricted by sanctions.

IRAQ
GDP growth:	6.2%
GDP:	$91bn (PPP: $130bn)
Inflation:	6.1%
Population:	31.3m
GDP per head:	$2,910 (PPP: $4,150)

Violence increased in the wake of the withdrawal of US troops from Iraq's cities in mid-2009, but to nowhere near the level at the height of the post-invasion conflict. Even so, the Iraqi armed forces will face a difficult year as bombings designed to widen sectarian divides continue. Nuri al-Maliki, the prime minister, will seek re-election in January, though his decision to remain aloof from a new Shia coalition reduces his chances.

To watch: Yankees' home run. President Barack Obama has said he'll keep a campaign promise to pull American combat troops out of Iraq by August, though up to 50,000 are likely to remain in support roles.

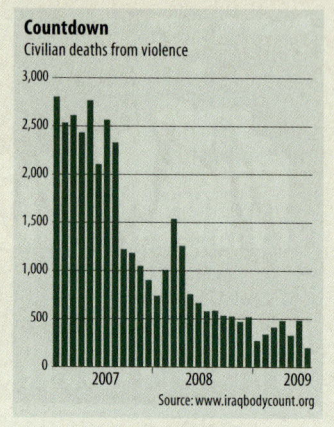

Countdown
Civilian deaths from violence
Source: www.iraqbodycount.org

ISRAEL
GDP growth:	2.3%
GDP:	$199bn (PPP: $207bn)
Inflation:	2.9%
Population:	7.6m
GDP per head:	$26,300 (PPP: $27,400)

The prime minister, Binyamin Netanyahu, and his coalition partners have 74 seats in the Knesset (that is, more than half) but divisions within his government mean that his real authority is far weaker than that figure suggests. Likud, his own party, is holding up, but two senior coalition partners are in trouble. A legal case threatens the effectiveness of Yisrael Beiteinu, while the Labour Party is divided and offers only faltering support. The government will use public spending to boost growth, at the cost of a widening fiscal deficit.

JORDAN
GDP growth:	3.0%
GDP:	$23bn (PPP: $33bn)
Inflation:	5.8%
Population:	6.4m
GDP per head:	$3,590 (PPP: $5,150)

A property boom and a heavy reliance on tourism meant the country was exposed to the global financial meltdown and ensuing economic slump, and the government will support domestic demand regardless of the impact on the budget. Reform efforts will concentrate on the economy rather than politics, where King Abdullah will continue to dominate, with the support of the armed forces.

KENYA
GDP growth:	2.7%
GDP:	$38bn (PPP: $66bn)
Inflation:	6.5%
Population:	40.9m
GDP per head:	$940 (PPP: $1,610)

The coalition government, combining President Mwai Kibaki of the Party of National Unity and his prime minister and main political rival, Raila Odinga of the Orange Democratic Movement, will look pretty wobbly, much as it has since its formation in 2008, although it will probably survive. But disagreements over key appointments and policy priorities will get in the way of effective government. An improved global environment will bring economic growth back to 2.7% after the 2009 slowdown.

LEBANON
GDP growth:	3.3%
GDP:	$32bn (PPP: $48bn)
Inflation:	3.9%
Population:	4.3m
GDP per head:	$7,480 (PPP: $11,210)

Managing the sectarian jigsaw of Lebanese politics will remain at the top of the agenda after Saad al-Hariri, emphatic winner of mid-2009 elections, abandoned efforts to build a government in September. Mr Hariri blamed opposition forces sponsored by Iran and Syria for blocking him. His opponents said his own mistakes sealed his fate. In contrast to the stuttering political process, competent economic policy will deliver 3.3% growth.

To watch: Judgment day. The tribunal investigating the 2005 killing of a former prime minister, Rafiq Hariri, is likely to point the finger at Syria.

LIBYA
GDP growth:	5.1%
GDP:	$55bn (PPP: $121bn)
Inflation:	5.4%
Population:	6.5m
GDP per head:	$8,350 (PPP: $18,550)

Colonel Muammar Qaddafi, the world's longest-serving ruler since the death in mid-2009 of President Omar Bongo Ondimba of Gabon, will extend his record by another year—and is on track to establish dynastic succession to one of his sons when the time comes. The colonel's aim of improving ties with the West will continue to be weakened by his idiosyncratic leadership style and policy decisions. Nevertheless, the country's oil wealth ensures that the rapprochement will carry on. Economic growth, which held at 4% in 2009 despite the global slowdown, will accelerate to 5.1% in 2010.

MOROCCO
GDP growth:	3.4%
GDP:	$99bn (PPP: $151bn)
Inflation:	2.6%
Population:	32.3m
GDP per head:	$3,060 (PPP: $4,670)

Moroccans may not like laws that make it a major crime to question the legitimacy of the monarchy, but they do like the king, and Muhammad VI, a decade on the throne, faces no substantial threat to his authority. Nevertheless, poor standards of living and high unemployment, combined with the lack of popular representation through a weak parliament, will keep discontent on the boil—and keep security forces busy suppressing dissent and neutralising Islamist factions. Fiscal stimulus and a bumper harvest helped the country avoid recession in 2009, and will contribute to a small improvement in 2010.

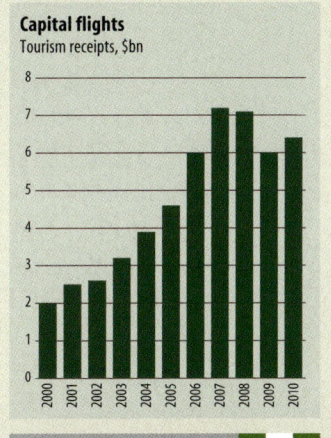

Capital flights
Tourism receipts, $bn

NIGERIA
GDP growth:	5.2%
GDP:	$167bn (PPP: $348bn)
Inflation:	8.5%
Population:	152.2m
GDP per head:	$1,100 (PPP: $2,290)

The government of President Umaru Yar'Adua will face the difficult choice between pushing ahead with a programme of important but unpopular market reforms and courting interest groups which favour the state-led model and the subsidy structure that characterises it. The job will be all the more difficult because of the impact of the global slowdown on Nigeria's economy, where the hard-hit international oil market is a mainstay. However, strong performance in non-oil industries helped the country steer well clear of recession in 2009, and rallying global demand will help push the growth rate to 5.2% in 2010—slow by recent standards but far from disastrous.

SAUDI ARABIA
GDP growth:	3.3%
GDP:	$472bn (PPP: $622bn)
Inflation:	4.0%
Population:	26.2m
GDP per head:	$18,020 (PPP: $23,740)

After the first recession in a decade in 2009, economic policy will focus on restoring growth, by distributing credit through the government's lending institutions, and increasing subsidies and other public transfers. The policies, combined with an improving global outlook, will drive growth to 3.3%. The price of oil will climb to an annual average of $74, 19% up on 2009. Politics will see no big change, with King Abdullah bin Abdul-Aziz al-Saud in control and democratic reform off the agenda.

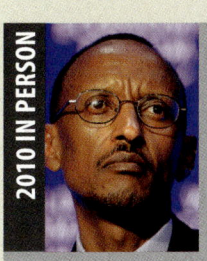

2010 IN PERSON

Fifteen years on, the ethnic bloodletting that took close to a million lives in 1994 is still the main thing most outsiders know about Rwanda. If the country now begins to break free of that legacy, much of the credit must go to **Paul Kagame**, the first directly elected president since the genocide and all but certain to win re-election in 2010. Mr Kagame, either on the throne or behind it since 1994, could work on his sense of inclusiveness (he is particularly intolerant of internal dissent), but few doubt his commitment to propelling his country into the modern era and raising the living standards of his people. Nevertheless, Rwanda remains at a fork in the road, and whether it takes the path to reconciliation and progress or to authoritarianism and repression will be decided during Mr Kagame's second term.

SOUTH AFRICA
GDP growth:	3.1%
GDP:	$275bn (PPP: $498bn)
Inflation:	5.7%
Population:	49.1m
GDP per head:	$5,610 (PPP: $10,140)

Preparations for the soccer World Cup, to be hosted by South Africa, have already given a boost to the economy through infrastructure spending. There is more to come as football fans from around the world descend on the country's big cities. But the economic headwinds will be strong, and maintaining living standards will remain a challenge for the government of President Jacob Zuma. Unemployment will stay alarmingly high, above 20%, causing a lot of social unrest.

To watch: Rounders? If the FIFA World Cup doesn't appeal, try the International Fellowship of Cricket-loving Rotarians' World Festival, which will be held in Durban in March.

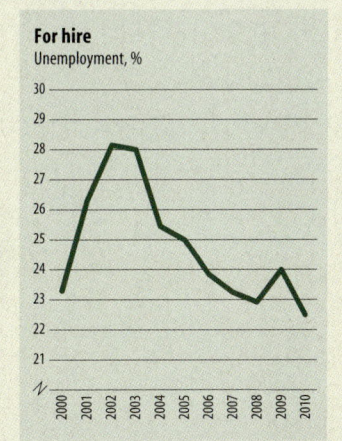

For hire
Unemployment, %

TANZANIA
GDP growth:	5.0%
GDP:	$23bn (PPP: $59bn)
Inflation:	8.0%
Population:	45.0m
GDP per head:	$500 (PPP: $1,310)

Jakaya Kikwete, the president, is likely to win the election due in late 2010 even though many voters believe they have not benefited much from the strong economic growth of recent years. His anti-corruption campaign will help his cause, and he remains personally popular. Donor-funded construction will contribute to stronger economic growth.

UNITED ARAB EMIRATES
GDP growth:	4.1%
GDP:	$269bn (PPP: $191bn)
Inflation:	4.2%
Population:	5.6m
GDP per head:	$48,280 (PPP: $34,310)

The economic downturn forced Dubai to adopt a more cautious and rigorous way of doing business, but its ruler and the UAE's prime minister, Sheikh Mohammed bin Rashid al-Maktoum, is expected to maintain his pro-business approach to the administration of the emirate. Politics will remain broadly stable, and significant reform is unlikely in the coming years. A gradual increase in oil output and the launch of several large energy projects will help the economy to start growing again.

ZIMBABWE
GDP growth:	1.9%
GDP:	$1.5bn (PPP: $1.9bn)
Inflation:	4.6%
Population:	12.6m
GDP per head:	$120 (PPP: $160)

The struggle between Robert Mugabe's Zimbabwe African National Union-Patriotic Front and Morgan Tsvangirai's Movement for Democratic Change, which theoretically share power in a unity government, will dominate politics. With each side seeking to undercut the other's power base, progress towards restoring economic stability will be halting and the threat of violence will be ever-present. By-elections were frozen until late-2009 under the power-sharing deal, but clashes over vote-rigging are inevitable as the election cycle resumes.

To watch: Cheaper by the dozen. Monthly inflation, which was estimated at 231,000,000% in mid-2008, was down to 1% in August 2009 after the local currency was replaced by the dollar. It will remain negligible in 2010.

CIMA
Chartered Institute of Management Accountants

'The CIMA qualification has given me the professional framework to add value to any decision making process, not restricted to finance, which is particularly valuable in a market as dynamic as China.'

James Bruce FCMA
Unilever, Greater China
Vice President Finance

CIMA *m*AKES BUSINESS SENSE

CIMA is the most relevant international accountancy qualification for business. Chartered Management Accountants are financially qualified business leaders operating in all areas of the organisation. They create value by applying leading edge techniques with a commercial and forward looking focus, adapting to the changing needs of the business.

Download the global employer pack today
www.choosecima.com/unilever

FINANCIAL MANAGEMENT   BUSINESS MANAGEMENT   FORECASTING   STRATEGIC INSIGHT   ACCOUNTING   PERFORMANCE MANAGEMENT   REPORTING   DECISION MAKING   TRANSACTION PROCESSING   ETHICS   PROJECT APPRAISAL AND MANAGEMENT   CHANGE MANAGEMENT   BUDGETING   ENTERPRISE GOVERNANCE   RISK MANAGEMENT   PARTNERSHIP MANAGEMENT   STRATEGY   SYSTEMS AND PROCEDURES   CORPORATE FINANCE

The world in figures: Industries

Automotive 113	Energy 114	Health care 115	Property and construction 116	Telecoms 116
Consumer goods 113	Entertainment 114	Information technology 115	Raw materials 116	Travel and tourism 116
Defence 113	Financial services 114	Media 115		
E-commerce 114	Food and farming 115			

For an interactive version of these pages, go to: www.economist.com/theworldin

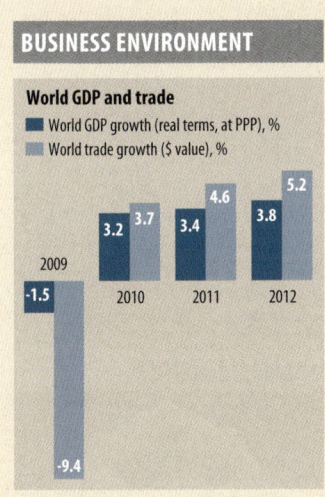

BUSINESS ENVIRONMENT

World GDP and trade
- World GDP growth (real terms, at PPP), %
- World trade growth ($ value), %

Year	GDP	Trade
2009	-1.5	-9.4
2010	3.2	3.7
2011	3.4	4.6
2012	3.8	5.2

The worst of the economic downturn may be over, but the Economist Intelligence Unit expects still subdued growth in 2010. Global output will expand by only 3.2% (on a purchasing-power parity, or PPP, basis), well below the 5% recorded in 2007. What growth the world can muster will come from large stimulus programmes, improving private-sector confidence and increased financial stabilisation. Even so, richer countries—where most of the damage was done—will expand by a mere 1.7%. Emerging economies will grow by a more encouraging 5.2%.

China, as ever, will lead the developing world. Rising spending, especially on infrastructure, will help the economy to grow by around 8.6%. What is good for China is good for Brazil: a vibrant Middle Kingdom will lift demand for Brazilian commodity exports.

Global trade will remain weak in 2010, growing by 3.7%. The Doha trade talks will resume but will yield little as governments safeguard fragile domestic economies. Protectionist legislation will be less of a threat, but countries may raise trade barriers legally, as tariffs in most countries are below WTO limits.

Interest rates will stay low. Although credit will be more available for larger firms, smaller fry will still go wanting.

2010 forecasts unless otherwise indicated. World totals based on 51 countries accounting for over 95% of world GDP.
Source: **Economist Intelligence Unit**
london@eiu.com

AUTOMOTIVE

CLOUDY — FAIR ▲ — SUNNY

After surviving the most difficult year in its history, the global auto industry will start to recover in 2010. Global car registrations will rise by 4.7%, led by Asia and the US. Sales will shrink, however, in western Europe, where a combination of state support and savage production cuts will ensure that much of the industry survives in more or less its current form. In the US, a smaller, leaner General Motors (owned by the US and Canadian governments, bondholders and a big union) should return to profit within two years. Chrysler (controlled by Fiat, a union and the US government) will also be in a stronger position once demand recovers. Ford could be in the most trouble if credit remains scarce.

With sales in Japan and most of Europe still under pressure, the brightest spots for carmakers will be China, Latin

Passenger-car registrations
m

Asia and Australasia	17.5
North America	11.3
Western Europe	10.7
Latin America	3.1
Eastern Europe and Russia	2.7
Middle East and Africa	0.7

America and India, where car sales will climb by 13%, 5% and 8%, respectively. Eastern Europe's prospects remain bleak.

Despite lower oil prices, carmakers are investing in fuel-saving technologies. Uncertainty over which ones will work best means R&D will be spread widely. By the end of 2010, electric cars won't be just for trips to local shops. By 2015, a faster crowd—Lamborghini and Ferrari—will have joined the game.

The industry's troubles have not put off new players. Geely, China's biggest privately owned car firm, plans to launch nine new models by end-2010 and up to 42 by 2015, when output will reach 2m.

To watch. The two-wheeler. GM and Segway are developing a two-wheeled, highly manoeuvrable vehicle aimed at drivers in congested cities. Dubbed the PUMA (Personal Urban Mobility and Accessibility), the prototype seats two, runs on batteries and can perform zero-radius turns. Once parked, more wheels drop down to keep the 136kg vehicle from falling over.

CONSUMER GOODS

CLOUDY ▲ — FAIR — SUNNY

Rich-country consumers, battered by job losses and depressed home prices, will remain tight-fisted, putting further pressure on retailers to think globally. China—no surprise—will be the biggest prize among emerging markets, with retail-sales volume likely to rise by almost 9%. The government is keen for China's consumers to spend more, to lessen the country's unhealthy reliance on exports and investment. Globally, retail sales will climb by a mere 1.7%.

The appetite for discount brands will remain strong. The world's largest retailer, Wal-Mart, which opened its first store in India in partnership with Bharti Group in 2009, plans to open a further ten by 2011. The largest footwear retailer in the US, Collective Brands, will open its first shops in Russia and across the Middle East in 2010 under its Payless ShoeSource brand.

For manufacturers, product innovation will be essential. Consumer-electronics firms expect a surge in demand for high-definition (HD) televisions ahead of the 2010 FIFA World Cup. Super-thin, ultra-sharp OLED (Organic Light-Emitting Diode) HDTV screens will hit the market in a big way in 2010, aimed at early adopters. With video-game consoles now a saturated market, manufacturers will find it hard to eke out profits from a once-booming sector. Japan's Nintendo, maker of Wii, expects to sell 26m units globally in the 12 months to March 2010, scarcely more than the previous year. A price war with Microsoft's Xbox and Sony's PlayStation 3 looks unavoidable.

To watch: E-reader wars. The Facebook generation will move from hardbacks to online e-readers as prices start to drop. New devices will allow easy access to blogs and shopping sites, as well as books. The Eee Reader, from Taiwan's Asus, will have two screens, a hinged spine, a web cam and a microphone for Skype.

DEFENCE

CLOUDY — FAIR ▲ — SUNNY

US defence spending will exceed half a trillion dollars in 2010, even as the war in Iraq winds down. The cost of fighting in Afghanistan will, for the first time, exceed that in Iraq: $65bn to $61bn. Yet none of this is included in the baseline defence budget of $534bn (a 4% increase on 2009). US military spending will be around 40% of the global total, seven to eight times more than China's, the secretive number two.

To help with the fight against the Taliban and al-Qaeda, Pakistan will receive $1.5bn in military and financial aid during the next five years. Israel alone will receive $2.8bn in 2010, partly to finance the Arrow ballistic missile defence system, designed with Iran in mind.

Encouraged by a thaw in relations with the North, perhaps, but driven by economic imperatives, South Korea will boost spending on defence by 3.8% in 2010, about half the increase initially announced.

Russia will spend Rb470bn ($16.4bn) on new weapons and infrastructure in 2010, part of a military budget of around $35bn. Although Russia will devote 40% of spending to its navy, the combat-readiness of ground forces, especially in the volatile region near Georgia, will be a focus.

To watch: The US navy wants to use high-powered lasers against small boats manned by terrorists wielding rocket-propelled grenades. Northrop Grumman has a $98m contract for the project, and by the end of 2010 should have installed a prototype of the laser on a ship for testing on remote-controlled vessels.

Industries The world in figures

2010 IN FOCUS

Whatever the shortfalls of the UN climate-change summit in Copenhagen, the global carbon market, which was unfettered by recession, will advance in 2010. According to Point Carbon, a private firm, 4.1 gigatonnes were traded in the first half of 2009, up 124% in volume terms. Indeed, recession helped to spur the carbon market as industry increased trading of surplus CO_2 allowances, even at lower carbon prices. The European Union still dominated the world carbon market in 2009, accounting for 75% of its value, so the introduction of a US emissions-trading market will turbo-charge growth. Warnings of a carbon-derivatives bubble are already being heard.

E-COMMERCE

CLOUDY — FAIR — SUNNY ▲

After contracting by 3.1% in 2009, US retail e-commerce sales—excluding travel, digital downloads and event tickets—will grow by 5.5% in 2010, to $135.2bn, according to a research firm, eMarketer. Pent-up demand will boost sales further in 2011, with growth peaking at 11% a year later. Beyond that, the maturity of the market will be reflected in a gradual decline in growth rates—a trend that was obvious before the recession. Even so, Forrester Research, another consultancy, predicts online sales will grab an increasing share of total retail spending in the US, rising to 8% by 2012 from 6% two years earlier.

The real commercial power of the online world lies not in transactions but in information-gathering. Store sales influenced by online research will be three times greater than e-commerce purchases, says eMarketer.

Around 2.2bn people will be using the internet by 2013, 17% of them in China, Forrester notes. The burgeoning e-commerce industry in the world's most populous country will grow by 28.3% year-on-year in 2010, according to IDC, another research provider. Given the lower start-up costs for an online shopfront, the number of Chinese users trading on e-business platforms could reach 100m by 2012.

Latin America will have to harmonise its laws to make the most of e-commerce. But, even so, its online sales, including travel and tourism, will reach $30bn in 2010, according to Visa, up from $11bn in 2007. Brazil's online sales will rise by 40% in 2010, helped by a relatively limited choice of goods in traditional stores.

To watch. E-books go mainstream. Although they will account for less than 3% of overall book sales in 2010, downloading books will become almost as popular as music and video downloads over the next few years as book-reading software improves.

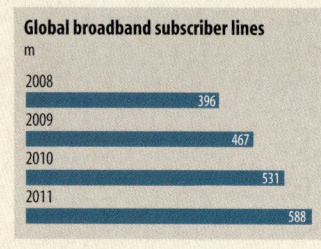

ENERGY

CLOUDY — FAIR ▲ — SUNNY

Green energy may be all the rage, but coal continues to power the world's biggest emerging markets. Demand from China and India will make coal the fastest-growing fuel in 2010, with world consumption rising by 3.3% from the year before. "Chindia" will account for more than 80% of that growth. Coal demand in more developed countries will decline as cleaner energy technologies become economically viable. China will be less eco-conscious. The world's largest consumer of coal will have about 700,000MW of installed coal-fired capacity by 2011, around 38% of the world's total.

Global demand for oil will rise by only 1.1% in 2010 because of sluggish economic growth. But oil prices will recover as the world economy emerges from recession; North Sea Brent, the European benchmark, will average $74 a barrel, up from $62 in 2009.

In the US, the Obama administration's green initiatives will be subject to continuing compromise in Congress. The twin goals of an emissions cap and a fully fledged carbon market are likely to succeed. Sales of liquid biofuels will continue to grow by double digits in 2010 in wealthy economies, but their impact will remain limited. The International Energy Agency (IEA) says it will be another 20 years before biofuels worldwide make up even 5% of the total liquid-fuels market. Overall, the IEA expects that primary energy demand met from renewable sources will rise to 10% in 2030 from 7% in 2006.

To watch. Pee power. The most common energy source in the universe, hydrogen, is difficult to produce, store and transport. Scientists at Ohio University have found that cheap quantities of hydrogen gas are released when they put a specially designed nickel electrode into a pool of urine and apply an electrical current. Converting the urine of one cow can supply hot water for 19 houses.

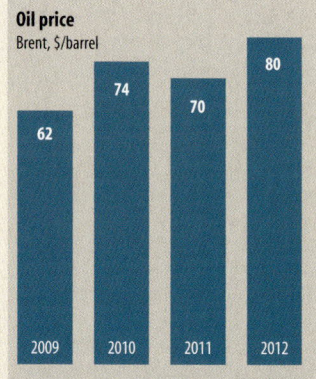

Oil price
Brent, $/barrel

Year	Price
2009	62
2010	74
2011	70
2012	80

ENTERTAINMENT

CLOUDY — FAIR ▲ — SUNNY

After contracting slightly in 2009, global spending on entertainment will grow by only 0.4% in 2010 before picking up to a still-lacklustre 3.2% in 2011, says PricewaterhouseCoopers (PwC). Some regions will perform much better, though: if Japan is removed from the Asia-Pacific mix, the region will enjoy a compound annual growth rate (CAGR) of 7.1% through to 2013. The real shift will be in the way consumers pay for their entertainment. Worldwide, end-user spending through mobile digital platforms will account for 78% of market growth over the forecast period.

Streaming mobile music services and full-track downloads will lead the way. They will be helped by an ever-expanding variety of applications and content, all-inclusive data packages, consumer-friendly front ends and expanding handset storage capacity. Worth $2.5bn in 2009, the market will grow to nearly $5.5bn by 2013, according to Juniper Research.

India's Bollywood is projected to grow at a CAGR of 11.6% over the next five years, according to PwC, and will be worth 185bn rupees ($4bn) by 2013. India's television industry will enjoy only slightly slower growth, at 11.4%, but will be worth much more. More than half of that revenue will come from distribution deals at home and, increasingly, from abroad. Meanwhile, the Motion Picture Association of America projects that international markets will account for two-thirds of the total box office of Hollywood films.

To watch: Another dimension. Some 20 films will be released in 3D format in 2010. As more cinemas convert to the technology, it will go mainstream within three to five years. The Blu-ray Disc is likely to be the preferred medium for at-home 3D consumption. Glasses-based technologies will dominate the market for 3D-capable displays, but will soon be superseded by autostereoscopic ("glasses-less") offerings.

FINANCIAL SERVICES

CLOUDY ▲ — FAIR — SUNNY

Big Western banks will continue to stabilise in 2010, but profit margins will remain thin, in part because regulators will insist on stricter capital requirements. Coupled with weak economic growth, the world's financial sector will shrink further as demand for new borrowing remains soft. Interest rates will remain low by historical standards for much of 2010 as central banks give the global economy a chance to regain its footing.

After dropping by 9.5% in 2009, new bank loans will rise by 5.9% globally in 2010, which in inflation-adjusted terms will amount to less than it looks. Saturated markets and tighter regulations at home will encourage large, global banks to shift their attention to emerging markets, where the financial meltdown had less impact. The need for conventional financing and simple savings products remains strong in most developing economies.

The year will also be a good one for asset managers, thanks to ageing populations and the sharp decline of final-salary pension schemes. Exchanges will scramble to capture some of the trading and clearing activity in the enormous over-the-counter derivatives market; governments are pushing for more of this activity to be conducted on centralised, public exchanges. After a terrible 2009, private-equity firms will find more quality buy-out opportunities in 2010, but the share of equity in deals will be higher than in previous years.

Global broadband subscriber lines
m

Year	Lines
2008	396
2009	467
2010	531
2011	588

The world in figures Industries

2010 IN FOCUS

The target date for achieving universal access to HIV prevention, treatment, care and support is 2010. The deadline is unlikely to be met, but there should be slightly better news on AIDS in Africa, thanks to increasing access to anti-retroviral drugs and the marginalisation of various high-profile "AIDS deniers" who threatened to derail some prevention programmes. Thus UNAIDS's 2010 "Report on the Global AIDS Epidemic" should be able to highlight success stories in countries as diverse as Botswana (where the mortality trend is declining) and Ethiopia (where AIDS deaths are being cut), although Africa will remain the world's worst-affected region.

To watch: Securitisation 2.0. Unbowed by the subprime mortgage debacle, bankers will find new assets to bundle, slice and sell on. Some of the securities gaining momentum may feature life-insurance policies and carbon credits.

FOOD & FARMING

CLOUDY — FAIR — SUNNY

International land-lease deals between countries with money and those with underused farmland will punctuate the growing debate over long-term food security in 2010. Critics say the deals amount to a neo-colonial land grab, with environmental downsides as well. The six member-states of the Gulf Co-operation Council, which will spend over $10bn on food imports in 2010, will pursue their goal of turning Africa into their "bread basket" with the help of Mozambique, Senegal, Sudan and Tanzania. Indeed, the Ethiopian Central Statistics Agency says the country's 13.3m smallholders will open up more than 1m hectares of virgin land to outside investors.

The Economist Intelligence Unit predicts a rise of 4.4% in commodity prices for food, feedstuffs and drinks, helped by increased demand for animal feed in emerging markets. The star performer will be sugar, whose price will go up by 15% in 2010. Demand from developing countries will be partly responsible, but so will the use of sugarcane for biofuels and a poor crop in India in 2009.

The recession has curbed coffee consumption in emerging markets, where it is considered a luxury, but Western retail sales will hold up well as consumption at home replaces the café culture. That's good news for Brazil, which will produce 43.5m bags of coffee in 2010, according to the US Department of Agriculture, ahead of its earlier forecast of 39.1m bags.

Food companies with strong brands and low-priced items will surge in 2010. A US giant, HJ Heinz, reckons its revenue will grow by 4-6%, implying sales of its namesake ketchup and other packaged items of $10.6bn-10.8bn. About 60% of that will come from non-US markets.

To smell: Bovine flatulence. By adjusting how much starch, sugar, cellulose, ash, fat and other elements are contained in cattle feed, scientists at Canada's University of Alberta reckon they can provide beef producers with the know-how to reduce cow emissions by as much as 25%. That's good news for both farmers and those worried about greenhouse gases.

HEALTH CARE

CLOUDY — FAIR — SUNNY

Long-awaited reform of the US health-care system will take place in 2010 but record-high levels of public debt—incurred to fight the financial crisis—will crimp its breadth and depth. Global life expectancy, meanwhile, will reach 72.5 years in 2010, bringing the number of people 65 and over to 523m, or 7.6% of the population. This will drive up costs and raise the old-age dependency ratio, reducing the amount of tax available to fund health-care systems everywhere.

Governments and insurers will redouble efforts to hold down costs, putting a greater emphasis on public health and preventive care. Insurers will offer lower premiums in return for evidence of healthy lifestyle choices, such as gym membership and health checks.

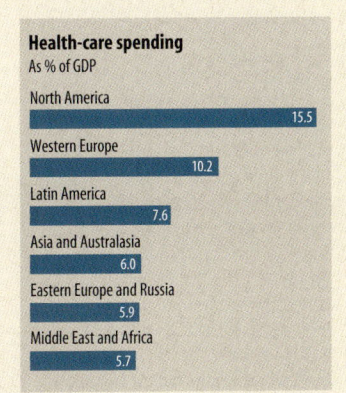

Some of the world's biggest-selling drugs will lose patent protection in 2010. According to EvaluatePharma, an unprecedented $133bn in sales will lose patent protection between 2010 and 2012, affecting Pfizer and Eli Lilly, among others. Their loss will be the generic drug manufacturers' gain—sales of generics will outstrip the total drug market's 5.1% growth (in dollar terms) in 2010.

The World Health Organisation expects the global swine-flu pandemic to last through 2010 and beyond, affecting up to one-third of the world's population by the end of 2011. So far, most cases have occurred in developed countries with good health-care systems, but the death toll could rise rapidly as swine flu spreads to places where public health care is poor.

To watch: Clean genes. Dozens of incurable hereditary diseases may soon be preventable. Researchers at the Oregon National Primate Research Centre removed hereditary material from a rhesus monkey's egg with defective DNA, then inserted it into a healthy egg stripped of its own hereditary package. They produced a healthy baby monkey.

INFORMATION TECHNOLOGY

CLOUDY — FAIR — SUNNY

The global IT industry skipped a heartbeat in the recession of 2009 but will go back to what it does best in 2010. Global IT spending will advance by 4.4%, led by pent-up demand for software and services. PC sales will romp ahead by more than 8%, aided by demand for sleeker netbooks and laptops.

This IT wealth will not be evenly spread. There will be only 17 PCs for every 100 people in the Middle East and Africa in 2010, compared with more than 97 in the US and Canada. Although PC ownership in Asia will be less than 19 per 100 people, the gap between the fastest-growing Asian economies and the West is starting to narrow. China, for example, will increase its total IT spending by 13.3%, to $80.2bn, in 2010 and will surpass Germany's IT spending by 2011.

The World Semiconductor Trade Statistics organisation expects chip sales to bounce back in 2010, rising by 7.3% to $209bn, and by a further 8.9% in 2011. It forecasts growth in all regional markets by 2011, but Asia-Pacific will continue to be the best performer, mainly because Western electronics manufacturers will be sourcing more of their production there.

To watch: Biocomputing. E. coli, better known as tummy bug extraordinaire, has found a new role as the brains of a bacterial computer dreamed up by scientists at Missouri Western State University and Davidson College. So far, the critter-based computer can count and solve complex equations.

Personal computers
Per '000 people

North America	974
Western Europe	688
Eastern Europe and Russia	393
Latin America	295
Asia and Australasia	189
Middle East and Africa	167

Health-care spending
As % of GDP

North America	15.5
Western Europe	10.2
Latin America	7.6
Asia and Australasia	6.0
Eastern Europe and Russia	5.9
Middle East and Africa	5.7

MEDIA

CLOUDY — FAIR — SUNNY

The recovery of advertising spending will be helped in 2010 by the Winter Olympics, the FIFA World Cup and the US mid-term elections. After contracting by 8.5% in 2009, global advertising spending will grow by 1.6% in 2010 and by 4.3% in 2011, according to ZenithOptimedia.

Among the larger economies, 62 of 79 will enjoy ad-spend growth in 2010, although North America will shrink a further 2.4% to just under $159bn, after contracting by 10.3% in 2009, according to Zenith. Western Europe will fare little better, edging up just 0.2%. Fast-growing China will be the world's fourth-largest advertising market in 2010, having overtaken Britain, and India will close in on the top ten. North American and west European markets combined will still account for nearly 60% of the global pie.

Zenith predicts that online ad spending will account for 13.8% of worldwide advertising in 2010—up from 10.5% in 2008—and be worth $63.1bn. Harnessing the advertising potential of social media will be key, however, as conventional search ads won't deliver especially good results.

Traditional media such as magazines, newspapers, television and radio will continue to lose advertising share. Magazines will fare somewhat better than newspapers, as it is difficult to

Industries The world in figures

2010 IN FOCUS

Ringtones are so last year. Ringback tones—clips of songs heard while waiting for a call to be answered—are already huge in Asia and are poised to become the next big thing for mobiles in the rest of the world. Ringbacks are generally cheaper than ringtones, but buying 15 seconds of sound for favourite contacts adds up to real revenue. According to UK-based Juniper Research, revenue from ringbacks will surpass ringtone sales in 2010. They will also provide marketing opportunities: operators will offer customers free airtime credit if they subject callers to a branded music clip.

reproduce online the leisure experience of reading a magazine. In the two years to 2010, print advertising in US magazines will plummet by 22.8% to $9.8bn before rising by 14.3% to $11.2bn by 2013, according to PricewaterhouseCoopers.

To watch: In-game advertising. It's a tricky way to reach consumers, but marketers love the novelty of it. Though starting from a low base, Jack Myers Media Business Report reckons in-game advertising will grow by 28% in 2010.

PROPERTY & CONSTRUCTION

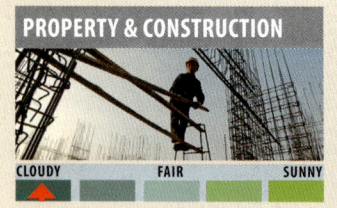

CLOUDY — FAIR — SUNNY

After a 16% drop in 2009, US non-residential construction spending will slip by another 12% in 2010, according to the American Institute of Architects. Commercial projects such as hotels, shopping centres and corporate offices will be hardest hit, but the so-called "institutional market"—schools, hospitals and infrastructure works—will fare better as public stimulus funding becomes available. Although the construction industry accounts for just over 5% of all non-farm payroll employment in the US, it has suffered more than 20% of job losses since the recession began, and will continue to suffer in 2010.

House prices in the UK's hard-hit residential property market will rise by 2% by the end of 2010, and by a further 3.6% in 2011, according to the Centre for Economics and Business Research. In China, the property bust of 2008 will be a distant memory. With house prices in Beijing, Shanghai and Guangzhou already back to 2007 peaks, residential investment in 2010 should once again easily account for 10% of GDP growth.

Expatriate workers will continue to leave the United Arab Emirates as the property and construction sectors contract. As a result, Dubai's population will shrink by 2% in 2010, says UBS. But Jumeirah, a Dubai-based hotel giant, won't be fazed, sticking to plans to launch 30 new hotels around the world before 2012. Asian cities will attract most of the new investment in lodging.

To watch: Brad Pitt. The A-list Hollywood superstar is working with Los Angeles-based architects GRAFT on an 800-room, environmentally friendly five-star hotel and resort for Zabeel Properties, a developer, in Dubai. It's not Mr Pitt's first foray into architecture: his charity, Making It Right, is building 150 sustainable homes in an area of New Orleans ravaged by Hurricane Katrina.

RAW MATERIALS

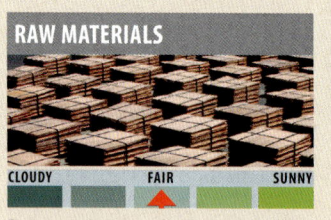

CLOUDY — FAIR — SUNNY

Base-metal prices will recover in 2010, as government stimulus packages support a modest recovery in demand. Investment in mining will remain subdued in the wake of the credit crisis.

Steel prices will edge up to average $517 a tonne as supply remains tight, although demand will remain below 2007 levels as the world limps out of recession. With the auto industry in the doldrums, tyremakers will have fewer orders to fill, causing a further slide in rubber demand. Global copper consumption will rise by 3.1% in 2010 on stronger demand from the world's cable-makers.

This will be good news for Chile, which accounts for around one-third of global copper production. The Chilean Copper Commission expects national output to rise by 6.3% to 5.8m tonnes in 2010. Gold's glittering run has been propelled by skittish investors who remain concerned about the health of the world's financial system. This demand won't entirely offset the continuing weakness in the jewellery market around the world. Gold prices, as a result, will ease back slightly to average $900 a tonne in 2010, from $950 in 2009.

To watch: The space elevator. A group of Japanese scientists is working on creating an incredibly long, thin and very strong carbon filament that would link Earth to a satellite in orbit. Once fixed, the cable could convey cargo and people into space more cheaply and easily than rockets. The price tag? $10bn.

TELECOMS

CLOUDY — FAIR — SUNNY

Through good times and bad, the world's love affair with the mobile phone remains undimmed. There will be 80 mobile-phone subscriptions for every 100 people in the world in 2010. Penetration will be highest in Europe (132%), where competition among operators is intense.

Smart-phones will be the fastest-growing category of handsets, even in poorer countries, where they often serve as a substitute for PCs. India and China, where more advanced third-generation (3G) mobile-phone networks are being rolled out, will see strong growth, given their lack of fixed-line infrastructure. According to Pyramid Research, 17% of Indian mobile-phone customers will be using 3G technology by 2013.

After fits and starts, m-commerce will flourish in 2010. Nokia, the world's largest handset-maker, will roll out an m-payment system that will allow users to transfer money, buy train tickets, pay bills or top-up their phone. Mobile banking, primarily an emerging-market trend, will move into the developed world. Music fans in South-East Asia will help the region account for more than a third of global spending on entertainment bought over the phone. Globally, this business will grow by 28% in 2010 to more than $40bn, according to the Mobile Entertainment Forum.

Mobile-phone subscriptions
per 100 people, globally
- 2009: 73.5
- 2010: 80.0
- 2011: 85.2
- 2012: 89.6

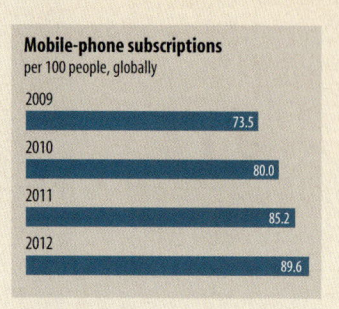

To Watch: Cloud phones. The lowly telephone handset will become a web-enabled, touchscreen device with applications such as a calendar, SMS and e-mail retrieval. It will also connect to users' mobile phones, so contacts and voicemail messages can be shared.

TRAVEL & TOURISM

CLOUDY — FAIR — SUNNY

International tourist arrivals will grow by 2.2% in 2010, according to Euromonitor International. Hotel revenue will rise by 1%, as will air travel—better than in 2009, but too little, too late for many operators.

With airlines struggling, Boeing will cut production of its long-range, wide-body 777 jet by 28%, having shelved planned increases in production of the 767 and 747. On the bright side, the company will deliver its first 787 Dreamliner to All Nippon Airways of Japan.

Revenue per room at US hotels will climb by 1.6% in 2010 after a 15.7% drop in 2009, according to PricewaterhouseCoopers. A modest rise in business travel will help. Indeed, the National Business Travel Association forecasts a 1.2% compound annual growth rate in global business travel during the five years through to 2013. Iranian business travel will increase by almost 9% as Russia's contracts by 4%.

China's tourism receipts will be aided by the biggest-ever World Expo, opening on May 1st in Shanghai. Some 70m people will attend. The soccer World Cup will make an even bigger difference to South Africa, where the government expects a tourism bonanza worth $2.1bn.

To watch: "Spaircraft". Thomson, a British holiday operator, is joining forces with Russian-based Pollof Air to develop a commercial jet that can leave the Earth's atmosphere, potentially cutting ten-hour flights to as little as 45 minutes. The 270ft-long Spaircraft will be able to travel at 70,000ft and circumnavigate the globe twice on just one tank of fuel.

EIU's industrial raw-materials index
% change in $ prices
(Rubber, Fibres, Metals, Industrial raw materials; 2009–2013)

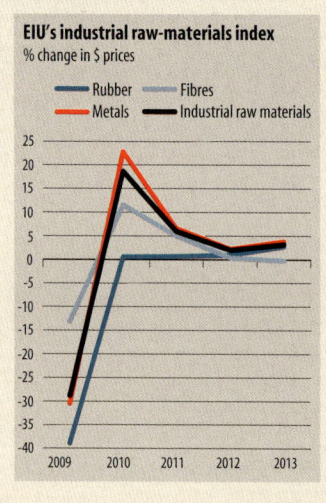

EDHEC Business School, for talented people

Master in Management
2-year programme driving you from knowledge to competencies

Masters of Science
1-year specialised programmes to become an expert

Financial Economics Track	Business Management Track
> MSc in Finance	> MSc in Marketing Management
> MSc in Corporate Finance	> MSc in Strategy & Organisation Consultancy
> MSc in Capital Markets	> MSc in Entrepreneurship
> MSc in Risk and Asset Management	> MSc in Legal and Tax Management
> MSc in Management Control	> MSc in Arts and NGOs Management

Meet EDHEC Business School
at the Campus France Nordic Tour in November
Copenhagen Nov 16th, Oslo Nov 17th,
Stockholm Nov 18 & 19th, Helsinki Nov 20th 2009
Find out more:
International.admissions@edhec.edu
www.edhec.edu

EQUIS ACCREDITED

Accredited by Association of MBAs

EDHEC BUSINESS SCHOOL

**SKYTEAM TAKES YOU WHERE YOU NEED TO GO.
SKYTEAM MILES TAKE YOU WHERE YOU'D REALLY LIKE TO GO.**

SkyTeam offers you the advantage of accumulating and redeeming your Frequent Flyer Miles on all members airlines. Now, SkyTeam Miles allow you to go where you've always dreamed of going. To find out more please visit **skyteam.com**

Caring more about you

AEROFLOT Russian Airlines AEROMEXICO. AIRFRANCE / KLM Alitalia CHINA SOUTHERN CZECH AIRLINES DELTA KOREAN AIR

SKYTEAM ASSOCIATES AirEuropa Kenya Airways

Business

Also in this section:
The jargon of 2010 120
E-books go mainstream 122
Can e-readers save newspapers? 122
Tracking online habits 124
Prepare for a dot.surge 125
Ubiquitous technology 126
Carol Bartz: Leadership in the information age 127
Big Pharma and generics 128
Falling out of love with business 129
Clean-energy competition in Asia 130
Sergio Marchionne: A green revolution for the car industry 131

Coming out of the dark

Robert Guest WASHINGTON, DC

There is light at the end of the tunnel, and it is not an oncoming train

Business will be easier in 2010, though that is not saying much. Companies have suffered a long and ferocious beating. Many have expired. But the tougher ones will emerge leaner and stronger, and ready to seize the opportunities that a gradual recovery will offer.

America was the first to stumble, and it will be among the first to pick itself up. After a painful bout of cost-cutting and job-shedding, executives in the United States are confident that business will soon start to recover, according to a survey by McKinsey, a consultancy. Asians are optimistic, too, especially in China. Firms in the euro zone are the gloomiest. The global recovery will not be quick, however. There is still a risk of a double-dip recession. And it is clear that business will not be the same after the crisis as it was before.

Firms will be warier of leverage. Those that borrowed too much will suffer and possibly die. Those with stronger balance-sheets will gobble up their rivals or seduce their customers. Entrepreneurial firms will displace market leaders, as they have in past downturns. And firms will boost their profits the old-fashioned way: by becoming more productive.

The trend towards bigger government and more regulation will continue, especially in America, where public spending as a share of GDP is growing fast. The United States government will still prop up and meddle in the financial sector, stabilising the system but also cramping innovation. Federal fingers will remain on the steering wheel in Detroit. And government will become the biggest customer for many industries. More companies will open offices in Washington, DC, to be close to the action.

The United States Congress will institute a cap-and-trade system for curbing carbon emissions, thus making it more likely that China and India will follow suit. But the toughest curbs will be pushed several years into the future. So energy prices will rise only slowly at first. But American firms will anticipate future price increases and scramble to adapt. Energy consumers will strive for greater efficiency. Producers of wind, solar and other alternative sources of power will invest heavily. Subsidies may spur the construction of new nuclear plants. Engineering, information-technology and consulting firms, such as GE, IBM and Accenture, will work hard to develop smart electricity grids at home and elsewhere.

Health-care reform in America will have both domes-

> More companies will open offices in Washington, to be close to the action

2010 IN BRIEF
Boeing hopes at last to deliver its **787 Dreamliner**—two years later than promised.

Robert Guest: Washington correspondent, *The Economist*

The jargon of 2010

Leo Abruzzese

Way beyond English

Hard times beget harsh language. Reckless loans led to the *credit crunch*, then to *meltdown*. When the jargon of the 2008-09 recession wasn't harsh, it was often mystifying: *credit default swaps*, *collateralised debt obligations* and *quantitative easing*. What vocabulary will executives need to familiarise themselves with next?

The recovery will spawn its own jargon in 2010. Policymakers will spend the year planning *exit strategies*—ways to withdraw from the markets and companies they rushed to rescue. Hopes of a sustainable recovery will depend on *deleveraging* by both consumers and firms, an effort to pay off the debt that piled up during the boom. The post-recession economy may have a different dynamic from the pre-crisis one; there is talk of an *economic reset* to a *new normal*.

Corporate boards will be preoccupied with risk management or, as it will be fashionable to say, *early warning*. Early-warning antennae should twitch when they detect the word *smart*, signifying a return to old ways but with lessons learnt: bankers are already talking about *smart securitisation*. Virtuous financiers will extol the importance of making a difference through *impact investing*. And, naturally, executives everywhere will have to keep up with the latest carbon jargon.

Tech-savvy types will dazzle as usual. In particular, *virtual reality* will in 2010 make way for *augmented reality*: overlaying the real world with digital information, typically with the help of a smart-phone.

The most-used piece of jargon in business will not be a word or phrase but a letter: *W*. No, not George W. Bush, but a w-shaped economy, in which the recovery peters out in the second half of the year as stimulus-spending fades, then resumes in 2011.

Really clever CEOs, however, will want to show a subtle understanding of the fastest-growing emerging markets. They will like to lace their presentations with references to Chinese culture. In a year of conflicting signals for business, the Chinese word for "contradiction", *maodun*—which, bosses will sagely point out, contains both a spear and a shield—may come in handy. ■

Leo Abruzzese: editorial director, North America, Economist Intelligence Unit

---

tic and global consequences. The government will make sure that more Americans are insured, and it will regulate private insurance more tightly. To restrain costs, it will squeeze not only hospitals but also drug firms and suppliers of medical devices. The returns from innovation in medical technology will decrease, affecting inventive firms throughout the world that rely on the American market to recoup their research costs. Public funding for research will only partly compensate for this.

Consumption patterns will change in 2010. America will remain the biggest economy by far. But over-stretched American consumers will no longer drive global growth as strongly. Firms bent on expansion will increasingly look towards emerging markets such as China, India and Brazil. Chinese productivity growth actually accelerated between 2008 and 2009, to a startling 9%. Russia will seem less inviting, despite its hydrocarbon wealth, because of fears about the rule of law.

Most consumers will still be short of cash, so firms that make cheap stuff well will thrive. Luxury-goods firms will flounder. Purveyors of basic necessities, such as Wal-Mart and Procter & Gamble, will do well. People don't stop brushing their teeth just because there is a recession, notes John Quelch of Harvard Business School. Asian firms that make cheap cars and washing machines for Asia's emerging middle class, such as Tata, Hyundai and Haier, will make inroads into Western markets.

Innovation, which slowed only slightly during the recession, will accelerate again. Firms that continued to invest in research during bad times, such as Google, Intel and Toyota, will reap rewards. America will remain the world's biggest innovator, but many Asian firms will draw closer. Manufacturers will sell more goods directly to consumers over the internet, bypassing traditional retailers. Data-intensive businesses will move more of their computing into the cloud. Social-media firms such as Facebook and Twitter will attract millions of new users but reap only slender revenues. Nanotechnology and genome research will yield fresh marvels.

The trade spats of 2009 will not, with luck, escalate into a full-blown trade war, but protectionist sentiment will rise. Governments that co-operated effectively to contain the financial crisis will have to co-operate again to keep trade flowing. Much will also depend on China's continued willingness to lend money to a still-profligate Uncle Sam.

President Barack Obama wants to raise taxes to ease America's budget deficit, but he has promised to soak only the rich. He will wait until after the mid-term elections in November 2010 to break this promise. If American growth stays slow, the public debt burden will become unsustainable and inflation will revive.

Public distrust of business will remain high. To allay it, firms will have to become more transparent. And they will have to adapt to a world where big changes happen quickly. Bad publicity travels at the speed of light. A big scandal can destroy a firm in an instant. The collapse of one financial enterprise can threaten the whole system. Governments cannot stop every foundering company from going under; nor should they. So firms will need sharp reflexes in 2010, tempered by caution. ■

2010 IN BRIEF

According to Airbus, **airline traffic** grows by as much as 4.6%, after a decline of perhaps 2% in 2009.

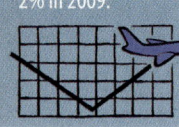

LLOYD'S
THE WORLD'S LEADING
INSURANCE MARKET

GREY
MATTERS.

In the grey area of emerging risk, get the facts in black and white from the world's sharpest minds.

Terrorism. Climate change. Pandemic. Whatever the threat, it is vital you understand emerging risk to successfully lead your business forward.

Lloyd's 360 Risk Insight brings together the views of business, academic and insurance experts, giving you access to an online resource, a programme of events, reports and research.

We are driving the global risk agenda as it takes shape, providing practical advice to help your business turn risk into opportunity.

Prepare for tomorrow's risks today.

LLOYD'S
360°
RISK
INSIGHT

Get the latest thinking and analysis on emerging risk at:
WWW.LLOYDS.COM/360

Business

The plot thickens

Tom Standage

E-books will move further towards the mainstream

Rather than being a thriller that grabs you from the first sentence, the tale of the rise of electronic books (e-books) is more like a novel that takes a while to get into its stride. But things have now started to become more exciting, and there are further plot twists and revelations coming. If you saw an e-book device for the first time in 2008 and first played with one in 2009, perhaps you will buy one in 2010.

Amazon catalysed the e-book market with its appropriately named e-reader, the Kindle, launched in 2007. It followed this up in early 2009 with the smaller, cheaper and more elegant Kindle 2, which costs $259, and the larger Kindle DX, which is designed to display newspapers and textbooks. Now that the Kindle is available outside America, users around the world can buy e-books from Amazon's growing selection, which materialise on the slate-like device's grey-scale screen within a few seconds, thanks to the Kindle's built-in wireless connection. Clicking buttons on the edge of the device turns the virtual pages.

There was a flurry of other e-book deals and announcements during 2009. Google launched a mobile version of its Google Books site, making hundreds of thousands of books available on mobile phones. Amazon launched a Kindle application for Apple's iPhone and iPod touch, turning them, in effect, into mini-Kindles. Amazon also bought Lexcycle, the maker of Stanza, another popular e-reader application for Apple's touch-screen devices. People can then give e-books a try on Apple's devices, which might make them more inclined to buy a Kindle. To compete, Barnes & Noble, an American book chain, unveiled the Nook e-reader in October.

Plastic Logic, one of several firms preparing to launch e-readers in 2010, struck deals with Barnes & Noble and several newspapers, including the *Financial Times* and

Tom Standage: business affairs editor, *The Economist*, editor, *Technology Quarterly*, and author of "An Edible History of Humanity" (Atlantic/Walker)

2010 IN BRIEF
Foursquare promises to be the **buzz social network**, allowing users to give their physical location—and be joined there by fellow-users.

Can e-readers save newspapers?

Tom Standage

Eventually, maybe, but not in 2010

It is a seductive idea. As newspapers struggle with declining advertising revenues and the rise of the internet, a new technology arrives just in time to save them. E-readers hold out the prospect of allowing newspapers to shut down their expensive printing presses and switch to much cheaper electronic delivery. Already, people are prepared to pay to receive newspapers and magazines (including *The Economist*) on the Kindle, even though they seem reluctant to pay for news on the web. An e-reader can be taken anywhere, after all, and provides a better reading experience than a web browser. Might e-readers provide a new model for newspapers in the digital age?

Perhaps they will one day, but it will not be any time soon. For one thing, e-readers are not yet a mature technology and are still too expensive. In theory a newspaper could ask its readers to sign up for a two-year electronic subscription, say, and subsidise the cost of an e-reader. Several newspapers are said to be considering this model. But newspapers would still have to keep their pricey presses running to serve readers who choose not to go electronic, and subsidising the switch to e-readers would require huge up-front investment. Given most newspapers' parlous finances, this seems implausible.

A further problem is that even if the technology were ready today, most newspapers would have trouble switching because their old-fashioned technology and processes would stand in the way. FirstPaper, a secretive start-up backed by Hearst, a media group, hopes to address this problem by providing all the technological components, from back-end software to e-reader devices, that newspapers need to go electronic.

It seems most likely, however, that people will buy e-readers (or more general-purpose devices, such as tablet computers) to read e-books primarily, and will then also use them to read e-newspapers. Getting the news on an e-reader will probably become commonplace eventually, but it will not happen soon enough to rescue America's troubled newspapers. Expect more of them to fold in 2010, e-readers or no. ∎

Rentokil Initial, Jaguar Land Rover, Telegraph Media Group,

+1,999,997 other businesses have Gone Google.

"Going Google" means switching your company over to Google Apps – a web-based suite of communication and collaboration tools. Google Apps reduces IT costs and empowers today's employees.

Learn more at www.google.co.uk/gonegoogle.

© 2009 Google Inc. All rights reserved. Google and Google logo are trademarks of Google Inc.

Google Apps

USA Today. IRex, a European firm, launched an e-reader in America. Sony, the number two behind Amazon in the e-reader market, launched several new products, including a low-cost model for $199, a touch-screen model and its first e-reader with cellular connectivity. Sony also embraced the open standard for e-books, called EPUB, which only Amazon now refuses to support.

In all, 2009 was to electronic books what 2001, the year Apple launched the iPod, was for music players, says Sarah Rotman Epps of Forrester, a consultancy. "It was the tipping-point when this market really started," she says. E-books and e-readers had been around since the 1990s, but they are now taking off because the technology has improved, prices have fallen and consumers are, thanks to digital-music players, used to the idea of buying and consuming content in digital form.

At the end of 2009 there are expected to be around 4m e-readers in circulation in America, and 6m worldwide. A further 12m units will be sold in 2010, according to Vinita Jakhanwal of iSuppli, a market-research firm. Forrester has had to revise up its sales forecasts because of the sudden increase in interest in 2009. "It's happening faster than anyone expected," says Ms Epps.

All will be revealed

This fast-moving plot will thicken in 2010, in three ways. First, e-readers will continue to get better and cheaper. The first models with colour screens will become available, and touch-screens (a notable omission from the Kindle) will become more widespread. Asus, a Taiwanese manufacturer that popularised ultra-cheap "netbook" laptops, is expected to launch a cut-price e-reader. As prices fall, more people will be prepared to give e-readers a try, though, if music players are any guide, prices will have to fall below $100 to make e-readers a mass-market proposition.

Second, there will be a growing split between Amazon's proprietary Kindle and the open approach favoured by its rivals. There may also be a showdown between Amazon and publishers. Amazon is selling many e-books at a loss to stimulate Kindle sales, a tactic it can't keep up. It will either have to raise retail prices (which would annoy consumers) or ask publishers to cut their wholesale prices, which they are unwilling to do.

Third, and perhaps most important, will be the role of Apple. The company is widely expected to launch a tablet-style computer, akin to a giant iPhone, during 2010. It would make an ideal e-book reader. Apple might then decide to start selling e-books through its iTunes online store; or it might make Amazon the preferred supplier of e-books on the new device. Apple already has a similar arrangement with Google, which provides maps on the iPhone. In the past, Apple has repeatedly taken existing technologies, made them much easier to use and triggered mass adoption (as it did for window-based computing, digital-music players and internet-capable smart-phones). Whether Apple decides to act as kingmaker in the e-book market, or claim the crown itself, the next chapter in the e-book saga is sure to be a page-turner. ∎

> Most important will be the role of Apple

2010 IN BRIEF

India's Tata Motors launches its **Nano**, the world's cheapest car, in Europe.

Martin Giles: United States technology correspondent, *The Economist*

Search me

Martin Giles SAN FRANCISCO

A battle looms over tracking consumers' online habits

The issue has been simmering for quite some time. But in 2010 the debate over how advertisers, web companies and others monitor individuals' use of the internet will reach boiling-point. Politicians in America will debate legislation that would give consumers more knowledge of the information being collected about them online—and more control over how it is subsequently used. Advertisers and web companies will push back, arguing that they can be trusted to police themselves.

At least three trends will ensure that online privacy commands plenty of attention in the coming year. The first is the rise of so-called "behavioural targeting", in which websites gather detailed data about the surfing habits of users and crunch this information to help determine which adverts to show surfers. Although this approach is still less widely used than, say, contextual targeting, which automatically links adverts to search terms on services such as Yahoo! and Google, it will become more popular as firms try to squeeze greater returns from their advertising costs in a tough economy.

Another trend driving privacy concerns is the spectacular growth of online social networks, such as Facebook. These networks capture a large amount of personal information about users and are seeking to leverage these data to generate revenue. Canada's privacy watchdog has already taken Facebook to task for short-

> Advertisers are no doubt hoping their initiative will placate politicians

THE WORLD IN 2010 — Business — 125

comings in the way it handles user data. More regulatory scrutiny is likely in 2010.

The proliferation of web-enabled mobile phones such as Apple's iPhone is also ringing alarm bells among privacy champions. An explosion of demand for these devices—Apple has already sold 30m iPhones around the world—has opened up the prospect of advertisers tracking users' movements and serving them ads based on their whereabouts. For now, most advertisers and phone networks are wary of exploiting data in this way. But firms will still seek to profit from information gleaned from third-party applications that sit on top of smart-phones' operating systems. Together with new apps for social-networking services, these create another way of tracking consumers' digital habits.

Much of the information is used in ways that are beneficial to those who provide it. But it is often unclear to web surfers exactly what data are being gathered about them and how this is being used. Critics point out that users are frequently forced to provide data when visiting sites, rather than being allowed to choose not to.

In a bid to calm such concerns, industry groups representing advertisers in America will implement a series of principles in 2010 that govern how their members collect data online. Among other things, websites will have to display an icon that takes users to a page which describes the data being gathered about them and gives them an opportunity to opt out from the process. Surfers will also have to provide consent before sensitive data such as financial-account numbers can be collected. Mike Zaneis of the Internet Advertising Bureau, one of the groups promoting the principles, reckons they could be rolled out in the first quarter of 2010, assuming work on the technical standards that are needed to implement them proceeds smoothly.

The politics of privacy

Advertisers are no doubt hoping their initiative will placate politicians, who are becoming increasingly concerned about the lack of transparency around online monitoring. That concern has already translated itself into proposed legislation in America. A bill that tackles online privacy issues is being championed by Rick Boucher, the chairman of the House of Representatives' Energy and Commerce internet sub-committee.

Nor is all this purely an American concern. Although European countries generally already have in place stronger controls, there is a feeling that more may need to be done in the European Union too. An EU body called the Article 29 Working Party, including representatives from national data-protection watchdogs, is holding a public consultation on the issue, due to end on December 31st 2009. This could result in recommendations for more new rules. One way or another, 2010 is going to be a year in which those who scrutinise consumers online will be subject to intense scrutiny themselves. ■

2010 IN BRIEF

General Motors, now majority owned by the US and Canadian governments, celebrates its escape from bankruptcy with an initial public stock offering.

Change of addresses

Martin Giles SAN FRANCISCO

Prepare for a dot.surge

It may seem like an arcane subject, but the question of who should be allowed to use which names on the internet is about to become a big issue. In 2010 the Internet Corporation for Assigned Names and Numbers (ICANN), the non-profit body that oversees online addresses, plans to make two changes to its regime for top-level domain names—the characters after the final dot in web addresses. Both initiatives have significant implications for politicians and business folk.

The first change involves expanding the number of generic top-level domains such as com, biz and org. At present there are only 21 of these, whereas there are 280 specific addresses for countries and regions, such as dot.cn for China and dot.eu for the European Union. From next spring, if all goes according to plan, ICANN will accept bids from anyone who wants to create a new generic suffix. Those that are accepted could be in use by 2011.

In another shift in policy, ICANN will for the first time accept bids for top-level domains in scripts other than Latin—a long overdue move given that more than half of the world's 1.7 billion internet users have a non-Roman script for their written language. At the moment web users in, say, Russia must switch to Latin characters to type domain names; under the new approach they will be able to type an entire address in Cyrillic ones. Known as internationalised domain names, the new addresses will be available in languages such as Chinese and Arabic.

To get hold of a new, top-level domain, successful bidders must pay ICANN a one-off fee of $185,000 and show they can run a registry that manages the sale of full addresses using the suffix. They will also be subject to other tests. Ultimately the process could create hundreds, or perhaps thousands, of new domains. Companies will register their brands—think dot.nike or dot.virgin—while local governments will bid for addresses that can promote activities in their area. New York City, for instance, is said to be eyeing dot.nyc.

The new domains will be a marketer's dream. But some corporate lawyers fear they could also create a legal nightmare. Having spent much time and money securing as many existing web addresses as possible to protect themselves from cyber-squatters and crooks, companies now face the prospect of many more battles to protect trademarks online. "All we can do is guarantee that we will establish a fair process" for allocating the new addresses, explains Rod Beckstrom, ICANN's boss. This is likely to involve formal auctions of popular names. Some observers fear that, in spite of ICANN's efforts to ensure fair play, there will still be a domain-name free-for-all that will result in a plethora of legal battles. Dot.lawyer anybody? ■

Big SIS is watching you

Ludwig Siegele

Ubiquitous technology will make the world smarter

Remember "The Matrix", the 1999 film in which human beings are plugged into machines? These simulate reality to control humankind and harvest their bodies' heat and electrical activity.

Such a parallel universe is indeed emerging. Fortunately, it is not intended to subdue humans, but to allow them to control their environments better. Some computer scientists already talk of the birth of "societal information-technology systems", or SIS. In 2010 such systems will start to make their presence felt.

To grasp this trend, one has first to recognise that the world is exceedingly wasteful. Utilities lose more than 50% of water supplies around the world because of leaky infrastructure. In America alone, congested roads cost billions of dollars a year in lost work hours and wasted fuel. And if the country's power grid were only 5% more efficient, this would eliminate greenhouse-gas emissions equivalent to those of 53m cars.

The reason for such inefficiencies? The infrastructure is not intelligent: roads, power grids and water-distribution systems are all essentially networks of dumb pipes. Over the past few years momentum has been building to make them smarter. More recently, in attempting to overcome the economic crisis, the pace has picked up. Many countries have earmarked a big chunk of their stimulus packages for infrastructure projects.

The other main driver is technology. Until now, the internet has mainly been about connecting people. Today it is more and more about connecting things—wirelessly. Thanks to Moore's law (a doubling of capacity every 18 months or so), chips, sensors and radio devices have become so small and cheap that they can be embedded virtually anywhere. Today, two-thirds of new products already come with some electronics built in. By 2017 there could be 7 trillion wirelessly connected devices and objects—about 1,000 per person.

Sensors and chips will produce huge amounts of data. And IT systems are becoming powerful enough to analyse them in real time and predict how things will evolve. IBM has developed a technology it calls "stream computing". Machines using it can analyse data streams from hundreds of sources, such as surveillance cameras and Wall Street trading desks, summarise the results and take decisions.

Transport is perhaps the industry in which the trend has gone furthest. Several cities have installed dynamic toll systems whose charges vary according to traffic flow. Drivers in Stockholm pay between $1.50 and $3 per entry into the downtown area. After the system—which uses a combination of smart tags, cameras and roadside sensors—was launched, traffic in the Swedish capital decreased by nearly 20%.

More importantly, 2010 will see a boom in "smart grids". This is tech-speak for an intelligent network paralleling the power grid, and for applications that then manage energy use in real time. Pacific Gas & Electric, one of California's main utilities, plans to install 10m "smart meters" to tell consumers how much they have to pay and, eventually, to switch off appliances during peak hours.

Smart technology is also likely to penetrate the natural environment. One example is the SmartBay project at Galway Bay in Ireland. The system there draws information from sensors attached to buoys and weather gauges and from text messages from boaters about potentially dangerous floating objects. Uses range from automatic alerts being sent to the harbourmaster when water levels rise above normal to fishermen selling their catch directly to restaurants, thus pocketing a better profit.

Yet it is in big cities that "smartification" will have the most impact. A plethora of systems can be made more intelligent and then combined into a "system of systems": not just transport and the power grid, but public safety, water supply and even health care (think remote monitoring of patients). With the help of Cisco, another big IT firm, the South Korean city of Incheon aims to become a "Smart+Connected" community, with virtual government services, green energy services and intelligent buildings.

> The year will see a boom in investment in "smart grids"

What could stop the world from becoming smart? Surprisingly, the main barriers are not technological. One is security: such systems will be vulnerable to all sorts of hacker attacks. Another is privacy. Many people will feel uncomfortable having their energy use and driving constantly tracked. Bureaucracy will also slow things down. For SIS to work, in many cases several administrations and departments have to collaborate.

And then there is the worry that all these systems will one day gang up on their creators, as in "The Matrix". Last July computer scientists, artificial-intelligence researchers and roboticists met in California to discuss the risk. But the vendors of smart systems insist that the idea will remain just science fiction. "These systems are designed to operate only within certain boundaries," says Bernie Meyerson, of IBM's systems and technology group. "They don't go off into the weeds." ■

2010 IN BRIEF
Google Wave enters the mainstream, promising a revolution in office work and e-mail.

Ludwig Siegele: technology correspondent, *The Economist*

Leadership in the information age

Information will be the greatest opportunity for business leaders in the coming years—and perhaps our biggest headache. Since the dawn of the internet, all of us in business have been swept up by the Niagara of information that fills our daily life. Real-time updates from the Hang Seng index; online earnings calls; photos shared around the world seconds after they've been taken; customised maps and directions delivered to you even as you drive. It's all breathtaking.

But for leaders in business, the information surge has triggered its own unintended consequences, especially for those of us over 40. Today, new employees arrive on their first day with an alarming amount of know-it-all. They have already read about you, and the online critiques of your plans, strategies and management style. The bloggers and the tweeters—all receiving steady streams of in-house gossip—analyse, assess and ridicule every business moment. At some companies, insider information can barely be said to exist.

In this environment, traditional management is impossible, or at least ill-advised. The hierarchical, layered corporate structures in which company information was carefully managed and then selectively passed down the line have crumbled. The online era has made command-and-control management as dead as dial-up internet.

As someone who came up through the ranks of the often hidebound and highly deferential corporate world, I am glad to say good riddance to much of the old office culture. But as chief executive of a dynamic information business, I also see how debilitating the stream of news and reaction can be for an organisation if mishandled. Public companies in particular are so besieged by 24-hour commentary and instant opinion that many managers find themselves paralysed.

That's why the greatest mandate for leadership in business is the ability to cut through the information clutter and make clear decisions without apology. More than at any time, employees need—in fact, desperately want—unequivocal direction.

Although decision-making has always been the task of a leader, it has become harder. The online world has guaranteed that every remark about your business and every change you implement will trigger a viral frenzy of second-guessing. Borrowing from the black bag of politics, your competitors will also be spreading their own version of "opposition research", feeding the blogosphere with critiques of your leadership.

Learn to live with it. Leaders should not only grow a thicker skin but also understand how important they can be to their own team by interpreting both the news and the disinformation that swirls around them.

Whenever I speak to an audience—internal or external—I am struck by how many people want to know my reaction to some recent press story or the latest legislative debate. They want someone to tell them what it all means. These are wonderful opportunities for leadership. Employees, investors, customers and business partners are heartened by executives who can sift through the avalanche of opinion and clearly communicate what matters—and what doesn't—to the enterprise.

Of course, communication cannot be a one-way street. The central role of information in business life has made two other much neglected leadership tasks more urgent.

Get the idea?

The first is listening. It is a hoary cliché of management schools that a good boss knows how to listen. But this shouldn't be merely an exercise in empathy. Listening to your employees at every level is one of the best paths to new insights. Precisely because the internet has made information so plentiful, your own team is likely to be full of ideas that should be tapped into. A leader who is sequestered in a corner office is missing out on the rich discussions bubbling a few floors below.

The second obligation that information creates for executives is to identify and mentor thought leaders. In the past, seeking out "high potential" employees typically meant looking for those who could climb the next rung of the management ladder. That remains important. But equally pressing is finding those employees who, though perhaps not the best managers, have the ability to digest and interpret information for others. Grooming these in-house ideas people helps foster a culture of openness to fresh thinking—the greatest energy an organisation can have.

The deluge of information is only going to rise. Leadership will increasingly mean leveraging that information, clarifying it, and using it to advance your strategy, engage customers and motivate employees. Business stakeholders are interested not only in your products and services, but also in your ideas.

So, welcome the information flood. Those who learn how to keep their head above it will be the most effective leaders. ■

The best bosses will be those who learn to swim amid all the information swirling around them, argues **Carol Bartz**, *CEO of Yahoo!*

The online era has made command-and-control management as dead as dial-up internet

Business

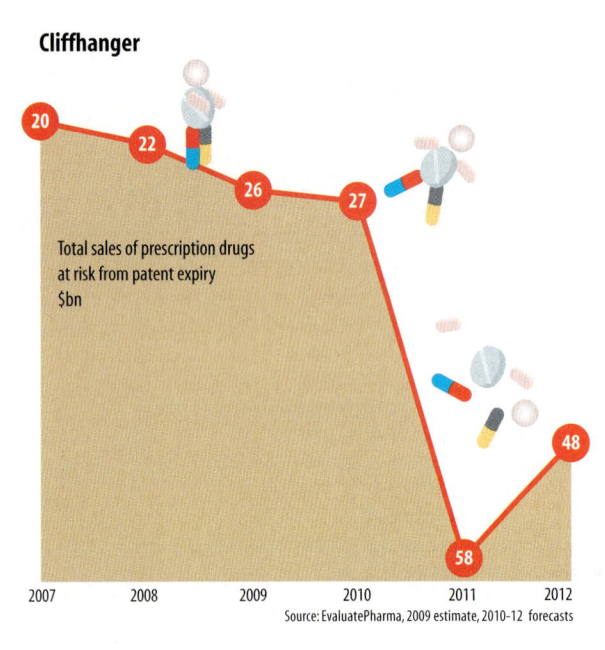

Cliffhanger

Total sales of prescription drugs at risk from patent expiry, $bn

- 2007: 20
- 2008: 22
- 2009: 26
- 2010: 27
- 2011: 58
- 2012: 48

Source: EvaluatePharma, 2009 estimate, 2010-12 forecasts

Generically challenged

Vijay Vaitheeswaran NEW YORK

The pharmaceuticals industry may yet find inspiration in its old nemesis, the generic-drugs business

This could be the end of the road for Big Pharma's failed business model. In recent years, the world's innovative drug giants have seen research productivity plummet even as the costs of research have soared. Share prices have taken a beating as the industry has failed to come up with enough promising blockbuster drugs to compensate for the revenue lost when old money-spinners lose their patent protection. Even the recent round of mergers and acquisitions instigated by large firms such as Pfizer and Merck, followed by the requisite cost-cutting and sackings, has failed to fix what ails the industry.

The heart of the problem is the looming patent "cliff" (see chart). EvaluatePharma, a consultancy, estimates that 13% of global pharmaceutical sales are at risk from generic competition in the coming two years. This matters because the price of a given drug falls by more than 85% within a year of patent expiry in competitive markets like the United States. Over the next year, company bosses had better come up with improved business models or else they will drive their firms right off that precipice.

And yet the industry's salvation could very well lie in the embrace of that very same nemesis—generic drugs. The coming year will bring dramatic moves by Big Pharma to learn from, copy and even get into bed with the rivals it once decried as copycats and scofflaws. The explanation for this startling turn of events is twofold: in the rich world, generic drugs are advancing as a result of government action, whereas in the developing world it is the booming middle class that is propelling them forward.

First, the developed world. In 2010 rich countries will boost the fortunes of generic drugs in two ways. In many such countries, from Japan to Germany, governments struggling to control health costs will introduce policies that favour the use of cheap generic drugs. The American precedent suggests this will be a powerful trend. From 1999 to 2008, the use of generic drugs saved America some $734 billion. And the boom is set to continue, with the American generics sector forecast to grow by over 9% a year to 2012.

Taking the medicine

But carrots will soon be accompanied by sticks. Regulators at America's Federal Trade Commission and at the European Commission have already expressed their displeasure at perceived antitrust violations involving Big Pharma's efforts to thwart competition from generics (through, for example, "pay for delay" deals that bribe rivals to put back the launch of generic pills). The year ahead could well see tough talk turn to regulatory action. This trend too should change attitudes at big firms, so that generics are not seen merely as pests to be tolerated or paid off, but rather as inspiration for a radically different business model.

That is especially true when it comes to the developing world, which is where the action is these days. In 2010 much of the revenue growth for the drugs industry overall will come from the leading economies of the poor world. IMS Health, another consultancy, calculates that the seven biggest emerging pharma markets made up more than half of the global industry's total sales growth in 2009. By 2012, nine of the top 20 markets will be emerging economies.

The trick to winning over the rising middle classes in such markets is not to peddle over-priced patented drugs on the Western model, cursing the local generics firms as rip-off artists. Big Pharma has tried that route for years with little success. Rather, the key is to pitch branded generic drugs. These are off-patent pills and potions that can be sold more cheaply than the on-patent variety, but which still command an attractive price premium in poor countries due to the proliferation in local markets of fakes and drugs of dubious quality.

> **The key is to pitch branded generic drugs**

In 2010 the big Western drugs firms will enter the branded generics markets in full force by joining up with local generics firms to get cheap access to this booming niche. A few pioneers have already headed down this path.

Some, like America's Pfizer, have experimented with licensing deals and alliances with Asian generics firms. Others have gone a bit further, as Britain's GlaxoSmithKline did with its recent acquisition of a share in Aspen, an African firm specialising in branded generics. Yet others go the full Monty, as Japan's Daiichi Sankyo did by gobbling up India's Ranbaxy Laboratories. Watch for a dramatic acceleration of this trend in the coming year—which could even lead to the end of the independent generics industry in India.

Taken together, these trends point to 2010 being a turning-point for the global generics business. Big Pharma is in big trouble, but it may yet find comfort in the arms of that erstwhile foe. ■

2010 IN BRIEF
After completing the Ras Laffan gas plant, **the world's largest structure**, Qatar produces a fifth of the world's liquefied natural gas.

Vijay Vaitheeswaran: health-care correspondent, *The Economist*

The end of the affair

Lucy Kellaway

Falling out of love with business

The love affair with business started in the 1980s and has grown into a mighty passion backed not just by money but by glamour and class. In 2009 the money ran out, but the mood was one of such chaos and confusion that it was hard to tell what was going on underneath. In 2010 it will become clear that the class and glamour are draining away from business too. It will be the end of the affair: business will be cool no longer.

> The decline of the MBA will cut off the supply of bullshit at source

Throughout this affair the business schools played the role of cupid. First, they made the study of business into an (almost) respectable academic discipline. More importantly, they made it socially acceptable, something even the poshest person could aspire to. What do the brightest and poshest students at Oxford and Harvard want to study? Business.

But in 2010, for the second year running, tens of thousands of overqualified MBAs will emerge with nowhere exciting to go. A very few will land jobs in investment banking, but those who want grand jobs in big companies or consultancies will be disappointed. Increasingly they will go crawling back to their old employers to do pretty much whatever they were doing before for pretty much the same money. As the efficacy of a business school is measured according to the salary one gets when one finishes, both students and employers will question whether it is really worth the $160,000 that a top MBA costs.

This is not going to be a little recessionary dip. It will be a more fundamental reappraisal. The magical myth of the MBA has for some time left the facts behind. In future, those who stump up will do so because they want to learn the skills, not because they think they are buying entry into a cool and exclusive club.

Some good things will follow from this. There will be fewer smart Alecs who think they know it all pouring into companies. There has been a bear market in management bullshit since the credit crunch began, but so far this has been on the demand side—managers have been too intent on staying in work to talk much jargon. In 2010 the decline of the MBA will cut off the supply of bullshit at source. Pretentious ideas about business will be in retreat.

But there will be bad things too: if fewer bright, ambitious people go into business, economies may suffer. Instead the talent will go increasingly into the public sector, the law, medicine—which are already bursting with bright people as it is.

While the decline of the B-schools will dent the glamour of business in general, the government will do its bit too with increasing regulation. Being a board director of a listed company in 2010 will never have been less fun: not only will the procedural side be more onerous, there will be even greater public hysteria over what directors are paid and even—in Britain at least—how much they claim on expenses. And with those at the top having such a grim time, it is unrealistic to expect any excitement at the bottom.

The onward march of the public sector may have some other unintended consequences in the private one. The coming year will be a vintage one for the cowboy, who will be quick to spot new loopholes and make a killing from them. It will feel a bit like the 1970s, when the endless recession and aftermath of the secondary banking crisis in Britain made it a high time for spivs and villains. In 2010 there will be a new cast of infamous billionaires—and they won't be MBAs bloated with theories. They will be the barrow boys quick on their feet and lacking any scruples. Their grubby success will make business look dirtier still.

You're hired!

The end of the affair will be felt strongly in our living rooms, where in the past decade we have gathered to watch phenomenally successful business programmes like "The Apprentice" and "Dragons' Den". These shows will start to look tired in 2010: they were premised on the idea of the business dream and on the glamour of a shiny boardroom table. The top of the business TV market was unwittingly called in 2009 when Gordon Brown made Sir Alan Sugar a lord and asked him to give advice—thus destroying the glamour of business TV at one stroke.

New television series are likely to take a grimmer turn and be modelled on the Argentine classic "Recursos Humanos", in which contestants competitively demean themselves in begging to be allowed a grotty job as a manual worker. Addictive viewing, possibly. Glamorous, cool or classy, certainly not. ∎

Lucy Kellaway: columnist, *Financial Times*

Asia's green-tech rivals

Kenneth Cukier *TOKYO*

Clean-energy competition in the region will be intense

The battle lines are being drawn in Asia over green technologies, as governments adapt their tradition of state influence on industry for an era in which eco-friendly products may spell export success. In China, Japan, South Korea and elsewhere, a big portion of fiscal-stimulus measures is dedicated to green projects. It is seen as a way to create new jobs, cut carbon emissions at home—and sell products abroad.

Globally, governments have budgeted as much as $500 billion for "Green New Deal" projects, estimates HSBC, a bank. Asia accounts for more than three-fifths of the total. Around 20% of this will have been spent by the end of 2009, with most of the rest to be lavished in 2010. Private capital is also pouring in.

Yet where the money is going varies across the region. Some countries are emphasising particular sectors (like solar power) or early-stage technology (such as fuel cells) with an eye towards building a future market. Other initiatives simply apply current technology to reduce domestic emissions (carbon-capture at power plants, for example). Only 15% of the spending is aimed at R&D, notes New Energy Finance, a market-research group.

China, by some measures, has the most ambitious policy. It has dedicated around $220 billion, or one-third of its overall fiscal stimulus, to projects such as wind, solar, hydropower and clean-coal technologies. This will help the country achieve its target of increasing the share of renewable energy to 10% by 2010.

In 2010 a generous subsidy will become available for low-emission cars in 13 big cities, including Beijing, Shanghai and Dalian. China will also subsidise 50-70% of the cost of large solar-power projects.

The emphasis on solar energy is as much a lifeline for floundering Chinese firms as it is an effort to reduce emissions. Without subsidies, solar is about four times more expensive than energy from the coal-powered grid. But Chinese firms have emerged as the biggest solar-panel producers in the world—almost all of it exported—just as the industry faces a massive supply glut that is forcing firms to close. By boosting domestic demand, China's programme has the added goal of absorbing the excess supply, and helping the firms to live.

South Korea has made green technology a cornerstone of national policy. The budget, about $60 billion to be spent by 2012, is smaller than China's but represents a whopping four-fifths of South Korea's total stimulus package. In 2010 tax incentives, subsidies, credit guarantees and spending programmes will begin to be showered on everything from hybrid cars to fitting buildings with energy-efficient LED lighting.

The country plans to spend around 2% of its GDP on green tech through to 2013, to reduce emissions and spur a new export industry. Sandwiched between China (with lower costs) and Japan (with superior technology), Korean manufacturers have much catching up to do in green-tech products. Bureaucrats hope to increase South Korea's global market share in these technologies from 2% to 8% by 2013.

Japan has long been a green-tech pioneer. It has set aside $35 billion of its stimulus, about 6%, for green tech, in areas such as subsidies for residential solar projects. Its green stimulus is smaller than its neighbours' as it already pours in funds from the regular budget: $22 billion for the environment and conservation in 2009, of which $7 billion was for clean energy including nuclear power. The new government has set ambitious targets for reducing carbon emissions. It also promises new spending in 2010 for low-emission cars and energy-efficient appliances.

Other Asian countries have green ambitions. Singapore has a war chest of $450m and in 2010 it will build a 55-hectare (135-acre) clean-tech office park and fund a solar-power research institute. Taiwan plans to spend $1 billion over five years developing solar, LED-lighting and renewable-energy technologies.

Any colour you want so long as it's...
What exactly counts as green technology? The figures include water and waste projects that are green, but not energy-related. Almost $100 billion of China's stimulus is for energy-efficient rail transport—which may reduce emissions, but is ultimately just a train system.

Still, the focus on green tech is a natural evolution for Asia's IT industries. LCD screens and semiconductor chips share the same materials and manufacturing processes as solar photovoltaic cells; many factories have simply been converted from one to the other. The battery technology for electric cars applies the intellectual property that was developed for electronic gadgets.

Whether the bureaucrats can channel the public largesse efficiently is an open question. Since the immediate purpose is to pump-prime the economy, the emphasis will be on dispensing the money rather than on the return on investment. ■

2010 IN BRIEF
Germany installs **smart meters** in new buildings.

Many panels make light work

Kenneth Cukier: Tokyo correspondent, *The Economist*

Rethinking the car industry

The car industry has been suffering the effects of the global economic crisis more than most. So profoundly, in fact, that it is being compelled to rethink its business model completely. Every crisis makes us discard our traditional way of looking at things. This one is forcing us in this direction but with the added complexity, long overdue, of environmentally focused solutions.

As far as the product is concerned, the innovation required in a period of crisis is not to invent something different. Rather, it is to adopt a different approach, to cease viewing the automobile as a stand-alone object and begin seeing it as a component in a much larger system. The industry has already been developing more fuel-efficient engines and other solutions which are more respectful of the environment. Fiat Group has embraced this path, with the lowest average CO_2 emission levels among the top brands in Europe. However, to make a true leap, we have to see this as a common challenge for the whole industry and for politicians.

Natural gas provides an eloquent illustration. Today, it is the only real, immediate alternative to petrol. It is the most eco-friendly fuel available in nature, the cheapest for customers—costing 30% less than diesel and half the price of gasoline. Yet in Europe use of natural-gas vehicles is derisory. One weak link in the chain can negate many of the advantages that innovation offers.

Three key factors will enable our industry to make the necessary changes: investment, creativity and courage. Even then, the pursuit of new technologies is not without risk.

Take hydrogen, for example. For many years, it was presented as a panacea to environmental problems. Our industry was accused of not putting enough effort into developing these alternative engines. Maybe in the future—in my view, the distant future—we will all travel using hydrogen power. But until we find a sustainable solution to stockpiling the fuel, it will remain an illusion: we will merely be shifting the problem elsewhere. It may provide us with super-clean cars, but we would also have enormous quantities of energy and polluting emissions, linked to producing the hydrogen itself, on our conscience.

Even with electric propulsion systems, certainly one of the most promising technologies, a distinction needs to be made. For those countries which depend heavily on electric energy that is imported or produced from oil, mass use of electric vehicles is not necessarily advantageous for the system as a whole. A courageous action would be to seize the opportunity to base our entire system on the development of renewable energy.

I believe that, even in the automotive field, public authorities can play an important role in building the future. In America, President Barack Obama formed an industry-focused task force whose mission is to transform the crisis into an opportunity. The aim is to influence an entire industry and the habits of consumers, while providing safeguards for the industry and promoting the shared objective of reduced emissions and fuel consumption.

American vision v European division

In Europe, too, many governments have given support to the sector, each in its own way. This has taken the form of incentives to stimulate demand, channelling it towards more eco-friendly alternatives, as well as direct financial support for domestic producers.

The objective, for both America and Europe, seems the same: to revitalise vital industries. But there is a real possibility that the results will be drastically different.

The American plan focuses on overcoming problems that have afflicted the automotive industry for years and on building a more sustainable future from both an economic and an environmental perspective. European plans, by contrast, are not addressing the underlying causes, because they lack a common vision. Individual states are acting unilaterally out of self-interest, rather than in the interests of Europe as a whole.

In Europe, the industry faces another major impediment: excessive regulation. That clearly represents a burden for carmakers, as it will increase production costs. But the most troubling aspect is that these rules often produce no concrete benefits.

Consider the European Union's regulation to reduce CO_2 emissions in new cars. It will cost carmakers a staggering €45 billion ($67 billion) a year, while reducing CO_2 emissions by only 0.0015% a year—a ridiculously small percentage with an absurd cost-benefit ratio.

My point is that technological evolution must also be viable in relation to the evolution of the market. Great crises can accelerate change. They provide the opportunity to confront structural problems with determination and speed, but only if we accept these actions as inevitable and necessary. Creating the conditions for virtuous change is the real challenge of our times. ■

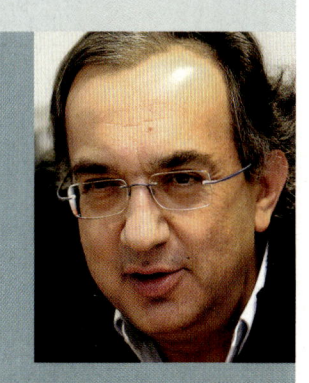

A green revolution for cars requires bold moves by politicians as well as the industry, suggests **Sergio Marchionne**, CEO of Fiat Group and Chrysler Group

The objective, for both America and Europe, seems the same: to revitalise vital industries. But there is a real possibility that the results will be drastically different

General Insurance
Life Insurance
Risk Management

Zurich HelpPoint®

One global insurance program for your expanding business. Even for places you've never been.

Zurich HelpPoint® is here when you need more than just insurance. So we offer the Zurich Multinational Insurance Proposition (MIP)*. It helps you keep global insurance programs compliant when you expand your business to a new market and expose yourself to new risks. The strength of Zurich MIP lies in a transparent and thorough set of solutions for writing and maintaining global insurance programs in over 170 countries. Our game-changing solution can help you sleep better at night, no matter the time zone. For more details about Zurich HelpPoint®, visit www.zurich.com

Here to help your world.

ZURICH®

Because change happenz®

Zurich Insurance plc, a public limited company incorporated in Ireland Registration No. 13460 Registered Office: Zurich House, Ballsbridge Park, Dublin 4, Ireland. UK branch registered in England and Wales Registration No. BR7985. UK Branch Head Office: The Zurich Centre, 3000 Parkway, Whiteley, Fareham, Hampshire PO15 7JZ. Authorised by the Irish Financial Regulator and subject to limited regulation by the Financial Services Authority. Details about the extent of our regulation by the Financial Services Authority are available from us on request. * patent pending

Finance

Also in this section:
China's economic bubble 134
Exit strategies for 2010 135
The lure of Africa 136
Dominique Strauss-Kahn:
Avoiding the next crisis 138
Big banks are back 140
Banking's ups and downs 141
Stephen Green: Finance must think globally 142

In the wake of a crisis

Philip Coggan

The credit crunch ripples on

After the panic, the relief. Some of the building blocks of the prolonged market rally that began in March 2009 will still be around in 2010. First, central banks, nervous about raising rates until they are sure the financial system has recovered from the trauma of the credit crunch, will keep interest rates low. Second, the scale of the recession means that it will be some time before inflationary pressures can emerge. And, third, with interest rates near zero, investors are bound to be tempted to move money into risky assets.

Corporate profits around the world took a big hit during 2007 and 2008, particularly in the financial sector. There should accordingly be scope for profits to rebound in 2010—by as much as 28.3%, according to forecasts compiled by Société Générale.

At the same time, the credit crunch has not disappeared. The number of banks on the Federal Deposit Insurance Corporation's "at risk" list has been increasing, not falling. In many countries commercial property is enduring a rise in vacancies and defaults, in a slow-motion replay of the housing crash. Private-equity groups still have to roll over debts they incurred in the boom of 2006 and early 2007.

Furthermore, investors' well-known tendency to discount the future, so helpful to the market in 2009, could be a pain to it in 2010. Central banks have introduced an extraordinary flurry of measures to deal with the credit crunch, including guarantees of bank debt and the outright purchase of assets. At some point, they will have to unwind those strategies. Even if that unwinding is delayed until 2011, investors may spend the second half of 2010 speculating about it.

Government bond markets could provide the trickiest test. Budget deficits have soared during the crisis, and are expected to hit more than 10% of GDP in both Britain and America. But bond yields have not soared. In part, this was because inflation stayed low and investors were risk-averse in the alarm of the recession. But central banks also helped by buying bonds. If the recovery reaches full speed, central banks will stop purchasing bonds, and may want to sell those they already own.

If bond yields are not to soar as a result, governments will need plausible plans to cut their deficits in the medium term. But those plans may be difficult to produce, given that there will be a general election in Britain and mid-term elections in America. And there is also a double risk. A move to curb deficits by rais-

> **Government bond markets could provide the trickiest test**

2010 IN BRIEF
The total assets of **Islamic banking** top $1 trillion.

Philip Coggan: capital markets editor, *The Economist*

ing taxes or cutting spending could stifle the recovery, as the Japanese did by raising the consumption tax in 1997. But if governments do not act, then markets may tighten policy for them, by pushing yields up sharply.

Currency markets may also be affected. Developed countries are hardly likely to default on their bonds. But creditors are still at risk if they are repaid in a devalued currency. Countries that appear to have lost control of their finances could see their exchange rates suffer.

Indeed, although government action has stabilised the global economy, a whole raft of questions remains unanswered. Has the long period of credit expansion—dubbed the "debt supercycle" by Martin Barnes of Bank Credit Analyst—come to an end? If so, will the result be a long period of sluggish growth? Can China and India carry the global economy on their own? Will another surge in oil prices dampen recovery, as it has so many times before? Will a more regulated economy, particularly in the financial sector, mean that profits form a lower proportion of GDP?

It may well be that medium-term economic growth will be slower as a result of the crisis. Some capacity has been destroyed and, in developed countries, the baby-boomers are now starting to retire, which will limit the potential size of the labour force. Japan has spent two uncomfortable decades adjusting to an era of slower growth and greying population.

All these issues can be summed up in one big dilemma. If the economy does not enjoy a typically vigorous rebound, then the equity market must come under threat. And if the economy does manage that upturn, then surely government bond prices will fall sharply.

This points to a potentially turbulent year. In the past, huge market setbacks have been followed, not by periods of calm, but by long stretches of volatility. The Great Depression included some of the best years ever for Wall Street, with shares rising by over 50% in 1933 and nearly 40% in 1935. But even though shares reached their bottom in 1932, investors still had to live through a flat year in 1934 and a 38% decline in share prices in 1937. In Britain, the bumper year of 1975, when equities more than doubled, was followed by a fall in 1976.

When a stone falls into a pond, the ripples persist for a while. The credit crunch was a whopping great boulder. ■

> **2010 IN BRIEF**
> As part of a two-year programme to **reduce public debt**, Britain sells off state-owned assets.

Blow, then burst

Thomas Easton HONG KONG

China may be inflating the world's next economic bubble

You often don't know about a bubble until it goes pop. But no country has ever puffed harder to inflate one than the Chinese authorities have done to ensure their economy does not collapse in the aftermath of the world financial crisis. As is always the case with bubbles, it is just a matter of time before they burst.

In 2008 and early 2009, demand for products from China's southern manufacturing belt dried up. Factories closed, and millions were fired. Managers of private factories in China complained bitterly about a lack of credit.

Then, all change: state-controlled banks began a massive lending binge. In the first half of 2009, new bank lending was 50% more than all of 2008's—in dollar terms, $1.1 trillion. The trillion-dollar question is: where did the money go, and what will it do?

There are no clear answers. Deposits in Chinese banks grew sharply (suggesting some of the money went nowhere). But between 50% (according to a big Chinese bank) and 89% (according to McKinsey, a consultancy) of the stimulus money will be used for big infrastructure projects.

Supporters of this spending make three points: dumping cash into an economy during a crisis can boost confidence and so growth; embarking on large projects when conditions are slow lessens unemployment; and the results may have indirect benefits since roads, railways, airports and wharves all help business.

But there is an alternative view. The fast growth in deposits is hardly a sign of a genuine need for funds. And China's banks have a suspect history. That their loans are politically driven does not mean that the loans will be bad, but it does raise the possibility that decisions had little to do with credit quality.

Wrongly applied credit can slosh around, drive up costs and create excess capacity. If this happens, the first evidence may emerge at the end of 2010, if only because some disasters will become impossible to ignore. At the moment, China is drawing global praise for maintaining growth amid a global slump. It would be ironic if, in the process, it is creating its own eventual crisis. ■

Thomas Easton: Asia business editor, *The Economist*

A house of cards?

Looking for a way out

Zanny Minton Beddoes WASHINGTON, DC

Ending the fiscal and monetary stimulus will be much harder than starting it

You will hear a lot about "exit strategies" in 2010. After saving the world economy from collapse with a combination of bail-outs, monetary loosening and fiscal stimulus of heroic magnitude, governments across the globe will want to retreat from this largesse as soon, and as smoothly, as possible. They will have trouble on both counts.

The scale of their task is staggering. From injections of public capital to state guarantees on bank debt, financial markets will enter 2010 wrapped in government support, a cocoon that involves scores of separate interventions and adds up to a potential government liability of trillions of dollars in the world's big rich countries. Monetary policy is looser than it has ever been across the rich world, with rates at or below 1% in the biggest economies. Thanks to "quantitative easing" and other unorthodox measures to pump in liquidity, central banks' balance-sheets are swollen—to well over twice their pre-crisis size in Britain and America.

Recession, bank rescues and fiscal-stimulus packages have sent budget deficits soaring, and those effects will linger. The big rich economies within the G20 group will face an average fiscal gap of 9% of GDP in 2010, barely lower than in 2009. At least three big economies—Japan, America and Britain—will have deficits in or close to double digits. On current trends, gross government debt in the big rich economies will reach an average of 106% of GDP in 2010, nearly 30 percentage points higher than before the crisis hit.

Which route to the exit?

Every policymaker knows that this situation is unsustainable. Once a solid recovery is under way monetary looseness will fuel inflation. And even if growth stays weak, today's fiscal deficits imply a pace of debt accumulation that will eventually lead to default. The problem in 2010 will be that even as the financial crisis fades, the world economy will remain enormously reliant on government support. In America, Britain and other former bubble economies, households will still be increasing their saving and paying down debt. Surplus economies, such as China, will not yet have rebalanced their economies enough to rely on private domestic spending. After a few months of vigour, largely driven by restocking and stimulus spending, global GDP growth will weaken to below its trend rate.

Balancing the need for short-term looseness and medium-term prudence in this sluggish environment will be the defining policy dilemma of 2010. Even in theory, the right mix of policies in any exit strategy ought to differ from place to place, depending on the circumstances. Countries whose public finances are in the worst shape, such as Britain, should focus their tightening on fiscal policy. Surplus countries would do better to increase interest rates and allow their currencies to rise. In practice, the decisions about whether to cut back state stimulus (or apply more) in 2010, and how to do so, will be driven by politics as well as economics. Three factors, especially, will play a big role: the behaviour of asset prices, investors' perceptions of sovereign-debt risk and public attitudes to budget deficits.

Asset prices will matter more than consumer prices because, thanks to high unemployment and ample spare capacity, core consumer-price inflation will remain low in both the rich world and emerging markets. So, too, will consumers' expectations of future inflation. Instead, the looseness of global liquidity will translate into asset bubbles, in things ranging from gold bullion to Beijing apartments. Asian assets will be particularly frothy so long as the region's policymakers prevent their currencies from rising against the dollar. Some commodity prices, too, will rise faster than is warranted by the pace of global growth. Central bankers' attitudes to these signs of asset-price inflation will drive their decisions on whether to start raising interest rates.

> **Balancing the need for short-term looseness and medium-term prudence will be the defining policy dilemma**

Investors' assessments of sovereign risk will become more volatile in the coming year, as the dramatic shifts in countries' relative fiscal health become clearer. The big increase in public debt will be overwhelmingly in rich countries and will be worsened by ageing populations. Whereas the average debt burden in big rich economies is headed for 114% of GDP in 2014, the average in big emerging economies will fall to 35% (see chart). As investors focus on that gap, the most profligate rich countries, such as Britain, will suffer.

Finally, the politics of stimulus will become more complicated in 2010. In some countries, such as Japan

Rich man's burden
Government debt of G20 countries as % of GDP

Advanced countries: 78 (2006), 78 (2007), 83 (2008), 98 (2009), 106 (2010), 114 (2014)
Developing countries: 38 (2006), 38 (2007), 36 (2008), 39 (2009), 40 (2010), 35 (2014)

2009 estimate, 2010-14 forecasts
Source: IMF *World Economic Outlook*

Zanny Minton Beddoes: economics editor, *The Economist*

The lure of Africa

Dambisa Moyo

Bond markets will discover its attractions

For African governments it is clear that aid flows will go down in 2010, and dramatically so. Donor governments have slashed their aid budgets, and with most facing unfavourable demographic shifts and large deficits, to depend on their largesse is no longer sensible.

The good news is that the bond markets offer a real opportunity for Africa's governments to be serious about financial discipline and transparency—and to escape from the yoke of aid.

The trend in asset allocation among the largest pools of international investment money suggests 2010 will mark a revival in African bond issuance. Although over the past 20 years investors have been overweight in equities, asset allocation is now tipping in favour of fixed-income bonds. Even at the retail level, flows into fixed-income funds have recently been in the order of five times more than into equity funds.

The drop in outstanding consumer and industrial loans made by European and American banks has been more than offset by the increase in corporate-bond issuance over the past year, demonstrating the strong demand for fixed-income products. If anything, the equity rally (on low trading volumes) since the spring of 2009 has masked this important trend.

Greater demand for bond products will contribute to credit spreads tightening across most bond assets. At some point soon the more traditional Western fixed-income products will look expensive, offering little upside for the investor. So it will be logical for investors to widen their search to the "frontier markets" of Africa.

Moreover, if inflation picks up in 2010, so will commodity prices, improving the creditworthiness of African governments. At the same time, sovereign-wealth funds, especially China's, will want to diversify away from Western markets. The result will be more debt issuance across Africa. The fact that relatively low-rated credits such as the government of Venezuela and the Eurasian Development Bank have been able to raise large amounts of long-duration money at competitive rates is a further signal that there is appetite for similarly rated African credits.

Today, 19 sub-Saharan African governments have recognised credit ratings. Yet only a handful have accessed the international-debt capital markets over the past two decades. This is bound to change in 2010. ■

Dambisa Moyo: author of "How the West Was Lost: Facing Up to America's Economic Decline and the Threat of China and the Rising Rest" (to be published by Penguin in 2010)

▶ and Germany, the new governments' priorities suggest bigger deficits for longer. Elsewhere, political incentives point the other way. Britain, for instance, is likely to have a new Conservative government, which will be keen to cut the budget deficit quickly, so that any attendant pain can be blamed on its Labour predecessor. In America there will be pressures in both directions. Continued high unemployment will bring calls for more government intervention, particularly as the country's midterm elections loom in November. But public concern about the size of the budget deficit and scepticism about the effectiveness of fiscal stimulus are both rising. Some opinion polls suggest people would prefer a weaker economy to higher deficits.

Faced with these pressures, central bankers will do a better job than finance ministers. Central banks' balance-sheets will remain unusually large, but tools, such as paying banks interest on their reserve holdings, will allow monetary policy to be tightened nonetheless.

There won't be much tightening in countries at the centre of the financial storm. The Federal Reserve and the Bank of England, especially, will keep rates close to zero throughout 2010. But elsewhere central bankers will react more swiftly to asset prices than they did before the crisis. Norway will be the first to join Israel and Australia in raising rates. Others, such as Sweden and Canada, will soon follow. Asia's central banks will also begin tightening in 2010, though their desire to keep their currencies cheap will, alas, lead them to move too slowly.

Fiscal policy will be more of a mess. Parts of the stimulus plans that have already been announced, especially the extra spending on infrastructure, will still be kicking in during 2010. But because few countries will develop sensible medium-term plans for their budgets in the year ahead, they will have little room to do more. Towards the end of the year, especially, the prospect of abrupt tightening will be a big risk, as stimulus programmes start to run out. Just as government spending tapers off, America is set to raise taxes sharply on high earners and investment income.

History shows clearly that this can be dangerous. In both America in 1937 and Japan in 1997, ill-timed tax increases sent fragile economies back into recession. The exit strategists of 2010 will have to avoid, if they can, the same peril. ■

2010 IN BRIEF
The Maldives adopts "**mobile money**", allowing people to send and receive money by their mobile phones.

YOUR RELIABLE FINANCIAL PARTNER WITH UNIQUE ABILITIES SINCE 1948.

SUSTAIN**ABILITY**
The most valuable bank in Turkey.*
The most valuable company in Turkey.*
Most widely recognized bank in Turkey.**

ST**ABILITY**
The highest standalone credit rating awarded to a bank in Turkey: **Baa1.*****
Prudent risk management infrastructure.
Robust capital structure and high capital adequacy ratio.

RELI**ABILITY**
Reliable financial partner of over **6 million** customers.
The **highest syndicated lending** received by an emerging market bank in 2009.****

PROFIT**ABILITY**
Net profit of **US$ 1.2 billion** in 2008.
One of the most profitable banks in Europe.

* Istanbul Stock Exchange, as of October 8, 2009
** Nielsen Turkey - Top of Mind Survey, 2008
*** By Moody's Baseline Credit Assessment, as of August 26, 2009
**** As of August 21, 2009

www.akbank.com

AKBANK

Reshaping the post-crisis world

Dominique Strauss-Kahn, managing director of the International Monetary Fund, explains how the world can avoid slipping back into crisis

As the global economy continues to recover from the worst economic downturn since the second world war, policymakers face both challenges and opportunities in 2010. The challenges include disturbingly high unemployment in the advanced economies, and the unfinished task of restructuring devastated financial sectors. In emerging and low-income countries, internal sources of growth will need to be found, as external demand and flows of foreign investment and credit remain weak. But there will also be opportunities to lay the foundations of a safer and more stable financial system, and so secure sustainable economic growth.

International collaboration will play a critical role in making the most of these opportunities. During the crisis, the rapid actions by policymakers across the globe—in particular, the co-ordinated fiscal stimulus—were crucial in averting a much deeper disaster.

However, collaboration will become more difficult. We already see differences emerging about when macroeconomic policies should be tightened. This is to be expected, given that the speed and nature of recovery will differ across economies. But if some countries tighten too soon, this could derail the global recovery. Given these risks, policymakers should be prepared to extend public support—through low interest rates, if inflation remains contained, but more likely through government spending—to stop the global economy slipping back into recession.

In the financial sector, enhanced international co-operation is needed to overcome possibly divergent national interests and so achieve meaningful reform in 2010. Making progress on this front is essential for shoring up financial-sector stability and for restoring the public's confidence.

A further rebalancing of global growth, supported by a strong recovery of international trade, will help sustain the recovery over the medium term. This process, which was kick-started by the crisis, will pick up speed in 2010. Many economies that have followed export-led growth strategies and run current-account surpluses will need to rely more on domestic demand and imports. Policies to support this adjustment include improving households' access to credit and strengthening social-insurance systems. Exchange-rate appreciation will probably be part of the adjustment process. These shifts will help offset the decline in domestic demand in economies that have traditionally run current-account deficits and are now suffering the aftermath of asset-price busts.

Policies to support supply-side reforms are also needed to boost growth in 2010. A speedy restructuring of the financial sector can accelerate the recovery of credit and capital markets and thus support investment and consumption. Labour-market reforms will help workers from crisis-hit industries to move to more vibrant parts of the economy. And product-market reforms—particularly in services—could create new jobs and boost productivity.

Turning to a longer-term issue, I see the world taking important steps in 2010 to strengthen the international monetary system. In the wake of earlier financial crises, many emerging-market economies stockpiled foreign reserves as insurance against losing access to international capital markets. But this accumulation of foreign reserves has been a destabilising force, contributing to the build-up of global imbalances (as the counterpoint in other countries has been large current-account deficits). It has also been costly, as countries could have invested these resources at home instead, for example in education or infrastructure.

Bolstering the buffers

I expect the IMF to play an increasingly important role as a global lender of last resort. In 2009 our membership decided to triple our lending resources to $750 billion and boost global liquidity via a $283 billion allocation of Special Drawing Rights (the international reserve asset issued by the IMF). But this may not be enough. As the crisis demonstrated all too clearly, the world needs very large liquidity buffers to deal with fast and hard-hitting financial shocks. The question of how much funding the IMF needs—and what form it should take—is certain to feature prominently in discussions on the future of the international monetary system in 2010.

A critical prerequisite for the IMF to serve as an effective global lender of last resort is further governance reform. The changes endorsed by the entire IMF membership at its annual meeting in Istanbul entail an important shift of voting power to dynamic emerging and developing countries. At the same time, they undertook to protect the voting share of the fund's poorest members. The implementation of these and other governance reforms will go a long way to bolstering the IMF's ability to serve its membership. ■

If some countries tighten too soon, this could derail the global recovery

Dubai.
Where one great experience leads to another.

Uncrowded clean beaches and year-round sunshine. Luxury hotels and restaurants, serving a variety of international cuisine. World-class shopping malls and gold & spice souks. Desert adventures and heritage attractions for a fascinating Arabian experience. In short, Dubai has fun and excitement in store for your entire family.

GOVERNMENT OF DUBAI

دائـرة الـسـيـاحـة والـتـسـويـق الـتـجـاري
Department of Tourism and Commerce Marketing

Discover Dubai

P.O. Box: 594, Dubai, United Arab Emirates. **Tel:** 00971 4 2230000, **Fax:** 00971 4 2230022. **Website:** http://dubaitourism.ae **e-mail:** info@dubaitourism.ae

The big boys' game

Lionel Barber

The bankers are ready to play, with stricter rules

After a near-death experience, the biggest banks in the West are breathing more easily. Life has been good to the survivors of the global financial crisis, especially those who escaped state ownership; and it will get better in 2010, despite tighter regulation and a blast of much-needed competition.

In 2010 we will witness the emergence of a banking super-league comprising Goldman Sachs, JPMorgan Chase and Deutsche Bank. Each will have the liquidity and appetite to dominate capital markets. These too-big-to-fail titans will be joined by Barclays, long seen as an accident-waiting-to-happen but now poised for a comeback.

Barclays will reap the benefits of two audacious gambles made at the height of the financial crisis: the purchase of the American operations of Lehman Brothers (if only Barclays had scooped up Asia, too); and the decision to snub British state aid in favour of private investors, notably from the Gulf. An independent Barclays, powered by its investment-banking arm, will command a place in the super-league, despite weaknesses in its British loan-book exposed by a still-fragile economy.

Yet life for the super-leaguers will become tougher. In 2009 the leading "bulge-bracket" banks generated easy profits (and handsome bonuses) buying and selling government bonds under central banks' quantitative easing (QE) and other stimulus measures. In 2010 these trades will fade away, just like QE itself. Regulation will tighten, as higher capital requirements are put in place. Competition will return, too, in investment banking, especially for talent.

After two years of convalescence, the walking wounded (Bank of America/Merrill Lynch, Citigroup and UBS) will slowly be on the mend. They spent most of 2009 on the sidelines, as regulators fretted about their capital ratios and dud assets. In 2010 the playing field will start to level out as lending recovers slowly and investment banks are weaned off emergency life-support systems.

The return to quasi-normality will challenge upstart corporate brokers and small-cap investment bankers such as Jefferies and London-based Evolution. In 2008-09 their growth (and staff) exploded as they sought to exploit the gap left by the bigger investment-banking players. In 2010 competition will intensify in the credit markets. "Someone is going to get hurt," predicts one City of London chief executive. "This is a big boys' game."

But a semblance of normality will not mean a return to the spellbinding leverage of the credit bubble. The days of easy pickings for hedge funds and their sponsor banks which traded credit-derivative insurance and other exotic debt instruments are over. But leverage will return and the securitisation market will be open for business, albeit in a more sober form. This will change the financial landscape in several ways.

First, reduced leverage and tighter credit will herald the end of the private-equity model of the past 20 years. This was epitomised by KKR's "Barbarians at the Gate" takeover of RJR Nabisco, the food-to-tobacco conglomerate which was stripped down and sold off. Private equity will shift to older models of long-term funding for small and medium-sized businesses epitomised by 3i and Alchemy Capital (albeit without the charismatic Jon Moulton).

Second, large private-equity players such as Blackstone, KKR and Carlyle, though bloodied, will continue to engage in leverage, provided they have committed capital. Those raising capital will still find it hard, even if lending picks up. Meanwhile, liquid hedge funds such as Citadel will muscle in on private equity's patch.

> Private equity will shift to older models of long-term funding

Third, expect a shift to private wealth managers at the expense of supermarket banks which stuffed clients with poorly performing funds (courtesy of Bernard Madoff) and AIG bonds. The shift will offer opportunities for the private Swiss banks (despite no let-up in the American-led campaign to water down Swiss confidentiality), established families such as the Flemings and even hedge funds such as GLG arguing that they can manage money better.

Risk will continue to be redefined in 2010. One of the effects of the financial crisis was to kick-start the corporate-bond market to help companies refinance. The demand for "risk mitigation" will gain pace, with more focus on clearing mechanisms, independent valuations and certainty in settlement to stop rogue traders.

And here we come to the bitter-sweet irony. Having spent the past couple of years worrying about derivatives as "financial weapons of mass destruction", regulators (and investors such as Warren Buffett) will have to accept that these hedging instruments are here to stay.

Governments will hedge against inflation, still a risk after the fiscal and monetary expansion to combat the crisis. Pension funds will hedge against longevity, increasingly important in planning for an ageing population.

A return to normality in 2010? Not quite. More like a return to sensible risk management. ∎

2010 IN BRIEF
France's leading banks close their branches and subsidiaries in **tax havens**.

Lionel Barber: editor-in-chief, *Financial Times*

Ups and downs

Andrew Palmer

The gap between weak and strong banks will grow ever wider in 2010

The financial crisis, like any good rollercoaster, started with a giddying ascent and a terrifying plunge. The ride is now slowing to a stop but 2010 will still produce some nasty moments for the banks.

First, the less-bad news. Rates of unemployment, corporate defaults and consumer delinquencies will have passed their peak in most countries by the end of 2010. House prices will have bottomed out in America, the place where it all began: national prices will at last hit a trough some 35-40% below their 2006 peak. Interest rates will remain extremely low, helping overstretched borrowers to meet payments and to refinance loans. Reviving economic activity will buoy transaction volumes at wholesale banks (although profit margins will come down from the extraordinary levels of mid-2009).

This slow turning of the credit cycle will not be enough to save some banks from being overwhelmed by losses. The first chapters of the financial crisis hit investment banks disproportionately hard; the closing ones will focus on commercial banks. Commercial property will remain the biggest single headache for many banks, particularly smaller lenders exposed to developers in depressed areas. The cull of smaller American banks will continue. The gloomiest estimates reckon that more than a thousand tiddlers will fail as a result of the crisis, many in 2010.

If survival is no longer the question facing bigger banks, three sources of misery will still weigh down the industry in 2010. The first will be the weakness of economic recovery, at least in the developed world. Higher savings rates will dampen demand for credit, both directly and indirectly. Various government stimulus programmes will be withdrawn during the course of 2010—one of the biggest, the Federal Reserve's purchases of mortgage-backed securities, is due to disappear early in the year. Housing markets will be weighed down by continuing foreclosures and the threat of another supply glut, as more homeowners are tempted to put their houses back on the market.

> The cull of smaller American banks will continue

The second source of concern for the banks will be the fragility of their balance-sheets. Governments' debt-guarantee programmes are being phased out, which means that banks will have to pay more for funding. And although capital levels are better than before, the quality of the loans and securities that banks hold is still unclear. Plans to transfer the most toxic assets from the banks have fizzled in many places. Some lenders have taken advantage of changes in accounting rules to reclassify trading assets as banking assets, which means that banks will take losses on those assets more gradually.

Many have routinely been extending borrowers' loan terms as refinancing deadlines approach: "Pay it back later" is preferable to "Don't pay it back at all". Some banks, notably in Spain, have swapped debt for equity, putting off write-downs but potentially storing up trouble ahead. Others have set aside too few provisions to cover losses that are still to come. All of which will leave weaker banks unable to take advantage of whatever rebound materialises in 2010.

The third drag on the banks will be the impact of regulation. Policymakers have already signalled the direction of reform: higher capital buffers to protect against losses; stricter rules on liquidity; and changes to bankruptcy regimes in the event of future bank failures. This will be the year when the devilish details are thrashed out. The Basel committee of bank regulators is hoping to agree by the end of 2010 on a new capital regime. Liquidity ratios are being mulled, too. Policymakers do not want to clamp down too early (higher capital charges on trading assets are an exception and will come into force in 2010), but the prospect of tougher rules will push banks to build up more capital.

Fun for some

In all, 2010 will be an anaemic year for the industry. But the overall picture masks a growing polarisation between strong and weak institutions.

Banks that have lots of capital will buy assets from banks that need equity or are still in the process of rebuilding themselves (for example, Citigroup or the Royal Bank of Scotland). Banks that have a strong presence in emerging markets will be in better shape than those that do not. Banks that have lots of deposits will take market share from those that rely on wholesale markets to fund loan growth (especially as the outline of new liquidity rules becomes clearer). Banks that have seen reputations sullied (UBS, say) will keep losing clients to those whose image has been burnished by the crisis (Credit Suisse). Getting off the rollercoaster is one thing; being able to get on the next ride quite another. ∎

White-knuckle ride
Write-offs, % of outstanding US loans
— Consumer — Residential property — Commercial property — Commercial and industrial
Source: IMF Global Financial Stability Report. 2009 estimate, 2010 forecast

---

2010 IN BRIEF

Foreign firms list on the **Shanghai stock exchange's** international board.

Andrew Palmer: finance editor, *The Economist*

People power

*Financial institutions able to think globally will benefit as the world economy shifts east and south, argues **Stephen Green**, chairman of HSBC*

By 2010, the working-age population of the developing world will exceed 3 billion. Thereafter, the total will continue to grow, reaching 4 billion within 30 years or so. Malthus would have been horrified. But there is good reason to take a more positive view of these demographics: 2010 will be a watershed year for the developing world, marking the beginning of a "demographic window" when its working-age population will be proportionally highest, and the potential for economic growth will consequently be at its peak.

Of course, to what extent these demographic changes result in economic growth depends on the complex interplay of a number of factors, from government policy to global economic conditions. The challenges are considerable: rapid economic growth will be needed to deliver employment, while social, political and environmental issues will have to be skilfully managed.

The consequences for financial markets will be wide-reaching. During the demographic window, the dependency ratio (the proportion of non-working to working population) is low and so the potential for consumption and savings is at its highest.

As they start to benefit from a regular income, millions of the "unbanked" will join the formal banking system. As they save and prepare for their retirement, workers will demand pensions, insurance and asset-management products.

Governments will seek to expand welfare systems and a better financial infrastructure will be required. The need for microfinance will also soar—a segment in which demand, according to some estimates, is already ten times greater than supply.

During this time of great change, fresh thinking, international co-operation and the sharing of expertise between industry, governments and society will all be required to build sustainable financial markets. In the wake of the global crisis, the financial-services industry now has another chance to prove that it can make a valuable contribution to social and economic development.

Today, 90% of trade transactions involve some form of credit, insurance or guarantee. Demand from businesses in developing markets for these products will grow and, as economies become larger and more sophisticated, they will also require access to fully functioning capital markets to ensure the efficient allocation of capital—including well-developed bond and equity markets. At the same time, global patterns of trade are shifting. Emerging economies are doing more business with each other and with the rest of the world, and the global recession has accelerated this trend. China is already overtaking Germany, ahead of schedule, not only as the world's largest exporter but also as the second-largest importer.

Banks will continue to play an important role in the financing of these new trade patterns, and those global providers able to deliver international connectivity for their customers will be tomorrow's winners. With their balance-sheets less damaged by the financial crisis, institutions in emerging markets may be best placed to benefit. By the end of 2008, China's five largest banks had a total of 78 overseas financial institutions under their direct control. As the economy improves we will see a further wave of international expansion, new listings and cross-border investments by emerging-market banks.

Multiple centres

Today, London and New York are the world's only two genuinely global financial centres. Nevertheless, as the developed world struggles with anaemic growth, other centres will encroach on their market share.

Asia now accounts for five of the world's top ten financial centres. Of these, Shanghai's rise is perhaps the most remarkable: its Pudong financial district is expected to accommodate a workforce of 200,000 in 2010.

Financial centres in emerging markets now have an exceptional opportunity to strengthen their position, whether as regional hubs, like Singapore, or as global specialists, like Dubai in Islamic financing. It is certain that some cities will join London and New York as truly global centres within a generation.

The scale of current demographic trends can be difficult to absorb. By some estimates, China's middle class is now larger than the entire population of the United States. Meanwhile, India is adding 10m new mobile-phone subscriptions every month, with the total about to reach half a billion.

A well-functioning financial sector will be a *sine qua non* for any developing economy. As a result, we can expect the world's financial map to be redrawn. Its centre of gravity will move east and south like that of the economy as a whole. For those institutions and financial centres that are able to think globally, the opportunities will be unprecedented. ■

Millions of the "unbanked" will join the formal banking system

LET'S
CONNECT
AFRICA

TO THE
WORLD

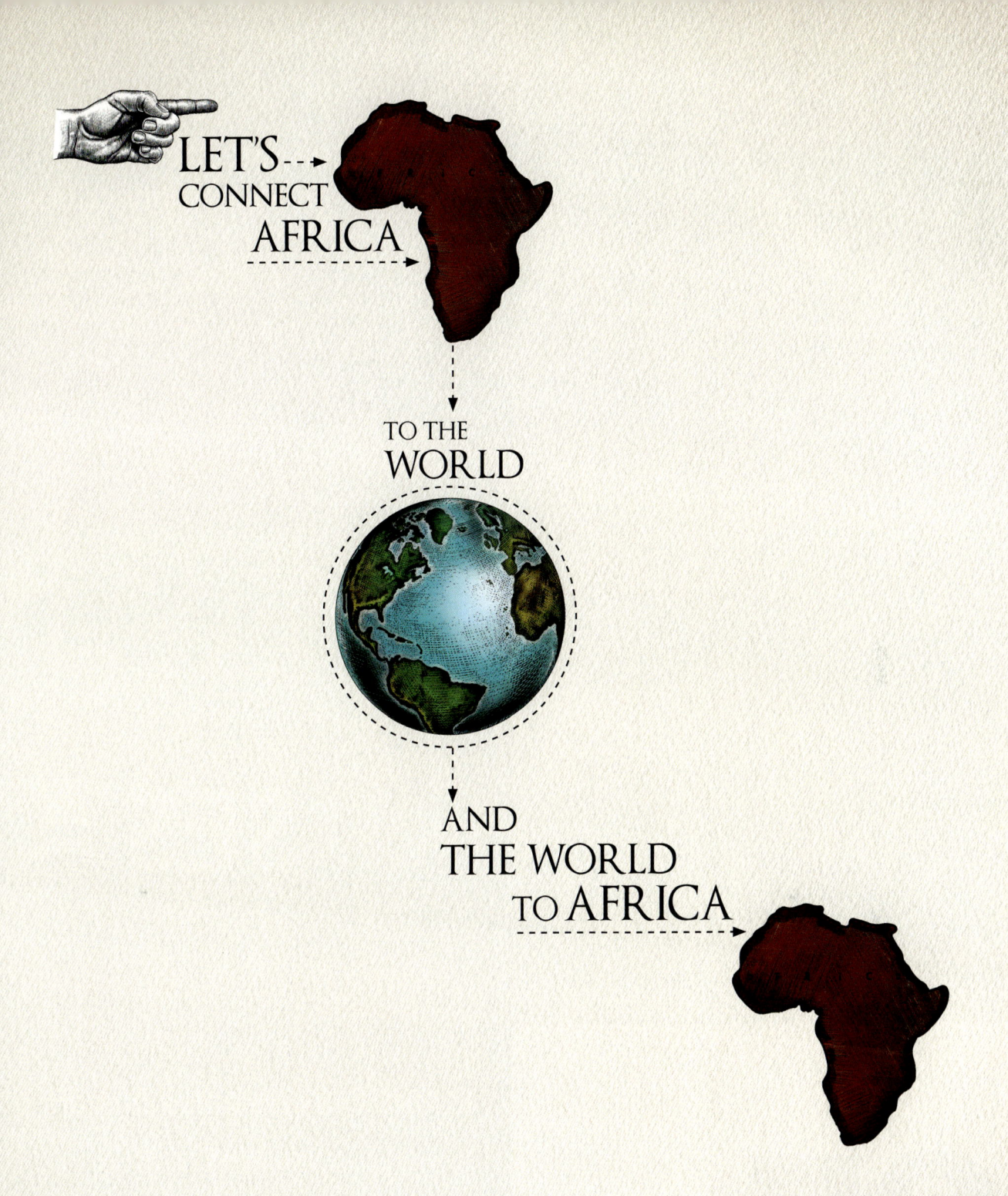

AND
THE WORLD
TO AFRICA

With international representation in over 30 countries around the world, we are able to combine our local market expertise and network with our emerging market capability to make the right connections.
www.standardbank.com/movingforward
Moving Forward

Standard Bank
Also trading as Stanbic Bank

thorised financial services and registered credit provider (NCRCP15)
Standard Bank of South Africa Limited (Reg. No. 1962/000738/06). SBSA 706922-6/09

One moment.
One satellite network.
Infinite connections.

Our 40 satellites reach 99% of the world's population, offering our customers regional strength and expertise on a global scale.

SES

25 YEARS

Bringing people together through the power of satellites since 1985.

In 2010 SES celebrates 25 years

Founded in 1985, SES launched its first satellite in 1988. Since then, we've expanded to become a global operator with a fleet of 40 satellites covering 99% of the world's population. Today, we are reaching out beyond our core markets of Europe and North America and investing in new capacity to meet the growing demand in Asia, Africa, the Middle East and Latin America. With our ongoing fleet expansion programme, SES will continue to be

Your Satellite Connection to the World.

www.ses.com

THE WORLD IN 2010   145

Also in this section:
The Arctic's melting ice 146
The next green revolution 147
Elon Musk: Commercial space travel ready for lift-off 148
The looming crisis in human genetics 150
Novel energy technologies 152
A solar-cycle surprise 153

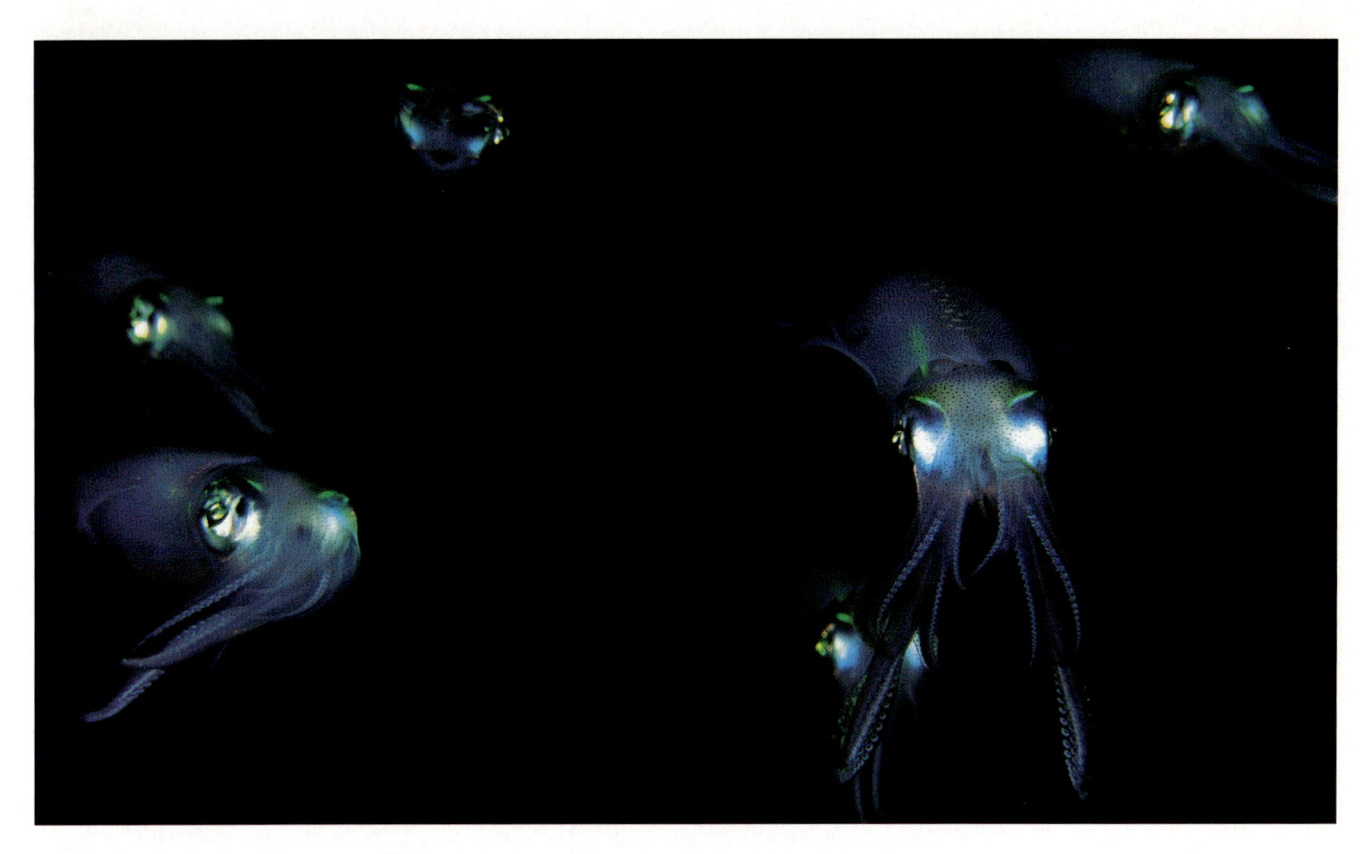

Science

Introducing the transparent ocean

Alun Anderson

The Census of Marine Life reveals wonders of the deep

Mankind's view of the planet's ocean life will be transformed for ever in 2010. That change will come from the insights gained in a ten-year, $750m project involving 2,000 scientists from 82 countries and the technological marvels they are using to see across vast reaches of the oceans and to track the travels of individual fish. Emerging from this is what Ron O'Dor, the Dalhousie University scientist who leads the Census of Marine Life, calls the "transparent ocean", revealing what is happening in the seas in three dimensions and over time.

The findings of the census will be released in October 2010 in London at a series of public events and scientific meetings. A website, the Ocean Biogeographic Information System (www.iobis.org), will give access to 20m or so records from the census; another, the Encyclopedia of Life (www.eol.org), will record photographs and details of 250,000 marine species. Over the decade, census scientists have explored every ocean realm from near-shore waters to the abyssal plains—which cover a greater area of the Earth than all its land. The frozen seas of the Arctic and Antarctic each had their surveys, too.

Many surprising discoveries will be described. Off the coast of New Zealand scientists found a "Brittle Star City", where tens of millions of these creatures live atop a sea mountain, holding their arms up into a swift current that brings them endless supplies of food. In the Pacific, a patch of water proved an unexpected home for thousands of white sharks which swim huge distances to spend half the year there. Why they travel to the "White Shark Café" no one knows. In the Bay of Biscay off France a mini-submarine found giant oysters 20cm (8 inches) across; in the Mediterranean another found gardens of sponges around a cold seep where methane leaks from the sea floor.

The diversity of the oceans that the census will reveal exceeds all expectations. So does the extraordinary performance of the new technologies which were pressed into service. Sophisticated ships, advanced sonar, robot submarines and genetic "bar-coding" techniques for fast species identification have all been brought into play.

Ocean Acoustic Waveguide Remote Sensing is an especially exciting advance. This sonar can scan thousands of square kilometres of the shallow-shelf seas at one time and see schools of fish moving within them. Compared with a conventional fish-finding sonar it is a ▶

2010 IN BRIEF
The **laser** celebrates its 50th birthday.

Alun Anderson: former editor-in-chief of *New Scientist*; author of "After the Ice" (Harper-Smithsonian/Virgin Books)

miracle, with a scanning rate that runs a million times faster. Its inventor, Nicholas Makris of MIT, has used it to watch herring hidden in the sea off the coast of Maine. As they headed for their spawning grounds, the 20m fish quickly came together in a school the size of Manhattan. It is the largest mass of life ever seen.

At the other end of the scale, individual fish weighing as little as 20 grams (0.7 ounces) are being tracked by attaching tiny electronic tags to them. The tags send out pulses of sound which can be picked up by undersea receivers. One project already has lines of acoustic sensors on the sea bed from Alaska to California. With them researchers have tracked individual salmon from Rocky Mountain streams all the way to Alaska and can see where they go and where they die on their 2,500km (1,550-mile) migration. Another sensor line runs off the Canadian coast. Others will follow around the world.

Technologies like these have enormous implications for the world, especially in the light of another census project. Not all researchers were at sea; others trawled through historical records, read whalers' diaries and even studied photos of prize fish taken by Floridian anglers to work out the state of the oceans in earlier times.

Their stories are telling us that the oceans were far more productive in the past. Life in the oceans is growing less abundant and big, full-grown adult fish much rarer. There were 27,000 southern right whales off the coast of New Zealand in the 1800s, 30 times as many as there are now. The Florida trophy fish have shrunk from an average size of 20kg to just 2.3kg in only 50 years.

The Gulf of Maine provides a particularly vivid example. Records from the 1880s show that 70,000 tonnes of cod used to be caught each year. Now the take is closer to 3,000 tonnes. The recent data might suggest that cod stocks could be rebuilt to obtain 10,000 tonnes in a year but the older records show that the oceans can be far more productive. "We have the potential to recover that productivity for the benefit of humans, not just so the fish will be happier," says Andy Rosenberg, an expert on the gulf's fisheries from the University of New Hampshire.

> A future in which fisheries are more productive starts to look possible

That is the big message which will be coming from the census on top of its maps of ocean biodiversity and the new understanding of what lives where and why. In the transparent ocean scientists have the tools to say where fish are, how many of them there are and where they are going. Couple that with knowledge of past riches, and a future in which fisheries are more productive and the oceans much better managed starts to look possible—and very valuable. As the census results become known in 2010, expect an end to simple "doom and gloom" and a much bigger debate over the future potential of the seas. ∎

2010 IN BRIEF

As species die by the day, the United Nations proclaims the **International Year of Biodiversity**.

On thin ice

Alun Anderson

An imminent answer to an Arctic riddle

For the past three years, the vast cap of shining-white ice covering the Arctic has melted away in summer to an area that would have been unbelievable just a decade ago. At the end of the winter, the frozen seas cover 15.7m square kilometres (6.1m square miles), an area more than one and a half times that of the United States. By September the ice regularly used to melt to 7m square kilometres. But since a great collapse in 2007 the figure has been closer to 4.3m square kilometres. Every summer an extra area of ice six times the size of California has been disappearing. As well as this reduction in area, scientists believe that, hidden beneath the surface, the ice is growing ever thinner, setting up the Arctic for another sudden, catastrophic collapse. The big question now is when the ice will disappear totally each summer. There will be an answer in 2010.

Another year of observations, better computer models and—the Holy Grail of ice scientists—maps of the thickness of the ice from a new European satellite called Cryosat-2 should reveal in 2010 how long the Arctic ice has left. Estimates range from 2013—terrifyingly soon—to 2050 for the first year when the Arctic is free of ice in summer.

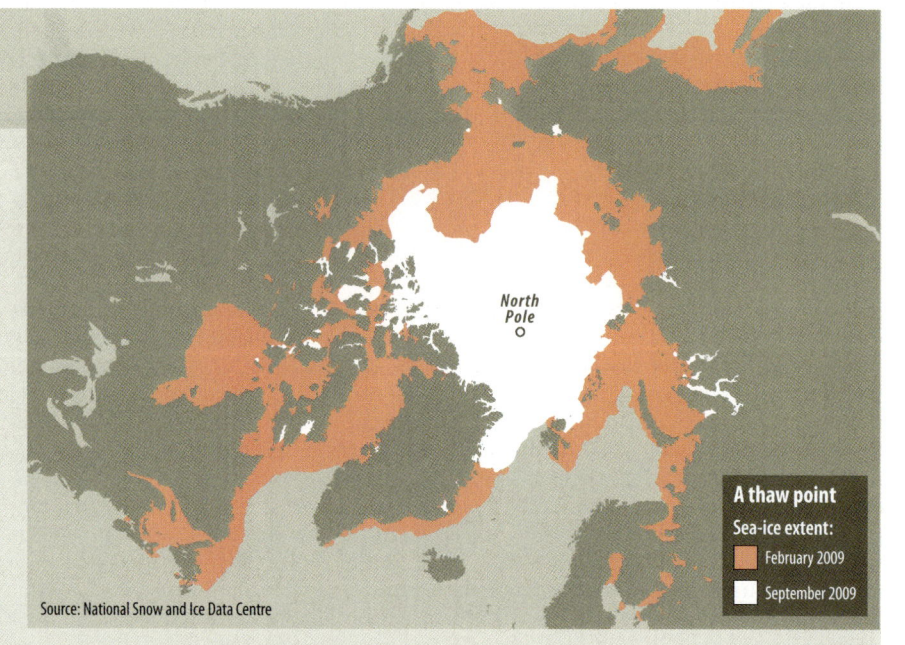

When that happens, it will be the biggest and fastest change to the Earth's surface ever made by human influence. The ice, poised between freezing and melting, is an especially sensitive indicator of the planet's temperature. When it disappears, it will be a disaster for all the Arctic life that depends on ice, from the polar bears that walk on it to the tiny creatures that live within it.

And it will be a disaster for the planet. That great dome of ice reflects sunlight back into space throughout the 24 hours a day of polar summer sunshine. When it turns sea-dark and soaks up the sun, global warming will really take off. ∎

A thaw point
Sea-ice extent:
- February 2009
- September 2009

Source: National Snow and Ice Data Centre

The new NUE thing

Matt Ridley

Nitrogen-use efficiency, the next green revolution

Imagine you could wave a magic wand and boost the yield of the world's crops, cut their cost, use fewer fossil fuels to grow them and reduce the pollution that results from farming. Imagine, too, that you could both eliminate some hunger and return some land to rain forest. This is the scale of the prize that many in the biotechnology industry now suddenly believe is within their grasp in 2010 and the years that follow. They are in effect hoping to boost the miles-per-gallon of agriculture, except that the fuel in question is nitrogen.

In the 19th century, the world fed its expanding population by finding new acres to plough—in the prairies, the pampas, the steppes and the outback. In the 20th century, food supply more than kept pace with population by getting more out of each acre thanks to fossil fuels: tractors freed land to grow food that once fed horses, and fossil fuels fixed nitrogen from the air to make ammonium-based fertiliser. Yields doubled and doubled again. Today roughly half the nitrogen atoms in an average human body have come through an ammonium factory. Had they not, rain forests would have been even more devastated than they have been; and famines worse.

But about two-thirds of the nearly $100 billion of nitrogen fertiliser spread on fields each year is wasted. Either it is washed out of the soil by rain, and then suffocates the life out of lakes, rivers and seas by causing dense algal blooms—vast "dead zones" lie off the mouth of the Mississippi and in the Baltic Sea. Or it turns to nitrous oxide in the soil, a gas with roughly 300 times the greenhouse-warming potential of carbon dioxide, pound for pound. Some of that waste is avoidable with sensible agronomic measures: timing the application of fertiliser carefully, for example. Countries such as Denmark have halved their nitrogen inputs without hurting yields in recent years. By contrast, fertiliser subsidies encourage futile over-use of nitrogen in parts of China.

But there is now a high-tech solution too. One day in 1995 in Allen Good's laboratory in Edmonton, Alberta, a student made a serendipitous mistake: she forgot to add nitrogen when she watered some experimental canola (rapeseed) plants. Some of the plants had been given an "over-expressed" version of a gene from a barley plant for an enzyme called alanine aminotransferase in the hope of making them better at tolerating drought. Whereas the other plants suffered for lack of fertiliser, the plants with the over-expressed gene flourished.

A company called Arcadia Biosciences in Davis, California, acquired the licence to use the gene and signed agreements with other firms that are now testing it in rice in China, wheat in Australia and many other crops. The results, says the firm's chief executive, Eric Rey, are not just encouraging; they are astonishing. In experimental plots the plants often need less than half as much nitrogen to achieve the same yield—or get 25% more yield for the same nitrogen.

If (and it remains a mighty big if) the technology achieves even half this gain in average conditions once commercialised, probably from 2012, the effect could be dramatic. Food would get cheaper, reducing pressure on rain forests and other wild land. Water would get cleaner, reviving fisheries and nature reserves. Greenhouse-gas emissions would fall by the equivalent of taking all the cars in America, Germany and Britain off the road.

Environmental pressure groups will scoff. But they scoffed at insect-resistant biotech crops too. There is now unambiguous evidence that wherever genetically modified insect-resistant cotton and maize are grown, insecticide applications have been reduced—by up to 80%. Since such crops came in, some 230m kg of insecticide-active ingredient have not been used that otherwise would have been. That saves not only wildlife, but also money.

The organic movement will scoff, too, saying synthetic fertilisers can be replaced by manure and legumes. But both require land. According to Vaclav Smil, author of the book "Enriching the Earth", to replace existing synthetic fertiliser with manure would require quintupling the world's cattle population from 1.3 billion to maybe 7 billion-8 billion; where are these to graze?

Genetically modified crops are proving to be an unmitigated environmental miracle. Herbicide-tolerant plants are now grown with minimum tillage, which reduces the soil erosion that results from ploughing. Drought-tolerant plants are nearing the market and salt-tolerant ones are not far behind. Within a decade there may be crops that are no-till, insect-resistant, omega-3-enriched, drought-tolerant, salt-tolerant and nitrogen-efficient. If they boost yields, then the 21st century will see more and more people better and better fed from less and less land. ■

> Genetically modified crops are proving to be an unmitigated environmental miracle

2010 IN BRIEF

The **American pika**, a cousin of the rabbit, becomes the first animal in the continental US to qualify for endangered-species status as a result of global warming.

Matt Ridley: writer on science and evolution; author of "The Rational Optimist" (to be published by HarperCollins in 2010)

Space, the fiscal frontier

Commercial space travel is ready for lift-off, says **Elon Musk**, CEO and chief technology officer of SpaceX

For the first time in its history, NASA has decided to turn over the transport of space-station cargo to the commercial sector. In December 2008, following a competition between SpaceX, Orbital Sciences and a joint venture of Boeing, Lockheed and ATK, NASA awarded 12 "space freighter" missions to my company, SpaceX, and eight to Orbital. You will see the first SpaceX demonstration flights, a prelude to operational missions, in 2010.

There is no realistic alternative to private enterprise advancing the cause of space if you believe it is important for life as we know it to become multi-planetary. Only the private sector is capable of improving the cost and reliability of space transport to the degree necessary to establish self-sustaining life on Mars. At current public-sector costs and reliability, even if the world already possessed rockets and spacecraft that could take humans to Mars, we would bankrupt the global economy and suffer loss of life that is intolerable in the modern era.

Some may be surprised to hear me assert that the commercial sector would improve reliability so dramatically, thinking perhaps that companies would make unsafe decisions to achieve low cost. Not at all—it is very unprofitable to kill customers! The airline and car industries are almost entirely private and both have incredibly impressive safety records. In fact, you may be surprised to learn that your probable lifespan would actually be higher if you lived every minute of it on a commercial airliner.

Historically, transporting cargo to and from the International Space Station has been done primarily by the space shuttle, but it is due to retire in late 2010, or in early 2011 if a short extension is granted. NASA is working on a new rocket system derived from the space shuttle, but that will be ready only in 2017. Moreover, the cost of using it to service the space station would require a dramatic and improbable increase in NASA's budget.

It is worth noting that cargo transport to the station is the shuttle's main duty. In effect, therefore, NASA has decided that the successor to the space shuttle will be commercial rockets and spacecraft. The significance of this decision has yet to permeate the public consciousness.

I'd like to be clear here that NASA played a critical role in fostering development of the commercial systems by providing much of the funding, as well as expert guidance. A great deal of credit is therefore due to the foresight and hard work of people at NASA. That said, the space agency should not be blamed for any missteps along the way, of the sort that almost always happen with new rocket developments. The design is that of SpaceX and we—particularly I as chief designer—should rightfully take responsibility for errors.

Whatever bumps along the trajectory there may be, I am confident that NASA's support for commercial companies will prove to be critical to humanity's future in space. It is not simply an option, it is the only option.

Flight of the astronaut

Although the course for cargo is set, the White House has not yet decided to have the commercial sector transport astronauts. However, it augurs well that a panel of industry luminaries recently convened by the White House and led by Norman Augustine, a former CEO of Lockheed, has come down firmly for it.

It is up to Barack Obama to make a final decision based on the options presented by the panel, but none of the options considered viable includes the default path, the shuttle-derived *Ares I* rocket and *Orion* spacecraft, to service the space station. The panel pointed out quite reasonably that the NASA budget allows for either *Ares I/Orion* or the space station, but not both. However, since *Ares I* is capable only of reaching low Earth orbit and the space station is the only habitable thing in low Earth orbit, *Ares I* by itself would be a road to nowhere.

Moreover, the panel said that *Ares I/Orion* would be ready to fly to the space station only in 2017, six years after the space shuttle retires. That would mean a long sole-source dependency on Russia's *Soyuz*, for which NASA is already paying $50m per seat. Whatever price is charged after the shuttle retires will depend on the kindness of the Russian government.

In contrast, SpaceX will be ready to transport astronauts within three years of receiving a NASA contract, at a price per seat of $20m. We are not alone. United Launch Alliance (ULA), a joint venture between Boeing and Lockheed, has publicly promised to be ready in four years. Orbital Sciences is also confident of getting the job done in a similar time-frame.

NASA will pick probably two or three companies for this task in 2010, heralding the dawn of a new era in human spaceflight. ∎

> *NASA's support for commercial companies will prove to be critical to humanity's future in space*

Servers that cut energy costs by 95%? Cool.

ALTERNATIVE THINKING ABOUT SERVERS:

The next generation of HP ProLiant servers radically cut your operating costs.

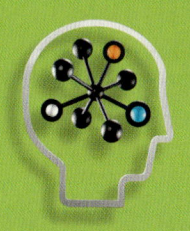

HP ProLiant servers let you radically cut the costs that matter most—energy, management and administration costs. So you can dramatically boost server performance and improve your bottom line.

- Cut energy and cooling costs up to 95%
- Consolidate the power of 13 servers into 1, so you have 92% fewer servers to manage
- Triple the capacity of your data center with HP Dynamic Power Capping

Technology for better business outcomes.

HP ProLiant DL385 G6
- Six-Core AMD Opteron™ 2400 Series Processor (up to 2)
- 16 DIMMs sockets for up to 128GB of memory
- HP Insight Control cuts management costs by up to $48K per 100 users over 3 years*

AMD Opteron 64

See how HP innovation radically shrinks your server purchase costs and operating expenses at **hp.com/eur/ROIG6**

* White Paper sponsored by HP, Gaining Business Value and ROI with HP Insight Control, #218069, May 2009.
Copyright © 2009 Hewlett-Packard Development Company, LP. AMD, the AMD arrow logo, AMD Opteron and combinations there of, are trademarks of Advanced Micro Devices, Inc.

Science

The looming crisis in human genetics

Geoffrey Miller

Some awkward news ahead

Human geneticists have reached a private crisis of conscience, and it will become public knowledge in 2010. The crisis has depressing health implications and alarming political ones. In a nutshell: the new genetics will reveal much less than hoped about how to cure disease, and much more than feared about human evolution and inequality, including genetic differences between classes, ethnicities and races.

About five years ago, genetics researchers became excited about new methods for "genome-wide association studies" (GWAS). We already knew from twin, family and adoption studies that all human traits are heritable: genetic differences explain much of the variation between individuals. We knew the genes were there; we just had to find them. Companies such as Illumina and Affymetrix produced DNA chips that allowed researchers to test up to 1m genetic variants for their statistical association with specific traits. America's National Institutes of Health and Britain's Wellcome Trust gave huge research grants for gene-hunting. Thousands of researchers jumped on the GWAS bandwagon. Lab groups formed and international research consortia congealed. The quantity of published GWAS research has soared.

In 2010, GWAS fever will reach its peak. Dozens of papers will report specific genes associated with almost every imaginable trait—intelligence, personality, religiosity, sexuality, longevity, economic risk-taking, consumer preferences, leisure interests and political attitudes. The data are already collected, with DNA samples from large populations already measured for these traits. It's just a matter of doing the statistics and writing up the papers for *Nature Genetics*. The gold rush is on throughout the leading behaviour-genetics centres in London, Amsterdam, Boston, Boulder and Brisbane.

GWAS researchers will, in public, continue trumpeting their successes to science journalists and *Science* magazine. They will reassure Big Pharma and the grant agencies that GWAS will identify the genes that explain most of the variation in heart disease, cancer, obesity, depression, schizophrenia, Alzheimer's and ageing itself. Those genes will illuminate the biochemical pathways underlying disease, which will yield new genetic tests and blockbuster drugs. Keep holding your breath for a golden age of health, happiness and longevity.

In private, though, the more thoughtful GWAS researchers are troubled. They hold small, discreet conferences on the "missing heritability" problem: if all these human traits are heritable, why are GWAS studies failing so often? The DNA chips should already have identified some important genes behind physical and mental health. They simply have not been delivering the goods.

Certainly, GWAS papers have reported a couple of hundred genetic variants that show statistically significant associations with a few traits. But the genes typically do not replicate across studies. Even when they do replicate, they never explain more than a tiny fraction of any interesting trait. In fact, classical Mendelian genetics based on family studies has identified far more disease-risk genes with larger effects than GWAS research has so far.

Why the failure? The missing heritability may reflect limitations of DNA-chip design: GWAS methods so far focus on relatively common genetic variants in regions of DNA that code for proteins. They under-sample rare variants and DNA regions translated into non-coding RNA, which seems to orchestrate most organic development in vertebrates. Or it may be that thousands of small mutations disrupt body and brain in different ways in different populations. At worst, each human trait may depend on hundreds of thousands of genetic variants that add up through gene-expression patterns of mind-numbing complexity.

> They simply have not been delivering the goods

Political science

We will know much more when it becomes possible to do cheap "resequencing"—which is really just "sequencing" a wider variety of individuals beyond the handful analysed for the Human Genome Project. Full sequencing means analysing all 3 billion base pairs of an individual's DNA rather than just a sample of 1m genetic variants as the DNA chips do. When sequencing costs drop within a few years below $1,000 per genome, researchers in Europe, China and India will start huge projects with vast sample sizes, sophisticated bioinformatics, diverse trait measures and detailed family

A plethora of papers
Number of scientific publications on genome-wide association studies

Species studied
· Human   · Others

Source: Web of Science, Thomson Reuters

2010 IN BRIEF

After a false start in 2008, CERN's Large Hadron Collider, under the Franco-Swiss border, hopes to discover the **Higgs boson**, without which matter would not exist.

Geoffrey Miller: evolutionary psychologist, University of New Mexico; author of "Spent: Sex, Evolution, and Consumer Behavior" (Viking)

intelligent life

A SISTER PUBLICATION OF **The Economist**

LIFE. CULTURE. STYLE.

Intelligent Life is the quarterly lifestyle and culture magazine from *The Economist*. It covers the arts, style, food, wine, cars, travel and anything else under the sun, as long as it's interesting. It shares *The Economist's* fondess for crisp prose, dry wit and free thinking. But rather than covering politics and economics, it is about life in general and making the most of your time off, from tailoring to museums, hotels to philanthropy, choosing wine to going green.

We mix our *Economist* writers with leading authors such as A.S. Byatt, Julian Barnes, Douglas Coupland and William Boyd. We have regular columns from Ed Smith on sport, Tim Atkin on wine lists and Linda Grant on style, with photography and illustration to match the elegance of the writing.

SUBSCRIBE NOW

We would like to invite you to subscribe at a special rate of £10 and have *Intelligent Life* delivered to your door every quarter.
Visit **www.economistsubscriptions.com/intlife**
or call **+44 (0)114 220 2404**. Quote code: TBKR
Also available at all good newsstands.

Dreamers or doers?
Bocconians.

The mission of Università Bocconi has never changed since 1902: to create a management class of excellence. As ethical and motivated as its own faculty. Renowned in the international business community for its commitment to research, Università Bocconi brings talented young people to Milan, the home of Italian business. Students will find one of the broadest selections of graduate and postgraduate courses in Europe at Università Bocconi and at SDA Bocconi School of Management. One day these men and women will be part of the Bocconian community. Dedicated people working for the good of the world. Bocconi. Empowering talent.

Ogilvy & Mather

BACHELOR: INTERNATIONAL ECONOMICS, MANAGEMENT AND FINANCE.
MASTER OF SCIENCE: INTERNATIONAL MANAGEMENT • MARKETING MANAGEMENT • FINANCE • ECONOMICS AND MANAGEMENT IN ARTS, CULTURE, MEDIA AND ENTERTAINMENT • ECONOMIC AND SOCIAL SCIENCES • ECONOMICS AND MANAGEMENT OF INNOVATION AND TECHNOLOGY.
PHD: BUSINESS ADMINISTRATION AND MANAGEMENT • ECONOMICS AND FINANCE • INTERNATIONAL LAW AND ECONOMICS • STATISTICS.

Master Programs
http://contact.unibocconi.it/international/
Call center: +39 02.5836.3535
Call by Skype : unibocconi_1

Università Commerciale Luigi Bocconi

Bocconi

2010 IN BRIEF

The first cheap **inhalant measles vaccine** begins human trials in India.

structures. (American bioscience will prove too politically squeamish to fund such studies.) The missing heritability problem will surely be solved sooner or later.

The trouble is, the resequencing data will reveal much more about human evolutionary history and ethnic differences than they will about disease genes. Once enough DNA is analysed around the world, science will have a panoramic view of human genetic variation across races, ethnicities and regions. We will start reconstructing a detailed family tree that links all living humans, discovering many surprises about mis-attributed paternity and covert mating between classes, castes, regions and ethnicities.

We will also identify the many genes that create physical and mental differences across populations, and we will be able to estimate when those genes arose. Some of those differences probably occurred very recently, within recorded history. Gregory Cochran and Henry Harpending argued in "The 10,000 Year Explosion" that some human groups experienced a vastly accelerated rate of evolutionary change within the past few thousand years, benefiting from the new genetic diversity created within far larger populations, and in response to the new survival, social and reproductive challenges of agriculture, cities, divisions of labour and social classes. Others did not experience these changes until the past few hundred years when they were subject to contact, colonisation and, all too often, extermination.

If the shift from GWAS to sequencing studies finds evidence of such politically awkward and morally perplexing facts, we can expect the usual range of ideological reactions, including nationalistic retro-racism from conservatives and outraged denial from blank-slate liberals. The few who really understand the genetics will gain a more enlightened, live-and-let-live recognition of the biodiversity within our extraordinary species—including a clearer view of likely comparative advantages between the world's different economies. ■

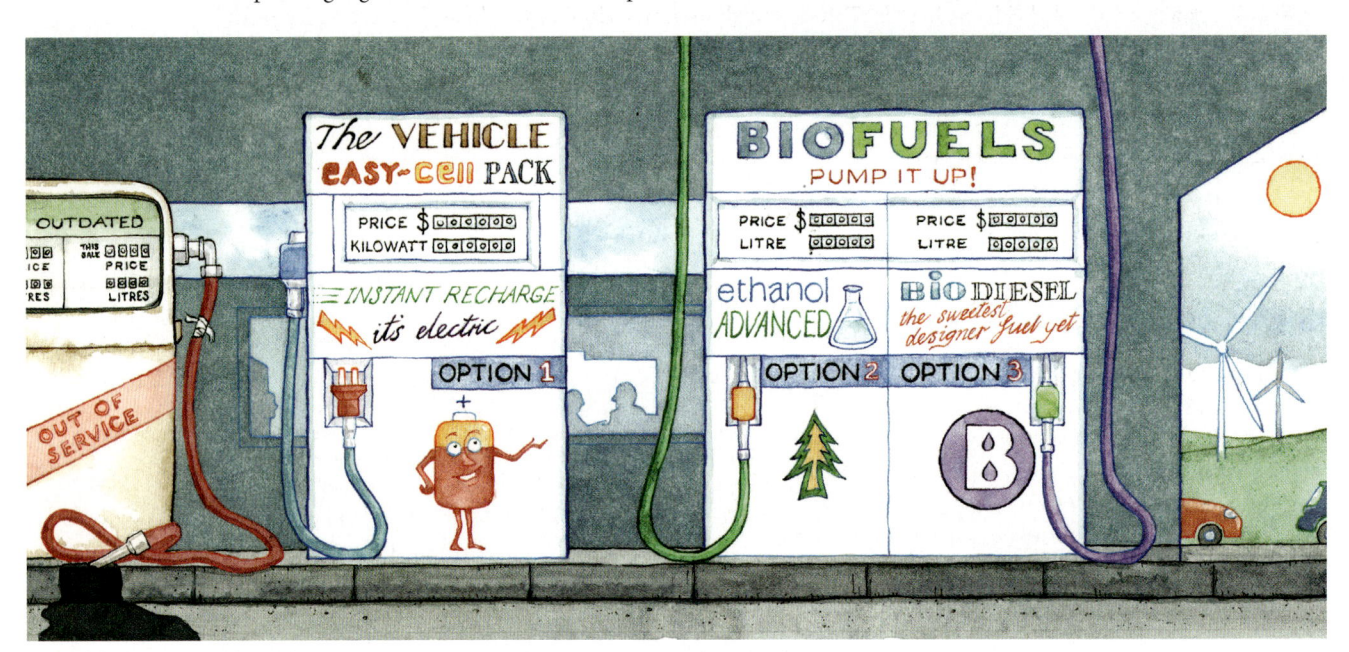

The coming alternatives

Geoffrey Carr

Novel energy technologies will continue to advance

"What does not kill me will make me stronger." That should be the motto of the alternative-energy industry in 2010. The past year has been a rough one. People are less disposed to make costly gestures towards environmental protection in a slump. But, for the bold, there is opportunity. In particular, solar-energy researchers will chase the hitherto-mythical beast called "cheaper than coal", which will enable them to compete in the electricity-generation market without subsidies, while battery engineers will chase that equally elusive creature, the vehicle cell-pack which can be recharged as rapidly as a petrol tank.

They will be assisted in their quests by the activities of Steven Chu, Barack Obama's energy secretary.

Dr Chu, a physicist with a lot of experience in energy research, has been sowing the ground with money in 2009, and in 2010 will expect to start reaping. A world that has lived for more than two centuries on cheap fossil fuels has seen little need to spend heavily on basic research into alternatives, but that means a lot of potentially fruitful lines of investigation remain unpursued. Now the anti-recession fiscal stimulus should uncover, via Dr Chu's largesse to the laboratories of America's universities, a host of ideas that venture capitalists may turn their attention to when the economy rebounds.

Even commercially, though, the news is not all bad. China, for example, is often portrayed in Western media as the uncaring über-polluter of the future, because of its massive coal-fired power-station programme. But it also has one of the world's biggest wind-power programmes. By the end of 2010, the country's wind-generating capacity will be about 20 gigawatts—equal to Spain's and only slightly behind Germany's and America's. The aim is to have 100 gigawatts by 2020. That is an eighth of China's present electricity-generating capacity. It must,

Geoffrey Carr: science and technology editor, *The Economist*

of course, be remembered that wind turbines do not turn all the time. Nevertheless, a study published in *Science* reckons that at current prices, which are guaranteed into the future by the government when a wind farm is built, wind could replace a quarter of China's coal-fired power stations.

The coming year will also see the opening shots in an inter-green war. This will be caused by the introduction of the first mass-market (or so their manufacturers hope) electric saloon cars in America and Japan. China's attempt to be first, in the form of BYD Auto's F3DM, has not gone well. Sales are pitiful. But the Chevrolet Volt and Nissan's Leaf are built to much higher standards by well-established companies. None of these cars relies solely on its batteries for power. All have petrol-driven generators to keep the wheels turning if the batteries run flat. But unlike existing hybrids, such as the Toyota Prius, in which the petrol engine drives the car directly, these so-called plug-in hybrids are pure-electric vehicles when it comes to turning the wheels.

The war will be between supporters of electric vehicles and those of biofuels, for these, too, will begin

The year will see the opening shots in an inter-green war

to leap forward. At the moment, "biofuel" means either ethanol made by the fermentation of sugars from cane or maize, or biodiesel from processed plant oils. In 2010 "advanced" ethanol—made from straw, wood chippings and suchlike, using new technological tricks such as genetically engineered bacteria to do the fermenting—will start coming out of pilot plants. So, too, will "designer" biodiesel, made from sugar but turned into hydrocarbons that should be even better than fuels from oil.

Greens who accept the need for personal motorised transport at all may thus have difficulty choosing. Electric cars themselves are zero-emission, but their overall environmental credentials depend on how the electricity is generated in the first place. If it comes from coal, they are still better in global-warming terms than traditional cars—but not by as much as they could be if the power were wind, solar or even (whisper it not) nuclear.

Biofuels, meanwhile, will remain controversial. Their carbon comes, via photosynthesis, from the atmosphere, so they do not contribute directly to global warming when they are burned. But their indirect environmental "bads"—competition with food crops, the need to clear virgin land to grow them, and the energy costs of processing them—all cause anguish. Tricky. ∎

2010 IN BRIEF

Anti-nuclear campaigners bemoan President Truman's decision, 60 years ago, to develop the **hydrogen bomb**.

Where have all the sunspots gone?
Alison Goddard

The sun will surprise scientists

Something odd has happened to the sun. Four centuries after sunspots were first seen—by Galileo—they have disappeared almost entirely. In 2009 weeks and sometimes months went by without a single sunspot being discerned. In 2010 they will return, or so say most solar scientists. Others wonder whether the sun may be going through an extended period of inactivity.

Sunspots are a bit of a mystery. They are transient tangles in the sun's magnetic field that are slightly cooler than their surroundings and so appear as dark patches in the photosphere—the surface layer of the sun. They tend to appear in pairs (on opposite sides of the sun) that persist for a fortnight or so before fading.

Normally the number of sunspots peaks every 11 years, coinciding with the times when the sun's magnetic field is at its strongest. As the field wanes, the number of sunspots falls to a trough or minimum, at which point the sun's magnetic field reverses direction and starts to regain its strength. As it does so, sunspots begin to appear close to the poles of the sun. When the magnetic field is at its strongest, and sunspots at their most plentiful, they cluster close to the equator.

Back in 2008 solar scientists saw a high-latitude, reversed-polarity sunspot, suggesting the start of a new solar cycle. Since then, however, there has been little activity. Reliable predictions of sunspot numbers are impossible to make until the solar cycle is well established, usually three years after the minimum. So with luck the sunspot riddle should be solved in 2010.

Scientists from America's space agency, NASA, reckon that the next peak will come in March or April 2013. However, their colleagues at the National Solar Observatory in Tucson, Arizona, have found that the magnetism of sunspots (the strength of the knot that they form) has been declining over the past couple of decades. If this carries on, solar magnetic fields will become too weak to form sunspots, which will vanish completely in 2015.

In the past, sunspots have disappeared for decades. Between 1645 and 1715, they were rare. There were several years in which none at all was sighted and others in which fewer than ten were spotted. Giovanni Cassini, an Italian astronomer, described a sunspot that appeared in 1671 as the first he had seen for many years. John Flamsteed, the first Astronomer Royal, observed one in 1684, after a gap of ten years. This 70-year period of low solar activity has since been dubbed the Maunder Minimum (after an astronomer called Edward Maunder, a sunspot specialist).

Whether the sun has taken that particular path or will return to normal will become clear in 2010. Not only astronomers will be interested in the answer. The Maunder Minimum coincided with a period of exceptionally cold winters in Europe and North America and, perhaps, elsewhere. What happens if global warming meets solar cooling? Expect a hot debate. ∎

Alison Goddard: science correspondent, *The Economist*

Obituary

Bringing space down to Earth
Ann Wroe

America's space-shuttle programme will soon be gone, or on life support

Government-sponsored exploration always has two stages. The first is tentative, dangerous and glorious, a voyage into the unknown perched on some untried piece of engineering, ending with proud footsteps in the alien dust and the planting of the flag. The second is a matter of manifests, warehouses, timetables, the rotation of crews and the mending of forts. The new and extraordinary becomes familiar and even, in some ways, dull.

So it was with America's space programme. After the wonders and terrors of *Apollo*'s race for the moon, the shuttle was space made everyday. Richard Nixon announced it in 1972 with all the drama of a CEO reading out the company report. Space was to become "familiar territory", ready for "practical utilisation". In his unlovely word, it would be "routinised".

The shuttle's great novelty was that the orbiter was reusable, like a bus or a train. Though garlanded with names from the glory days—*Endeavour, Enterprise, Discovery*—its business was commuting. The huge, showy booster rockets fallen away, it was just a little glider or an aeroplane. Its far bright lights would streak across the sky and its sonic ba-boom! would rumble out, regular as a flight to Chicago. NASA meant each one to last ten years or 100 flights, and though bad weather put paid to that, the five spaceworthy orbiters made more than 130 flights. They acquired the patina of travel. Crews found that other people's lost washers and M&Ms would float out from behind the fittings.

As on any commuter vehicle, all sorts used it. The pleasure of eating rehydrated shrimp cocktail, or trying to stuff a urine bag, against gravity, into the wet-trash container, was open not only to five or six well-trained astronauts and pilots. Scientists also went with their experiments, engineers with their screwdrivers. A Saudi prince was included, who wanted to observe the moon at Ramadan; a teacher went, to show schoolchildren the live wonders of the stars. Mothers-of-three flew, and old men of 77.

Though garlanded with names from the glory days, its business was commuting

Politicians hitched rides on the promise that they would look kindly on NASA's budget requests. They needed to, for each shuttle never flew enough to make financial sense, and the craft needed so much fixing after each flight that they were never, truly, used again. Once on board, everyone would don golf-shirts and shorts and mug for the camera on the mid-deck, with the prettiest floating.

The work was less exciting. Much of it was servicing the space station, taking water, coffee, sleeping bags and spare parts in, and moving rubbish out; launching satellites, retrieving them, and making running repairs. The shuttle was essentially a hugely expensive freight service, a sort of UPS orbiting the Earth. It launched hollow spheres, covered with mirrors, to measure the density of the atmosphere, and took up a payload of flags for distribution to the heroes of September 11th. On most missions one or two astronauts would walk in space, carrying clumpy instruments in huge gloved hands, to tinker with the craft. Their logs were eloquently mundane:

> Godwin & Tani start a space walk to install insulation around the top of the ISS truss structure, they also made an attempt to secure one of four legs that brace the starboard station array but were unable to close the latch…they retrieved an errant electrical cover (lost during 2001 April 24 during the STS-100 mission), and positioned two switches to be retrieved and installed during the upcoming STS-110 mission.

The logs also included near-misses in the clutter of space: old rocket-stages, blankets and foot restraints, all orbiting past. The work was interrupted to take telephone calls from Ronald Reagan or whichever leader had a citizen on board. If not quite a day at the office, there was a fair approximation to the muddle of faraway Earth.

Mundane but miraculous

Yet it was desperately dangerous. The shuttle, at its launch, clung piggy-back on to 4m pounds of explosives. There was no escape route. Defective o-rings doomed the *Challenger* flight in 1986, and a chunk of insulating foam gashed the wing of *Columbia* on re-entry, in 2002. The dreadful fan-like tumbling of the debris from the sky was all the worse because *Columbia* carried a woman teacher and a black astronaut among its crew, America in miniature.

And this was also, for all its familiarity, a course in amazement. The shuttle enabled its astronauts to see, every 90 minutes, how the sun ignited a giant rainbow over the morning Earth. It allowed them to observe the still, fixed colours of the stars; to watch from the outside as lightning forked through a weather front; to measure the spiders' webs of cities against the immense blue of ocean and the matt black of far space. Much of the shuttle's business—launching the Hubble telescope, putting up satellites, mapping the Earth—could have been done by unmanned craft, at a fraction of the $174 billion the programme cost. But the shuttle threw space open as a place where ordinary men and women could not only live, work and fool about, denizens of the universe, but where they could also routinely slip the bonds of time, be humbled, and be astonished. ∎

Ann Wroe: obituaries editor, *The Economist*